Walt Disney &

Recollections of the
Disney Studios: 1955-1980

Walt Disney &
Recollections of the Disney Studios: 1955-1980

by Charles Tranberg

BearManor Media

2012

Walt Disney & Recollections of the Disney Studios: 1955–1980

© 2012 Charles Tranberg

For information, address:

BearManor Media
P. O. Box 71426
Albany, GA 31708

bearmanormedia.com

Typesetting and layout by John Teehan

Published in the USA by BearManor Media

ISBN — 1-59393-684-2
978-1-59393-684-6

Table of Contents

Back Story & Acknowledgements

Dear Reader:

    First and foremost I must tell you plainly and at the beginning that this is not a biography of Walt Disney. There is a great deal of discussion about Walt Disney provided. You will read his thoughts about his company and many of the films he produced and some of the personalities that worked for him. You will read the thoughts of many of those who knew him, worked for his studio or saw him around the studio and had a chance encounter. But as far as a substantive biography of the man— this is not it. I do list a bibliography which does list some wonderful biographies if you would like to pursue.

    What I have tried to do with this book is gather a round table of thoughts and opinions about the Disney Studio from those who worked at the studio from about 1955 until 1980. The book concentrates on the live-action rather than the animated films. From roughly the mid 1950's onward, Walt Disney put more time and effort into live-action films rather than the cartoon and animated features that established him in the late 20's and were hallmarks of his studio's output until the early 50's. One of the main reasons for the shift in emphasis was because of the increasing cost of producing animated features—and the dwindling profits they provided to the studio. As an example, *Sleeping Beauty* was produced in 1959 at a cost of $6 million and brought in $7.7 million at the box office— which with distribution, publicity and other costs kept it in the red for many years. On the other hand, *The Shaggy Dog*, a black and white slapstick comedy released the same year and produced for under a million dollars grossed over $9 million and became the third biggest box office hit of the year—and a huge profit maker for Disney.

It was also in the mid-1950s that Disney got involved in television—largely to help finance his dream of Disneyland. And in this book we will look at two groundbreaking TV events of the 1950's—the Davy Crockett phenomenon which spread like wildfire all across the country and inspired a hit song and passion for, of all things, coonskin caps. And then there was a daily kiddie show that made children everywhere want to be members of *The Mickey Mouse Club*.

In films, from 1959 onward the Disney formula was established. *The Shaggy Dog* was Disney's first live-action comedy, but it certainly wouldn't be his last. For the next twenty-years the backbone of the studio output would be modestly budgeted comedies, often containing unbelievable situations (e.g., a boy that turns into a dog, a formula called Flubber that causes a Model T to fly, a Volkswagen that has human emotions, a college student who becomes invisible, a duck that lays golden eggs, a mule that can kick field goals) that produced huge profits. Along the way Disney would still produce the occasional animated film and blockbuster (*Babes in Toyland, Mary Poppins, The Happiest Millionaire*) and heart-warming drama (*Old Yeller, Follow Me, Boys!, Rascal*), but, by and large, the mainstay of the studio output would be its formula comedies—often starring Fred MacMurray, Dean Jones, and sometimes Hayley Mills—and populated by a stock company of supremely talented character actors.

This was the Disney Studio that the baby boomers grew up with. The family-friendly company that parents could always trust in an increasingly R-rated world—and laugh and enjoy along with their children. This was the studio before Michael Eisner and before Touchstone, the division of Disney that, since 1984, has produced more mature films. Yes, we still have a Disney film division today that still produces product (some quite profitably) to a general market, but this is a Disney that is far removed from the Walt era and the decade or so following his death in December 1966. The Disney Studio of 1955-1980 was a small (as compared to Warners, Fox, MGM, Paramount or even Universal) independent studio which, as we find in many of the recollections told in this book, had the feel of a college campus more so than a movie studio. In those years the studio produced only an average of 5-6 motion pictures per year. Today the output just for Disney films division is closer to 12 releases per year—and not including the output from Disney subsidiaries such as Touchstone, Hollywood and Miramax films. The Disney Studios of today would be, in my opinion, completely foreign to Walt.

It is also my hope that in this book the reader will find out about some of the other unsung heroes of the Disney Studios. People like Roy

Disney, Bill Walsh, Bill Anderson, Robert Stevenson, Norman Tokar and Vincent McEveety—among many others. These are the people who, in many cases, made Walt's vision a reality and then, after his passing, continued the course—for better or worse.

In this book I highlight more than 40 Disney live-action productions. Naturally we will examine and get recollections about such classics as *Old Yeller, Pollyanna, The Absent-Minded Professor* and *Mary Poppins.* But it is also my hope that you will learn more about lesser known Disney gems like *Babes in Toyland, Emil and the Detectives, Savage Sam, Summer Magic, Follow Me, Boys! Blackbeard's Ghost* and *The One and Only Original Genuine Family Band.*

I would like to thank the following people for their time and contributions to this book:

Sharon Baird, one of the most beloved and talented of the original Mickey Mouse Clubbers.

Peter Brown, star of such TV series as *Lawman* & *Laredo* who charmingly played Hayley Mills' love interest in the underrated *Summer Magic.*

Mary Grace Canfield, a wonderful character actress who was personally selected for her grumpy role in the classic *Pollyanna.* She may be best known for her role as "Ralph Monroe" on the TV classic *Green Acres.*

Harry Carey, Jr., character actor extraordinaire and member of the John Ford stock company in films like *Three Godfathers* & *The Searchers,* who contributed to several Disney productions of the 50's and 60's including *Spin and Marty.*

Jonathan Daly, well-known film and TV actor of the 60's and 70's. He played James Stewart's son for one season on the delightful *Jimmy Stewart Show* and Lt. Whipple on the 1976-1978 Don Rickles series *CPO Sharkey*—he added his talent to several Disney films including *Rascal, Million Dollar Duck* and *The Shaggy D.A.*

James Drury, the star of one of TV's finest Westerns, *The Virginian,* who in 1960 lent his talent to three Disney films: the classic *Pollyanna,* the underrated *Toby Tyler,* and the visually beautiful *Ten Who Dared.*

David Frankham, the courtly English gentleman best known for his work in three Vincent Price films: *Return of the Fly, Master of the World,* and *Tales of Terror*. He also worked in *Ten Who Dared* and voiced Sgt. Tibs in *One Hundred and One Dalmatians* at Disney.

Arthur Hiller, distinguished director of TV and film—Hiller is a past president of the Academy of Motion Picture Arts and Sciences. Among his films are *The Americanization of Emily, Love Story, The Out-of-Towners, The Hospital* and *Silver Streak*. Hiller directed *Miracle of the White Stallions*; he gives us a director's perspective of working at Disney.

Eddie Hodges, as a child star, was the original Winthrop in the classic Broadway musical, *The Music Man*. He co-starred with Frank Sinatra and sang (the Oscar-winning) "High Hopes" with him in *A Hole in the Head*. At Disney he lent his considerable talent to *Summer Magic* and *The Happiest Millionaire*.

Ann Jillian, as a child actress, was 'Dainty' June in the film version of *Gypsy!* She grew into a three-time Emmy-nominated actress (*The Ann Jillian Story, Mae West & Ellis Island*) as well as three-time nominee for a Golden Globe (with one win for *The Ann Jillian Story*). She also starred in the TV series *It's a Living*. At Disney she was featured in *Babes in Toyland* and *Sammy, The Way Out Seal*. She kindly allowed me to use her Disney memories found at http://www.thecolumnists.com/jillian/jillian11.html and also answered some follow-up questions.

Tommy Kirk was one of the top Disney juvenile leads of the late 50's through mid 60's in films like *Old Yeller, The Shaggy Dog, Swiss Family Robinson* and *Savage Sam*. His memories, first provided for my book on Fred MacMurray, are among the most provocative.

Marta Kristen, beautiful Norwegian-born actress, is best known as Judy Robinson on the sci-fi hit *Lost in Space*. She took on the role of Lizbeth in the sequel to *Old Yeller, Savage Sam*. She literally choked when meeting Walt Disney.

Michael McGreevey was one of the Disney stock company with several Disney films to his credit including *Toby Tyler, Sammy, the Way Out Seal, Snowball Express* and his the Medford College trilogy: *The Computer*

Wore Tennis Shoes, Now You See Him-Now You Don't, and *The Strongest Man in the World*. McGreevey began his career at age 11 and soon was appearing as a regular in the TV series *Riverboat* as well as a variety of other series including *The Donna Reed Show, Lassie, Bonanza* and *Wagon Train*.

Roger Mobley, the popular star of the Disney *Gallegher* series, and the film *Emil and the Detectives*, also appeared in numerous episodic TV episodes in the 1960's including *Wagon Train, Route 66, The Virginian*, and *Dr. Kildare*. He was also a regular on the TV-series *Fury*.

Billy Mumy remains one of the most recognizable child stars of the 60's and early 70's with memorable performances on *Alfred Hitchcock Presents, The Twilight Zone* and *Bewitched*. His films include *A Child is Waiting* (with Judy Garland and Burt Lancaster), *Dear Brigitte* (with James Stewart) and *Bless The Beasts and Children*. He is best known as Will Robinson on *Lost in Space*. As an adult actor he has worked in the movie *Papillon* and the TV series *Babylon 5*. For Disney he appeared in *Sammy, The Way Out Seal, For the Love of Willadean* and starred in the film *Rascal*.

Maureen O'Hara, the legendary star of such classics as *The Hunchback of Notre Dame, Miracle on 34th Street, Rio Grande, The Quiet Man* and for Disney, *The Parent Trap*, was kind enough to allow me to use her taped comments about her Disney memories. I thank her secretary, June Beck, for helping to arrange this.

Fess Parker was a genuine Disney legend who became one of the most popular cultural icons of the 1950s through his portrayal of Davy Crockett for Walt Disney. He also appeared in a number of Disney films, including the classic *Old Yeller*. Later he was the popular star of the TV series *Daniel Boone*. Sadly we lost him in 2010—not long after he responded to my interview questions.

Robert Pine, terrific character actor who has made hundreds of TV and film appearances, continues to work to this day in popular series like *The Office* (playing Jim's dad) and *CSI*. He may be best known as Sgt. Joe Getraer on the 1977-1983 TV series *CHiPs*. His career stretches back to the mid-1960s and includes appearances on *The Lucy Show, Gunsmoke,*

The Virginian, Lost in Space, Mannix, Streets of San Francisco, Charlie's Angels & Magnum P.I. He played President John F. Kennedy in a 1987 TV movie, *Hoover vs. the Kennedys.* At Disney, Mr. Pine appeared in *One Little Indian, The Bears and I,* and *The Apple Dumpling Gang Rides Again.*

Elliott Reid graciously afforded me the opportunity to interview him twice, for my books on Agnes Moorehead and Fred MacMurray. At Disney he was Fred MacMurray's stuffy rival in three films: *The Absent Minded Professor, Son of Flubber* and *Follow Me, Boys!*

Peter Renaday was another popular member of the Disney stock company. You may not recognize the name, but you definitely will know the face. He appeared in over a dozen Disney films. Today he is a well sought after voice actor. His first encounter with Walt might have been his last day on the Disney lot!

Larri Thomas, beautiful dancer who appeared in such films as *Guys and Dolls* and *The Music Man*, also lent her talents to many episodic and variety TV series. At Disney she became Julie Andrews's stand-in on *Mary Poppins* and also appeared in the film as "the pretty lady" in the carriage who blows a kiss to Dick Van Dyke. She also danced in the films *The Happiest Millionaire* and *The One and Only Original Genuine Family Band.* Later on, she played the character of Henrietta Hippo on the popular children's show *The New Zoo Revue.*

Dick Warlock, a top film stunt man, worked stunts in numerous Disney films (as well as for other motion picture companies) and began a twenty-plus career as Kurt Russell's stunt double.

Beverly Washburn is the sweet and pretty actress who played Lizbeth Seary in the classic coming of age drama *Old Yeller.* Washburn has appeared on many TV shows and was a regular member of *The Loretta Young Show* stock company. *Star Trek* fans will remember her as Lt. Galway in the episode "The Deadly Years." She also appeared in the cult film *Spider Baby.*

Patrick Wayne, the star of the popular 1974 Disney outdoor saga *The Bears and I,* grew up as Hollywood royalty—the son of John Wayne. He appeared with his father in several films including *The Quiet Man, The*

Searchers, The Alamo, Donovan's Reef and *McLintock!* He later co-starred in the 1967-68 Western series *The Rounders* and appeared in such films as *Shenandoah, The Gatling Gun, Beyond Atlantis* and *Mustang County*—as well as dozens of episodic TV appearances.

Jan Williams began in the mail room at Disney and worked himself up to producer of such films as *The Shaggy DA, Herbie in Monte Carlo, The Cat from Outer Space*, and *Condorman*. He gives us a look at Disney from a producer's outlook.

Dee Dee Wood, with her ex-husband Marc Breaux, choreographed Andy Williams' TV series and a Judy Garland TV special. Then, Walt Disney gave her the opportunity of a lifetime—choreographing the dances in *Mary Poppins*. She also choreographed the films *The Sound of Music* and *Chitty Bang Bang Bang*. She has been nominated for two Emmy awards (one for choreographing the *Cher* TV series and she won an Emmy for her work as choreographer for 1987's *Liberty Weekend*).

Alan Young, Emmy Award-winning comedian and star of *Mister Ed,* also appeared in such films as *tom thumb* and the cult favorite *The Time Machine.* For Disney, he has voiced the character of Scrooge McDuck for several years and appeared in the film *The Cat from Outer Space.*

And last, but not least, a special thank you to my friend **Hank Jones**, who wrote the introduction to this book. I first became acquainted with Hank on my Fred MacMurray book and he has always been tirelessly helpful to me. He helped arrange some of the wonderful interviews I had for this book with people like Peter Renaday, Jan Williams and Jonathan Daly—all good friends of his. He is also a valued member of the Disney stock company: if you are a fan of the film *Blackbeard's Ghost*—and many are—you know him well as Gudger. He also gave memorable turns in *Herbie Rides Again* (remember Sir Lancelot?) and *No Deposit, No Return, The Shaggy DA, The Cat from Outer Space* and numerous others. In addition, he was a regular on the daytime *Tennessee Ernie Ford Show* on ABC in 1962 and appeared on such popular TV shows as *My Three Sons, The Patty Duke Show, The Love Boat* and *Mork and Mindy.* Today he is a noted genealogist. In addition to his writing the introduction to this book, he allowed me to quote extensively from his memoir, *The Show Bizz Part of My Life,* as well as answer additional questions I presented to him. A big Thank You, Hank!

I also want to say a big thank you to my friend Gary McFall who, as he did in my last book on screen great Robert Taylor, scanned dozens of photographs that are included in this book.

A further note: While I have included many interviews conducted with (as I call them) my round table (as listed above), I have also included recollections from other sources. I have provided a detailed source section and to further differentiate from the interviews I conducted, those comments that came from other sources will be *in italics.*

I hope you enjoy this look inside the Disney Studio.

– Charles Tranberg
Madison, Wisconsin

Foreword

"*Blackbeard's Ghost*!! I love that movie! I saw it when I was a kid with my folks. Now I show it on DVD to my own kids (and my grandkids too). It's one of my favorite Disney films."

How many times have I heard that over the years in one form or another when someone finds out I was lucky enough to be one of the many character actors working at Walt Disney Studios in the 60s and 70s. I guess we all were sort of an in-house stock company of familiar faces that the studio used over and over again in parts big and small. I've had complete strangers come up to me on the street and begin reciting some of my own dialogue from *Shaggy D.A.*, *Herbie Rides Again*, or *Cat From Outer Space* when at the time I didn't even know those lines myself very well in the first place. They were indeed special films that meant a lot to the people who made them and also to the folks that went to their local Bijou, purchased their ticket, bought their popcorn, and sat down alongside their friends and family and saw them. Writer/Director Peter Bogdanovich says good movies are really "pieces of time," and I think that phrase captures the unique qualities of these Disney movies that enthrall and touch so many of us.

There have been several excellent books published on the wonderful animated films made by Disney, honoring the imagination and the craftsmanship of those marvelous artists who created them. However, a comprehensive study celebrating just the live-action features of the studio alone has been lacking… until now. Enter Charles "Chuck" Tranberg, a fine writer and movie buff, who has several well-reviewed books to his credit, among them biographies of screen legends Fred MacMurray, Marie Wilson, and Agnes Moorehead. Chuck just happens to have a passion for the older Disney live-action films, and his love for them comes through on each and every one of these pages.

After exhaustively canvassing all the articles and literature out there on the subject, via e-mails, letters, and in-person interviews Chuck then rounded up many of us who had been part of those magical days and barraged us with questions. He drew us out about "what it was like then," "how we did that," and "what was so-and-so really like." Chuck was like Sherlock Holmes in finding out the story behind the story – how what we experienced off screen eventually led to what finally was seen on screen. As you'll see from these pages, quite often the drama behind the scenes was even greater than what was in the movie itself.

From the guys in the mailroom, to the stunt people, to the crew, to the wardrobe and makeup folks to directors, producers, major stars, and bit players—Chuck found us all and picked our brains—and more importantly our hearts—for memories of those fond Disney days when we showed up for work at the corner of Goofy Lane and Dopey Drive. This book reinforces that those pictures that we made were the sum of many parts: although the buck stopped with Walt, it truly was a team effort – and this fine book reflects just that.

In between acting in pictures and sit-coms, my favorite pastime has always been genealogy: climbing the family tree. Now in my later years, I enjoy writing books on the subject and whatever "hambone" I have left from my acting days comes out in the genealogical seminars I give around the country. As family historians, we say that to do our work correctly it's our job to take a skeleton of names and dates and put flesh and blood on it and make the person real—to make our ancestors come alive again. I think that's what Chuck Tranberg has done especially well in this volume. When you boil it all down, it's really all about the people, isn't it? You'll read first hand here about the special folks who made those Disney movies and what they were really like: their strengths, their foibles, their quirks, their genius—all of it. And as to the boss-man himself, not a mythical but a real picture of "Uncle Walt" emerges on these pages from those who knew him and felt his constant and overpowering presence.

There's a common thread I think you'll find as you read this book: how very much everyone involved in getting these vibrant and visually stunning live-action-features on the screen simply loved their work – just loved it! I've always said that working on the Disney lot was like going to summer camp! Everybody seemed to smile, because we all were so happy to be a part of the action there. In each of our own ways, we now realize that these wonderful movies are part of our own personal legacies—they'll endure and never be forgotten; so that means we won't either—and that's pretty nice!

We were and are truly blessed. ENJOY!

– Hank Jones

1

A Little about Walt

Walter Elias Disney was born on December 5, 1901 in Chicago. He was the youngest of five children, which included four boys and a girl. Soon after his birth, the family, headed by his father Elias and his mother Flora, moved the family to Marceline, Missouri. He spent much of his childhood there helping out on the family farm and working an assortment of odd jobs. The farm was close to the Santa Fe Railroad tracks and Walt used to enjoy watching the approaching trains—and dreaming of the far off places that the trains were traveling to. It was the start of a life long affection and appreciation for trains. Later, through his uncle, an engineer, he worked a summer with the railroad selling newspapers and refreshments to passengers.

Disney developed a knack for drawing caricatures and cartoons. Eventually the family moved to Kansas City and he took art classes at the Kansas City Art Institute. Along with his artistic bent, the young Disney became well-known for his story-telling ability and would, with the teacher's approval, tell stories in class while providing illustrations on the chalk board. In 1917 the family moved to Chicago after Elias bought a jelly factory. Walt began attending McKinley High School and taking night courses at the Chicago Art Institute.

When Walt was sixteen-years old the United States entered the First World War. In the fall of 1918, he attempted to enlist into the service, but was denied because he was underage. Undeterred, Disney joined the Red Cross and was sent to France. He was assigned to drive an ambulance. He decorated his ambulance with drawings of characters he created. It was while in France that Walt picked up the terrible habit that would eventually destroy his health—cigarette smoking. He became a life-long chain smoker.

Walt Disney at the Drawing Board.

When he returned to the United States, Walt had plans of being a political cartoonist. He was rebuffed in his efforts, and so he went into commercial art and began producing short animated black and white films in Kansas City, but the company soon went bankrupted. He later produced "The Alice Comedies" which was an innovative combination of live-action and animation about a little girl and her cat who have adventures in an animated world. These films proved successful and soon they received orders for more "Alice" featurettes from around the country. Walt, and his brother Roy, moved to California where they opened their first studio—in the rear of a Hollywood real estate office. Roy Disney was instrumental from these earlier days in helping Walt achieve his goals. He handled the business end while Walt was the innovator and creator. "I used to sleep in the same bed with my big brother, Roy," Walt once recalled to a studio employee named Charley Levy, "and I used to wet the bed. I've been pissing up his leg ever since."

The studio slowly grew thanks to the "Alice comedies" and in 1925; Walt married one of his employees, Lillian Bounds. Eventually they had two daughters, Diane and Sharon, who was adopted. It was in 1927, after the "Alice Comedies" had concluded, that Walt created and introduced a new animated character named Osgood the Lucky Rabbit. The Osgood character in fact looks a great deal like the character that Walt would soon introduce and become internationally famous—Mickey Mouse (actually Walt initially named him Mortimer, but Lillian suggested Mickey instead)—except with large rabbit-like ears. Osgood was produced for Universal Pictures and proved very popular. Walt soon asked Universal for an increase in the budget for the Osgood cartoons, but was turned down; in fact, Walt was rudely told that Universal owned Osgood and instead of an increase they wanted a budget cut of twenty-percent. Disney soon disassociated himself from Universal and along with his friend and animator, Ub Iwerks, they created Mickey Mouse—which was owned by Disney himself.

The first Mickey Mouse cartoon, *Plane Crazy*, was made as a silent cartoon, but sound in films was in demand, so the Disney's decided to make Mickey Mouse's film debut in the first synchronized sound cartoon, *Steamboat Willie*, which was released at the Colony Theatre in New York City on November 18, 1928. The cartoon—and Mickey—created a sensation. Mickey would become the symbol of the Disney Studio and Walt once famously said, "I have never loved anything more than that mouse." Walt saw Mickey as a Chaplinesque character—the everyman as a mouse. In fact, it can be stated that the two most popular characters in films at this time were Charlie Chaplin and Mickey Mouse.

The years ahead proved daunting and successful. Walt was an innovator in the use of color in his cartoons and created a series called "Silly Symphonies Cartoon Features." In addition to the popular Mickey Mouse cartoons he also created new characters such as Pluto, Goofy and Donald Duck. The quick-tempered duck would soon rival and then overcome Mickey Mouse in global popularity by the late 1930s. In 1932, the Disney Studio release of *Flowers and Trees* won the studio its first Academy Award. Also proving popular was the studios 1933 release of the Silly Symphony cartoon, *The Three Little Pigs.*

Next, Walt wanted to do what many thought was impossible—create the first animated feature film. Most people tried to dissuade Walt, telling him that nobody would sit for over an hour watching a cartoon. Walt felt differently and went on to make *Snow White and the Seven Dwarfs,* which cost the studio nearly $1.5 million—almost bankrupting them. When it was released on December 21, 1937, it proved to be a blockbuster. This led to other classic animated features: *Pinocchio, Fantasia, Dumbo* and *Bambi.*

With the success of the Disney Studio, Walt and Roy brought their parents out to California and set them up in a house. A terrible tragedy struck that remained with Walt for the rest of his life—his mother accidentally died from asphyxiation due to a bad furnace in the new home. Walt felt terrible guilt and agony over this.

In 1940, the Disneys opened a brand new studio located in Burbank and by this time the studio staff had increased to more than 1000. However, during the War years (1942-1945) most of the studio operations were geared towards war work with the studio producing training films and propaganda films for the US government. They also produced goodwill cartoons which were distributed throughout the world by the State Department. One was the 1945 feature, *The Three Caballeros,* which was yet another innovation of live-action and animation.

Prior to the war, a situation involving the studio and labor came to a head. In the thirties there had come a rise of several unions in Hollywood, such as the Screen Actors Guild and guilds which looked out for the interests of writers, directors and others in the industry. Soon animators wanted to get unionized. Warner Brothers, which operated the very popular Looney Tunes cartoons featuring Bugs Bunny, Daffy Duck and others, soon was unionized as were such others in the industry including those associated with Walter Lantz (Woody Woodpecker) and MGM (Tom and Jerry). But Disney tried to withstand. It's not that his animators were unappreciated—in fact, Disney was known for paying the best wages in the business to his animators. Despite the huge success of *Snow White,* the animators got no bonuses and were faced with lay-offs. The resources it took to produce that film was hitting the studio hard despite the money it was bringing in. The costs of making animated features were astronomical.

A strike was called. *Dumbo* was then in production. Disney bitterly resented it and fought it. The strike lasted five weeks and eventually was settled with the help of a federal mediator, which decided most issues in favor of the guild. The Disney studio was unionized. One consequence of the strike was Walt's changing political views. Prior to the strike he was considered moderately liberal, but after the strike he moved increasingly to the right on the political spectrum.

The post-war years saw the studio edging closer to live-action as opposed to strictly animated films, in addition to those that combined animation and live-action such as *Song of the South* and *So Dear to My Heart*. There were classic animated features such as *Cinderella,* but in 1950, the Studio released its first full-length live-action film not to feature animation—*Treasure Island.* During the war many Disney films were released in England and proved very popular and made a good deal of money. But the British government wouldn't allow the money made in England to be used anywhere except in England, so Disney (like other studios) began to make films in England using this surplus money. *Treasure Island* was the first and was followed over the next few years by *The Story of Robin Hood, The Sword and the Rose* and *Rob Roy-The Highland Rouge.* Meanwhile the studio made more animated features including *Peter Pan, Alice in Wonderland* (which proved disappointing at the box office) and *Lady and the Tramp.* They also continued with a series of "true life" wilderness films which proved exceptionally popular such as *The Living Desert* and *The Vanishing Prairie.*

By the mid-1950s many motion picture studios realized that television was here to stay and began selling many of their older films to TV to make an extra profit. Disney, on the other hand, felt that many of his classics could be re-released in theatres and make millions more. For example, *Twenty-Thousand Leagues Under the Sea* brought in $6.5 million in its initial release in 1954. When it was re-released in 1963 the film brought in another $2.5 million. *Snow White* grossed another $2.75 million on its *fourth* re-issue and the third time *Bambi* was released it brought in more money than its first two releases *combined.* However, when some Disney films demonstrated that they were not strong commercially in their first release they would usually be shown within a couple of years on the Disney television show. But as a rule one of the classic Disney animated or live-action films would be held back and re-released in theatres for a new generation to enjoy—to additional profits.

By this time, much of Walt's time and effort was moving away from the production end to establishing his dream of a family friendly theme park—Disneyland. To help finance this $17 million dream he needed to get a network of donors. Among those was the ABC television network, which agreed to partner with Walt on the theme park if he would help the fledging network by supplying programs. This led to Disney on TV and the weekly *Disneyland* TV-series, which introduced the phenomenal *Davy Crockett* and the popular children's series, *The Mickey Mouse Club*.

By the late fifties the studio was producing popular live-action films like *Old Yeller* and *The Shaggy Dog,* which Walt discovered cost less and brought in more than some of their animated films—especially after the lackluster box office performance of *Sleeping Beauty* in 1959. "We're through with caviar," Walt once declared of the days when expensive animated films like *Snow White, Fantasia, Dumbo* and *Bambi* ruled the studio output. "From now on it's mashed potatoes and gravy." The studio moved increasingly to modestly budgeted family dramas and slapstick comedies with the occasional blockbuster, especially *Mary Poppins* (1964) which was the most successful film the studio had ever produced and one of the most successful both critically and financially of the decade—and one that Walt spent decades wanting to make (more on that later).

In 1962, Hollis Alpert in *Woman's Day* described Walt's average work day:

> "Nothing makes him as happy as his work. He's up at six each morning and at his Burbank, California studio by eight-thirty. He makes a round of the stages where movie and filmed television shows are in production, visits the animation department where shorts take six months and a cartoon feature takes five years to finish, and spends most of the remainder of the day in his office where he has the final word on everything the studio does…Writers, directors, and production associates stream in for a continual round of conferences. His working day is finished at seven. Disney heads home for a quiet evening with his family, now augmented by several grandchildren of whom he is enormously fond and proud. An unostentatious man, he sums up the components of his success in four words—curiosity, confidence, courage and constancy."

Walt and friends.

One anonymous associate said of Walt, "He is the best compartment-ed man I've ever met. Walt can go into a meeting and discuss a true life adventure film, leave that to look over a scale model for a new Disneyland addition, go off to talk over the story line for a full length feature, spend most of the day on different projects. He can come back to a similar series of conferences a week or so later and take up each meeting at the precise point where it left off on his previous visit."

By the mid-sixties Walt was consumed with yet another innovative project—a mammoth 43 square miles of land in the center of the state of Florida where he wanted to produce a "Disney World" which would include a theme park, hotels and an Experimental Prototype Community of Tomorrow. By 1966 (he began the year as Grand Marshal of the Tournament of Roses Parade), Walt was 64 years old and his health was declining. An old polo injury had given him discomfort and pain for years and people around the studio could always hear Walt approaching due to a constant cough that seemed to grow worse as time went by—but Walt did nothing to cut down on his cigarette smoking. He seldom took vacations and got his greatest joy in work. His joy now was building Disney World. He would still be a presence at the studio and approve scripts and give input, but by and large the studio operations were taken over by others.

Walt also was instrumental in the development of the California Institute of Art, a college-level professional school of creative and performing arts. He held fundraisers for Cal-Arts and pigeon-holed friends and acquaintances to make contributions.

In late November 1966, Walt was admitted to St. Joseph Hospital, situated right across the street from the Burbank studio, for what had been announced as surgery to alleviate the pain caused by his old polo injury. However, x-rays showed a spot on one of Disney's lungs and an operation was ordered almost immediately. It was cancer. The lung was removed. The doctors confided to Lillian that they felt that at most he had from 6 to 18-months to live. She decided that Walt shouldn't know. He was of the opinion that he would recover. He got hope when John Wayne sent a telegram which said: WELCOME TO THE CLUB. In 1964, Wayne, too, had a cancerous lung removed and he now seemed fine and was hard at work making one picture after another.

After being released from the hospital Walt was seen around the studio. To many who saw him he looked like a dying man—weak and shriveled and his voice barely above a raspy whisper. A few days later he and Lillian flew to Palm Springs so that he could regain his strength in the heat of the desert. He had a relapse and a plane flew him back to Burbank. He re-entered the hospital and never left. Walt Disney, to the shock and sadness of the world, died on December 15, 1966. He was only 65 years of age.

In 2001, on the centennial of Walt Disney's birth, the *New York Times* wrote in an editorial:

And if Walt were still living in our world, he would have been 100 yesterday. He belongs in the company of 20th-century Americans like John Wayne and Ronald Reagan, whose sentimentalized versions of this nation have been profoundly influential, creating a portrait of American history and values so clear-cut as to make the actual history and values of America look incoherent.

What influence the man still had that 35 years after his death his life is still remembered and his influence is still felt.

Walt on Walt

I formed my work patterns early in life. At first I worked on my father's farm, and then I delivered newspapers in Kansas City for my father, who was a dealer. At 15 I was a news butcher on trains that ran to Colorado and all over. At 16 I was a night watchman in a jelly factory in Chicago.

I had to get up at 3:30 every morning. The paper had to be stuck behind the storm doors. You couldn't just toss them on the porch. And in the winters there'd be as much as three feet of snow. I was a little guy and I was up to my nose in snow. I still have nightmares about it. What I really liked on those cold mornings was getting to the apartment buildings. I'd drop off the papers and then lie down in the warm apartment corridor and snooze a little and try to get warm. I still wake up with that on my mind. On nice mornings I used to come to houses with those big old porches and the kids would have left some of their toys out. I would find them and play with them there on the porch at 4 in the morning when it was just barely getting light. Then I'd have to tear back to the route again.

I wanted to draw. The thing I wanted most was to be a political cartoonist. My father fancied himself as kind of a socialist, and he subscribed to socialist newspapers of the time. I studied their cartoons and tried to copy the style. After I got back from the war in 1919, I tried to get a job cartooning for the *Kansas City Star*. The editor liked my samples, but the paper already had a political cartoonist. I thought there must have been a better way to make cartoons, so I went to the public library and asked for all the books they had about cartooning. I found a better method.

If you keep busy, your work might lead you into paths you might not expect. I've always operated like the princes of serendip, who went on quests not knowing what they would find. That happens in science; some of our most important discoveries have come from scientists who were searching for something else.

I've always had a great deal of natural curiosity. Whenever I was curious about something I'd go to the library and ask for all the books they had on that subject. I'd read about everything, and then I'd ask questions from people who were experts in their field. When I started making cartoon films, I asked the older artists how they did things. Some of them didn't want to give me any secrets of their trade, but most of them gave me all the help I needed. I do the same thing today. If I'm curious about something, I pick up the phone and call someone who knows about it. I always get an answer. You'd be surprised how nice people can be when you show them you're really interested.

A person should set his goals as early as he can and devote all his energy and talent to getting there. With enough effort, he may achieve it. Or he may find something that is even more rewarding. But in the end, no matter what the outcome, he will know he has been alive.

Hell, I'm Disney, and I don't know (what a Disney picture is). I've produced every type of picture except sick ones. The truth of the matter is I try to make movies to please my own family. We don't aim at children specifically. When does any person stop being part child?

I am just an entertainer. I don't pretend to know about art. I make pictures for entertainment and then the psychologists tell me what they mean.

Always when I finished a picture, there was something final about it. I had to reach an end some time and send it out. I hate to see it again because I always find things I would like to do better.

I really don't concern myself too much with how the pictures do. Most of my thinking is two years ahead.

There is no way of pleasing everybody. I get squawks over almost everything we do. A lot of people were even unhappy over our treatment of "The Three Little Pigs." In the old fairytale the wolf ate them up. We put a happy ending on it. Many people didn't approve.

I don't like depressing pictures. I don't like pestholes. I don't like pictures that are dirty. I don't ever go out and pay money for studies in abnormality. I don't have depressed moods and I don't want to have any. I'm happy, just very happy.

My feeling is that picture makers make the kind of films they like themselves, that they are attracted to certain themes. I, myself, I just can't stand a downbeat story. I don't like to come out of the theatre feeling like

I want to cut my throat. I like to come out smiling, feeling happy. I like to see comedies. Tennessee Williams is not for me. That's not to say it isn't art. It's great art, but it's not for me.

I don't make films exclusively for children. I make them to suit myself, hoping that they will also suit the audience. The biggest grossers of all time have been pictures like *Gone with the Wind, Ben Hur, The Ten Commandments, Snow White, The Best Years of Our Lives*—so don't let anyone tell you that the public is sex-obsessed, because it is not. Of the pictures coming up, not one will have a downbeat theme. I've proved, at least to myself and our stockholders, that we can make money, lots of money, by turning out wholesome entertainment. My belief is that there are more people in America who want to smile than those who want to be artistically depressed.

All we are trying to give the pubic is good entertainment—that is all they want.

We have an organization of young men to whom nothing is impossible. We have licked every mechanical difficulty that our medium has presented. But one fear is constantly before us. The fear that our next effort will not be regarded by the public as highly as the last.

I don't go for that sloppy kissing in films. It's like watching one of those French peep shows. We have kissin' in our pictures—but only if there's a reason for it.

Our part in things is to build along the lines we are known for, with happy family stories and comedies. I've never thought of this as art. It's part of show business.

Producers too often are afraid to take a chance on new people because they want the insurance of recognized names. We've got to gamble more.

We like to have a point of view in our stories, not an obvious moral, but a worthwhile theme.

I can't laugh at intellectual humor. I'm just corny enough to like to have a story hit me over the heart.

All right. I'm corny. But I think there's just about a-hundred-and-forty-million people in this country that are just as corny as I am.

There's enough ugliness and cynicism in the world without me adding to it.

There's no magic to my formula. I just make what I like—good, human stories in which you can get with people and which prove that the better things of life can be as interesting as the sordid things.

I try to make happy, humorous pictures. Humor is a sort of international sixth sense. It makes life, with its intolerable burdens, tolerable. Often, I think humor is the closest of all human bonds.

I believe in the worthwhileness of the entertainment of the masses. My operations are always based on experience, thoughtful observation and warm fellowship with my neighbors at home and around the world.

We've got to make it more comfortable for people to go to the theater—as well as give them good pictures. Many theaters still have the same seats they had when I started in the business. Many of them have no air conditioning. They've got to gear to the jet age.

I am a patient listener, but opinionated to the point of stubbornness when my mind is made up.

I don't get ulcers. I give them.

"Childishness? I think it's the equivalent of never losing your sense of humor. I mean, there's a certain something that you retain. It's the equivalent of not getting so stuffy that you can't laugh at others."

One of the things I want to do is make a picture that shows the good side of teen-agers. I get so put out with all these pictures about delinquency. I thought that one about Marlon Brando and the motorcycles (*The Wild One*) was bad, and *The Blackboard Jungle* upset me for three days afterward. I think those pictures are a mistake. After all, 'monkey see, monkey do' kids get bad ideas when they see such things on the screen. And I don't think they show a true picture of the young people today. All in all, I think kids are a good bunch. There are some bad ones, but there always have been. I remember when I was a kid in Kansas City, a bunch of kids were breaking into houses and storing loot in the cellar of an unfinished church. The difference nowadays is that you always hear about such things. Everybody reads the papers, has a radio and TV set and goes to the movies: In my youth, the only communication was the newspaper…I don't want anything that preaches to kids about how to be good. I've had them take such things out of *The Mickey Mouse Club*, too, except for little things like 'words to grow by.' Preaching won't keep kids out of trouble. But keeping their minds occupied will.

Kids are too idle nowadays. Their parents don't think it's good for them to work when they're young, but that's a mistake. They have too much leisure, and they don't know what to do with it. I worked hard as a youngster, but knew how to enjoy myself, too. When I did get some leisure I used it to the utmost.

The American child is a highly intelligent human being — characteristically sensitive, humorous, open-minded, eager to learn, and has a strong sense of excitement, energy, and healthy curiosity about the world in which he lives. Lucky indeed is the grown-up who manages to carry these same characteristics into adult life. It usually makes for a happy and successful individual. In our full-length cartoon features, as well as in our live action productions, we have tried to convey in story and song those virtues that make both children and adults attractive. I have long felt that the way to keep children out of trouble is to keep them interested in things. Lecturing to children is no answer to delinquency. Preaching won't keep youngsters out of trouble, but keeping their minds occupied will.

I'm against censorship. I think we've progressed beyond that, in books and movies and all forms of expression. I don't think some small group of individuals should have the power to say what the citizens of a town can read and see. I believe the movie business can still function well by censoring its own product. I'm in favor of pressure groups, like the religious organizations, keeping an eye on what we do. They're a healthy influence. But outside censorship would be bad.

I agree that the American public wants sex in its movies, and I am in favor of sex. After all, I have five grandchildren. Where would they be if we didn't have sex? The point is that a large segment, maybe the largest segment of the American public, wants wholesome sex. It also wants humor, mystery and adventure.

I've done a lot of thinking about a model community—a city of tomorrow. I believe people still like to live like human beings. The automobile has moved into communities too much. We need to put people back as pedestrians. I'd love to work on a project like that. And I'd love to be part of building a school of tomorrow.

People who have worked with me say I am 'innocence in action.' They say I have the unself-consciousness of a child. Maybe I have. I still look at the world with uncontaminated wonder, and with all living things I have terrific sympathy.

I've got a lot of ideas. I haven't worked them out and I haven't proved them out. I can carry ideas around in my head for a long time.

When we do fantasy, we must not lose sight of reality.

I suppose my formula might be: dream, diversify and never miss an angle.

I feel what's wrong—there's been too much of me. I have been a slave driver…I sometimes feel like a slave drive the way I pound, pound, pound.

I'm never so filled up with my work that it causes me loss of sleep. I sleep like a baby. Once in a while, of course, such as before an important preview, I may stay awake and wonder how it's going to go over. But that's pretty rare.

Everybody can make their dreams come true. It takes a dream, faith in it and hard work. Yet, the work isn't all that hard because it's so much fun you hardly think of it as work.

In the last ten years we've gone into three big businesses—the feature field, the amusement park field and TV. If it were just animated cartoons, it'd be a cinch. This organization can't retire with me! I've gotta get it going so that it won't need me.

Some of us just wouldn't be satisfied with just carrying out a routine job and being happy. Yet I envied those people. I had a brother who I really envied because he was a mailman. But he's the one that had all the fun. He had himself a trailer, and he used to go out and go fishing, and he didn't worry about payrolls and stories and picture grosses or anything. And he was the happy one. I always said, 'He's the smart Disney.'

I don't even want to be President of the United States; I'd rather be the benevolent dictator of Disney Enterprises. I count my blessings every morning.

2

Encounters with and Thoughts about Walt

Julie Andrews: *He was a charming man with a twinkling personality, and he put in an enormous number of hours at his studio each week. Among all of his skills, one of his great talents was an almost phenomenal ability for picking nice people to work with. His studio had a special charm-it still does-and at first, you'd go there slightly cynical because of all the cartoons and fairy tales he'd produced, but once you were there you discovered that it was filled with nice people who were all very dedicated to Walt and to doing a good job. They made me feel very comfortable.*

Ken Annakin (director): *Walt was a great guy to work with, a great creator. As we now know with the books that have been written about him, right from the first he didn't regard himself as the greatest artist, but he could get other artists to produce ideas that he had. That's how he got started, and that's how he carried on once he had his studio and had his team around him.*

Of all the studio chiefs I have ever worked with, I have never known anyone who operated at conferences so magnificently as Walt. You would go into a story session with him, full of great ideas, and he would scratch his nose and say, 'This is just from the top of my head, but I think we should do this and this...' And it would usually be like listening to a new fairy tale, and we would break up the session happy and amazed that the solution to our story problems should be so simple—and different.

Harry Carey, Jr.: The first time I met Walt Disney was a great experience. A friend of mine was a script supervisor and used to be a stunt man. He called me up and says, 'Dobie, they are going to do a show at Disney called *Spin and Marty'*. He told me the story—it was about a kid's ranch where they are looking for a football player type of guy—but he thought it would work better if it was cowboy type. My pal later told me that he told the casting people at Disney that I was a 'good cowboy but a lousy actor.' But they said, 'send him over anyway!'

I go over to the studio and do a test with Tim Considine, who played Spin. I thought it went pretty well, but didn't expect to hear anything for a few days—so I went home. An hour later the phone rang and I was told that I got the part—they DID like the cowboy type better than the football

Walt on the *Spin and Marty* set with Harry Carey, Jr. on the left.

type. I was told that Disney, himself, was on the set and hired me on the spot. He didn't need to see any film because he liked what he saw with his own eyes. I hadn't even known he was on the set! He must have been somewhere in the back because I couldn't see him –and nobody referred to him. Hell, he probably didn't want to make me nervous.

I never did get to know him well at all. When I did run into him he was a very friendly man and very easy going. Some have written that he was wicked and a racist and whatever, but I never saw any of that. He never did visit the set too often. Oh, he might drop in once in a while, but as a rule—No. I mean he had a big studio to run and we were just a little television program, and he was supervising a great many things at the time—including Disneyland which had just opened.

Jonathan Daly: One day many years ago I had the honor of chatting with Mr. Disney himself as he strolled around the grounds of his studio which he referred to as 'The Campus." He and I bemoaned the violence and tasteless sex in movies. He influenced me with that conversation so much that I recalled our chat often as I wrote my plays and subsequent screen-plays. Walt was gracious and he built my favorite studio at which to work because he actually cared about creative people more than most.

James Drury: Walt Disney would come out on the studio grounds every single day and greet everybody from the animators to the guys who swept up the horse crap. He'd go on every set and know everybody's name. We wondered how the heck he was able to remember everybody's name—but he did. He was well loved and respected by those who worked for him.

Annette Funicello: *Mr. Disney knows what he wants and it turns out that's what the people want too.*

Eddie Hodges: One day my agent called and said that the Disney Studios were looking for a boy to play a Rebel soldier, Billy, in a TV-program based on the book, *The Drummer Boy of Shiloh*. They wanted to meet me and see if I would be interested. The project starred Kevin Corcoran as Johnny Shiloh and I was selected for the role. I met Mr. Disney one day and I was very excited. Soon, my agent said the Disney Studio felt that I would fit the role of Hayley Mills' brother in their upcoming project based on the book, *Mother Carey's Chickens*. I jumped at the chance to work for

Mr. Disney, or Uncle Walt, as we called him, because he was really down to earth and very nice to me.

Before I met Mr. Disney, I asked people what he was like. One said, 'He's as natural as an old shoe.' That put me at ease. He was always dressed comfortably—if you didn't know who he was, you wouldn't know he was important by looking at his clothes. He didn't' talk much, but kind of stayed off to the side. But, if he stepped forward and made a comment or suggestion or something, it was tended to immediately. He never made a big splash anywhere he went. I never saw him walk onto a sound stage and never saw him leave. That was a little eerie—he was a bit of a ghost that way. You always felt his presence, though—like he was a partner that was always there in spirit. I think he was concerned that his movies always reflected his sense of decency and morality. He did not like anything that was at all risqué in films, unless it was very mild, in good taste and never offensive. I respected that.

Marta Kristen: I auditioned for the role of Lisbeth in *Savage Sam.* The person to make the final decision about whether I was to play the part was, of course, Walt Disney. I met him at an arranged lunch along with the director, Norman Tokar, and a few of the other executives involved in the production. I was very nervous and could barely eat anything. I remember vividly, however, when I finally did put fork to mouth, Mr. Disney asked me a question and I started to choke. I was mortified! Once I had recovered, Mr. Disney was lovely, asking if I was alright, and continued talking to me as if nothing happened. I could have jumped up and given him a big hug, but then I was a polite MidWestern girl, and I would never have done such a thing.

Karl Malden: Disney didn't ask for much. He trusted filmmakers and the actors. He tried to get the best and, when he did, he let them do their work without much interference. I did one six-minute speech in one take (for *Pollyanna)*, and the next day, after he had seen the rushes, Disney came out to me and asked if I wanted a 16mm print of the film because of what I had done! Of course! And he delivered.

Michael McGreevey: Every day Walt Disney visited the set of every show shooting on the lot. If you were on location, he didn't usually show up, but I can recall several times seeing Uncle Walt (that's what he wanted you to call him) out at the Disney ranch. He would always stand off to the

Pretty Marta Kristen co-starred in *Savage Sam* (1963).

side and never intrude on the production. He'd just watch the shooting for a while, and then quietly slip away. I never officially met Mr. Disney. I never auditioned for him. But I did spend time with him—playing ping-pong. There were two ping-pong tables next to the commissary and I would always play after lunch. One day, Walt showed up and I played him. He occasionally would come by and we would play and talk. I never beat him—but I tried like hell and came close a few times. Years later, Kurt Russell told me that he had the same experience with Mr. Disney. Kurt claims that he beat Walt Disney at ping-pong, but I don't believe him.

Hayley Mills: *I seem to remember I was taken out of school in order to meet him. I was well aware of who he was of course, and I was thrilled at the idea, although I only knew vaguely at the time he was interested in me for a film. It happened that we had recently been given a very small and sleazy Pekingese called Suky by Vivien Leigh. She had given it to Mummy because it peed all over her carpets, and it peed all over our carpets, too. In our case, it just joined a lot of other dogs that were doing the same thing, so it really didn't matter. So I took this dog along with us and I met Walt Disney, who was lovely, very kind and very calm, and we spent most of the time on the carpet playing with the dog. My parents must have been terrified that he would start peeing there, too, but fortunately on this occasion he didn't. Then he showed us the sights of London from his balcony, served some champagne, and began talking to my parents. I didn't take much notice of that because, I suppose, it was all above my head. But shortly afterward, I learned I was going to Hollywood to play in* Pollyanna.

John Mills: *Walt Disney, apart from being a genius, was one of the most charming, immediately likeable men I have ever met. His enthusiasm for anything he was concerned with was enormous.*

Pola Negri: *Mr. Disney was a truly wonderful gentleman, fully aware of what I was going through and responding to my situation with warmth and sympathy…I was still hesitant to make a commitment. "To go through all that again—Mr. Disney, I don't think I have the strength." "I'll take the responsibility for making things easier for you," he responded. "If you come to London, you won't have to do anything but give your performance. I did and he was true to his word. It was a wonderful experience.*

Suzanne Pleshette: *I was just insane about him (Disney) and everybody thought we'd hate each other because I'm somewhat bawdy. On the first day of filming The Ugly Dachshund, I had to fall in the water during the party scene. So I said, ingenuously, 'Is it all right to have tits at Disney?' meaning, when I go in the water should I come up facing the camera or with my back to the camera because I was dressed in a white blouse. Walt had walked on the set and everyone was silent, thinking I was gonna be fired. Then Walt said, 'Yes! It's all right. Face the camera!' In another scene, the script said I had to fight with Dean and then start to cry. I said, 'My character wouldn't do that! She would kiss him and tease him to get her way.' Walt asked, 'What do you want to do?' I said, 'I wanna kiss and tease him.' 'You know,' he said, 'I can date the fall of the morality of the Studio to the day you walked on the lot."*

Peter Renaday: I had very little contact with Walt. But, by coincidence, on my first day on the lot as I was walking into the animation building (wondering if I would ever get to see Walt Disney in person), the first person I saw walking toward me was Walt! I had already been told that everyone is on first name basis, but I couldn't bring myself to say, 'Good morning, Walt!'—so I just gulped out, 'Good morning!' He returned the greeting, and—I think it was another month before I saw him again. He impressed me as being a man with a lot on his mind—friendly, but pre-occupied. (Later when I started appearing in plays with the Disney players—an amateur theatrical group made up of Disney employees—Walt would come backstage after the shows to greet the cast. I guess that was how he learned who I was!).

I did—almost—run into Walt in an unexpected place. There's a tunnel leading from the basement in the Animation Building under the street to the Ink and Paint Building. It was used to transport cells to Ink and Paint in rainy weather. We messengers used it to keep the office mail dry. The ramp from the basement to Ink and Paint had a switchback turn halfway through it. If the light was turned off, the ramp was pitch-black. One day I decided to see just how dark it would be. I turned off the switch in the basement and started feeling my way up the ramp. I had gone a few feet when I heard two people slowly feeling their way DOWN from the ramp from Ink and Paint. A very familiar voice was grumbling, 'Who the hell turned off the lights?' Fortunately for me, by the time Walt and his companion got to the bottom of the ramp and turned the lights back on, I had made the turn and escaped unseen. I might have had a very short career at Disney!

Suzanne Pleshette with Dean Jones in a scene from *The Ugly Dachshund*
© Walt Disney Productions

Larri Thomas: Walt Disney was on the lot a great deal—and he visited the set (of *Mary Poppins*) quite often. It was unusual for the studio head to do this—usually they were hidden away in their offices, but Disney liked walking around and he knew exactly what was happening on the set. When the boss came on the set it wasn't like at other studios where the crew acted as if the principal had entered the classroom—usually people would freeze, but not with Walt Disney. It was very relaxed and people enjoyed Disney and he enjoyed talking with the cast and crew. I hate to use the "F" word but the Disney Studios did have a family atmosphere. Dancers are usually at the bottom of the totem pole in Hollywood, but Walt Disney treated everybody at the studio as part of the Disney family—including us. I'll never forget in October 1966 when my daughter was born I was sent beautiful flowers with the Disney characters (Mickey Mouse, Donald Duck, Pluto) arranged around the basket along with a note for my new baby from Walt saying, "Welcome to the family." She was my daughter but because I was part of the Disney family (I continued to do films at the studio like *The Happiest Millionaire*—after *Mary Poppins*),

Peter Renaday (photo courtesy of Mr. Renaday).

so too was my daughter part of the Disney family. Then—just the following month—he died.

Dick Van Dyke: *Walt's great to work for. Nobody else gets into fantasy but Disney. He makes his own world, like Laurel and Hardy used to do, and everybody accepts it. He sets the rules and audiences are captivated by them.*

Dick Warlock (stuntman): I think it was around 1964 or 5 that I was called by Dick Ivey, one of the casting directors, to show up one morning at the Disney lot. I reported and was told to go to the wardrobe department. When I walked in the place was set up with a desk, an office background, camera, lights, etc. I thought to myself, I must be in the wrong place and I started to leave when a man hollered to me, "Are you Dick Warlock?" I said yes and he came up and told me that I was indeed in the right place. The man was Art Vitarelli. He was the director of this segment we would do for *Disney's Wonderful World of Color*. The show that this piece was being done for was called "Willy and the Yank" starring Kurt Russell.

The next thing I remember was being led over to the desk where sitting on the edge was Mr. Disney. Now I had watched this man for years on T.V. and here I was standing there being introduced to him. He was very gracious and I felt like I was talking to my dad. I was told what the scene was and we began the rehearsal. The camera was on Mr. Disney and as he starts to explain the upcoming show the camera pans off of him and around to me where I am in front of the wardrobe department counter putting on a rebel uniform hat. His dialog was, 'How can you make a man out of a 16 year old boy' and then he explains what the show is about... After the first rehearsal he called me over to him. He looked me in the eye and said, "Now you aren't going to upstage me are you?" I smiled, looked him the eye and winked as I said; "Would I do that" then I turned and went back to my start mark. We got the shot, I said my thanks and goodbyes and left.

By the time I arrived back at Mr. Ivey's office there had been a message sent to him to get everything he could get on me in the way of information about myself. I had no idea until about eight years later that Mr. Disney had told Mr. Vitarelli that he was going to make a star out of me. Yes, that's what he said. Mr. Vitarelli said that once Mr. Disney had passed away he was reluctant to tell me as it would serve no purpose because the powers to be at the studio at that time didn't feel the same way. As he sat

Dick Van Dyke starred in three Disney films in the 1960's.

me down in his office one day and told me the story he said he thought that I should know how that meeting with Mr. Disney might have turned out for me. I was thrilled that Mr. Disney thought of me in that way after such a short time together. However, I guess I was on a list someplace because I stayed there for nearly ten years. Mr. Vitarelli, or Art as came to know him, became a mentor and friend to me in so many ways.

Jan Williams (producer): I grew up in a home where I was born a half mile from the Disney Studio. I spent my summers on Catalina Island where I had a paper route, dove for coins when the steamer came in and finally got a paying job at Joe's Rent-a-Boat on the pleasure pier for twenty-five cents an hour. When I graduated from John Burroughs High in Burbank in 1962 I went to a number of different schools looking for my self. I studied art, restaurant management, business, radio announcing and, then, in the summer of 1963 my father got me a job delivering mail at Disney Studios. My father, Warren Williams, had been hired by Walt in 1937 to design and paint the titles for *Snow White*. Up to that point the animators had always done the titles but for the big feature, Walt wanted a pro and he had seen some of my father's orange crate designs and hired him for a seven week job. Dad designed the titles for all the features up until the point Disney went on television, the work-load grew and my dad found he had a title department to run. My dad stayed at the studio until he retired in 1974.

I went back and forth between various schools and various jobs at Disney. I worked the Disneyland Records warehouse across the street from the studio, I wrote liner notes for the albums released by that company. I did radio commercial voice-overs, pretty much what I could find to keep me busy.   I had been delivering mail for about a month and I was on the third floor, Walt's floor, when I was getting on the elevator and I heard a voice call out, 'hold that car!' I turned, it was Walt. He got on. I was dumbstruck. He turned and said, 'You're Warren's boy aren't you?' I gulped and told him that I was. The car hit the bottom floor—the door opened and as Walt walked out he turned and said, 'Welcome aboard.' After that I would see him occasionally on sets or at his house where, when I was in school, I had a night watchman job—keeping an eye on things during a massive remodel. I remember when I was in Traffice (the mail room), and I would get 'the money run' on a Friday afternoon. If Mac, the head of Traffice, called your name you headed out to accounting at the far corner of the lot and went up to the front desk and told them you were there for Walt. The gal would hand you an envelope which you took directly to Walt's office and handed to Walt's secretary, Lucielle. It was exciting because you never knew if you would see Walt or someone coming or going at his office. I never looked but was told the envelope contained a couple of hundred dollars, all brand new twenties, Walt loved new money.

Alan Young: My first association with the Disney organization was in 1955 when I appeared on the nationally televised live program the day

Disneyland opened. Well, it was amazing! I never saw anything like it. There was me, Art Linkletter, Ronald Reagan, Bob Cummings and all kinds of people making reports. It was thrilling. I never saw so many people—there were tens of thousands of people in the park on that opening day. It was done live so there were the usual technical flubs that went into that endeavor, but I was just amazed by the view—all the people and what Walt had created. Despite doing that program I didn't actually meet Walt Disney until years later. I was hot for a month and a half in the early fifties and had done a show which had been successful called *The Alan Young Show* and even got an Emmy for it. But as the years went by the writing fell off and we ran out of ideas and by the late fifties I was asked to come and see Walt Disney about a film role. I went to Walt's office at the studio and he told me that he decided to go with somebody else, but he still wanted to meet me because he had been a fan of my work—and that was that. The film was *The Shaggy Dog*, and the role of the postman/ dad went to Fred MacMurray—and it turned out to be a big hit.

Alan Young.

3

First Impressions of the Studio

Peter Brown: Walt Disney requested me from Warner Brothers, where I was under contract, to do *Summer Magic*, so I was loaned out after I agreed to do the film. Who wouldn't want to work for Walt Disney? Oddly enough I have a partner in my film company here in Phoenix whose name is Chuck Disney—his grandfather and Walt were brothers. I remember the first time driving onto the Disney lot, and going in for a wardrobe fitting. First, the guard at the gate looked at me and said, 'Good Morning, Mr. Brown, if you will follow the yellow-brick road painted in front of you it will lead you to your parking place which has your name on it. There will be a pretty girl waiting there to escort you to your dressing room.' I thanked him and drove to the pretty girl, who then escorted me to my room, which had a brass star with my name engraved on it mounted on the door. No cardboard one, but Brass! I thanked the pretty girl and went to my room—correction, my suite! On the bar was everything I was drinking at the time—good red wine, rum, and Coke, fresh limes and snacks, cheeses, crackers and a couple of bottles of chilled champagne. Whatta welcome! Someone had done their homework. There was even a personal note from Walt welcoming me to the Disney family.

Harry Carey, Jr: One thing I'll say for the Disney Studio is that there was less angst and stress—unlike some of the other big studios. You just didn't see that much of it. I think the reason for it came from the top. Disney had a relaxed presence around the lot and there wasn't somebody constantly looking at the clock. It was just very relaxed. I liked that.

David Frankham: Other studios were like concrete—one concrete building after another, but there was a hum of creativity through the Disney studios back then. You could hear the birds singing.

Annette Funicello: *Not too many years ago I found myself on a talk-show panel where I was greeted with skepticism bordering on disbelief when I described our wonderful life on the Disney lot. Only after I began working at other studios, with other producers, directors, and crews, did I realize how unique the Disney lot was. For one thing, any form of profanity was strictly forbidden. If Walt Disney learned that anyone—even an adult— had uttered so much as a 'damn,' you could be sure you wouldn't see him on the set the next day. Second, everyone who worked at Disney lived according to the same high moral standards of behavior. Respect, consideration, fairness—these were part of our everyday lives at the studio, and I think the work environment Walt Disney and his staff maintained for us was the key to why those qualities came through so clearly in the television show itself.*

Eddie Hodges: It wasn't extremely different at Disney, compared to other studios, except maybe there was a bit less pressure. Mr. Disney expected everyone to treat each other with respect and to be respectable. I did like the fact that there were people working there that had been there for years. The man who did our 'looping' or voice-overs in the sound studio was the man who was the voice of Mickey Mouse! The Sherman Brothers did our songs. My own stand-in was a munchkin in *The Wizard of Oz*. And there was a secret workshop where they were developing the animatronics President Lincoln and had the map of what was to be Walt Disney World in Florida—it was all hush-hush. It was exciting! Mr. Disney would show up on the set unannounced and everyone was delighted to see him. The crew called him "Walt." I was just in awe of him.

Hank Jones: The Disney Commissary was by far the best studio eating place in town! The food was SO good that it was a struggle to not stuff oneself at lunch so you still had energy left to do your scenes in the afternoon. You never knew who you'd eat with: everyone was so friendly and welcoming. The live-action actors sometimes would share a table with someone in the animation department: I remember being awestruck meeting some of the fabled "Nine Old Men" at the Commissary who were responsible for the animation classics like *Snow White, Bambi* and *Pinocchio*, like Frank Thomas and Ollie Johnston—what a treat to just be in their company.

Billy Mumy: I remember the Disney lot was great and it was different from the other lots. It had a friendly vibe. There were ping pong tables and basketball hoops outside the commissary—everybody played. The squirrels ran around the lot everywhere! The "streets" on the lot had names like "Dopey Drive." Other studio lots don't have street names. It did feel friendlier than other lots back when Walt was alive.

Hank Jones circa 1964.

One of the busiest child actors of the 60's, Billy Mumy.

Tommy Kirk: When Disney was alive the studio was very clean, very wholesome—almost squeaky clean. We had to walk on egg shells. It really was very Victorian because Disney himself was very Victorian. The studio was in many ways, compared to some of the other studios in Hollywood, an island of purity. Walt Disney didn't put up with a lot, too. I remember Bobby Driscoll, who was in films like *Song of the South* and *Treasure Island* and had been the voice of Peter Pan, was let go because of drug problems.

There was no Betty Ford Clinic back then. We all had a morals clause in our contracts. But there is no getting around that Walt Disney was a great showman and knew what the public wanted and gave it to them.

Roger Mobley: Back in the 60's the Disney lot had grass and landscaping and sidewalks while the other studio lots were all concrete. Disney's streets and lanes were all named after Disney characters too which was fun.

Jonathan Daly: I am a lucky man to have worked at Disney—and I'm sure others feel the same way. I've worked at all the studios, but Disney was the only one where you could feel the love. It was like working on a campus.

Tommy Kirk circa 1964.

Elliott Reid: Working at the Disney Studio was like a paid vacation. It was very nice when Walt was alive and very much in evidence. Disney was a very charming man and very friendly. One day I ran into him and said, 'Hi, Mr. Disney,' and he told me to call him Walt.

Richard Todd (Disney's *Robin Hood*): *The atmosphere in the Walt Disney Studios was quite different from any I had so far experienced in the film factories. Walt first of all took me on a brief tour of his empire, going round acres of sound-stages and rows of drawing offices, where animators were busy sketching. And everywhere he went he was greeted with 'Hi, Walt,' and he replied, 'Hi! Jack—or Fred—or Art—or Lou.' He seemed to know every single one of the workforce. Eventually, we arrived in his office, a large, paneled, comfy room with a bar at one end. Before we settled down to talk, Walt proudly showed me how, at the touch of a button, the bar became a soda-fountain for youngsters. He adored children, and delighted in surprising them.*

Dick Warlock: I enjoyed working on the Disney lot—it has been described as being like a college campus and that is exactly the feeling I had as I went through the gate. No other studio that I worked at had that same feeling.

Lesley Ann Warren (*The Happiest Millionaire*): *We did a scene that I didn't think was particularly good…and I swore. There was a death like silence on the set. And I was told not to do that again. A girl must be a lady at all times here. They even told me not to drink—which I don't do anyway.*

4

Fess Parker: Disney's First
Live-Action Superstar

Fess Parker (1924-2010) became a true American cultural hero in the middle 1950's. He became as much a part of that era as Elvis Presley or Marilyn Monroe. To millions of children he was THE hero that they looked up to—in buckskin clothes and wearing a coonskin cap, Fess Parker WAS Davy Crockett.

Fess was born in Forth Worth, Texas. He was named after his father ("Fess means proud"). He was a voracious reader as a child, "I certainly did know a lot from a very early age about Davy Crockett—having been born in Texas." He graduated from the University of Texas in 1950 and was encouraged by the actor Adolphe Menjou to pursue an acting career. He moved to Los Angeles and studied drama at USC. By 1952 he was working steadily in small roles in movies and on television programs.

At about that time, Walt Disney was developing *Disneyland* in cooperation with the ABC television network, which was then in its infancy. ABC was also a major stockholder in Walt's Disneyland theme park in Anaheim, California. The Disney-ABC deal was an 'I'll scratch your back if you scratch mine' type of venture with ABC putting up money for Disneyland if Walt would do an hour-long weekly series on their fledging TV-network. *Disneyland* helped put ABC on the map.

Walt chose Bill Walsh (1913-1975) to be the line producer of *Disneyland*. At the time Walsh had been with Disney for over a decade, and among his duties was writing the daily *Mickey Mouse* comic strip (drawn by Floyd Gottfredson). You will read the name of Bill Walsh many times in these recollections. Fess Parker recalls him as "Walt Disney's right arm as far as production was concerned." Walsh immediately set out develop-

35

Fess Parker.

ing the various shows and by June 1953 had presented a nine-page memorandum outlining the elements of the weekly series. It was Walsh who urged that Walt act as host and that he introduce each episode. Walsh felt that the show should leave a "clean, pleasant taste in the mouth—that bespeaks a friendly relationship between the show and the viewer—and establishes a contact between every member of the family as they sit before the viewing screen." In other words, Walsh was speaking Walt's language. One of the ideas Walsh mapped out was to do a multi-episode arc on a single frontier hero—in a way to help promote Frontierland at the theme park. Walsh and his associates wrote down a list of names of frontier heroes and put them in a hat and the first one pulled out was—Davy Crockett. Walsh later explained:

I thought it might be a good thing to do a series on vaunted American heroes, and we mulled over subjects like Johnny Appleseed, Daniel Boone, Wid Wagon Smith, Big Foot Wallace, and Davy Crockett. The first one we picked, by dumb luck, was Davy Crockett, who was someone at that time nobody had ever heard of.

Chosen by Walsh to direct was a veteran named Norman Foster (1903-1976). Foster had been a former newspaper reporter in his native Indiana who moved to New York in hopes of hitting it big, but instead got involved in the theatre, first as an actor and later as a director. He went to Hollywood and acted in several pictures including the 1933 Will Rogers film version of *State Fair*. He also was married, from 1928-1935, to Claudette Colbert. By the late thirties he was almost exclusively directing, mostly programmers at Fox, but solid ones like *Mr. Moto* and *Charlie Chan* (including one of the best, *Charlie Chan at Treasure Island*). He also directed such major films as *Journey Into Fear* (for Orson Welles), *Rachel and the Stranger* (featuring his sister-in-law Loretta Young) and *Tell it to the Judge* (with Rosalind Russell).

Next came finding the right actor to play Crockett. Several were considered and one in particular, Buddy Ebsen, thought he had actually been selected for the role. Ebsen explained in his autobiography, *The Other Side of Oz*:

He (Norman Foster) saw me in a TV program, and he called Disney and announced, 'I've found your Davy Crockett.' He borrowed a copy of the kinescope and showed it to Walt. Disney was half sold. Norman called me with the news and I celebrated. Then Walt happened to see a picture called *Them!* about giant ants. In it a young actor, playing a highway patrolman, is locked up as a suspected nut after describing his sightings of gigantic insects. It was only a two-minute scene, but when it was over Walt said, 'That's Davy Crockett.' That young actor's name was Fess Parker, and the rest is history.

Parker, himself, recalled his audition before Walt Disney:

I was twenty-nine when Walt Disney interviewed me for Davy Crockett. I brought my little guitar with me, even though I wasn't much of a singer. After Walt and I talked for a while, he said, 'Why don't you play me a little tune? I had written a song called 'Lonely,' about a guy who had broken up with his girl and was riding on a train. I did the sound of a train whistle in the song. I later found out that Walt's other passion in life was railroads. I suppose that didn't hurt my chances.

Ebsen, while missing out on Davy, got a considerable consolation prize, "Norman Foster was apologetic when he called to tell me I was not to be Crockett. I was crushed, of course, but then he called to tell me about the role of (sidekick) Georgie Russel."

Parker and Ebsen made a strong team with Ebsen investing the episodes and his character with some down-home humor which would be a hallmark of Ebsen's when he began playing Jed Clampett on the phenomenally popular *The Beverly Hillbillies* in the early 1960s. Ebsen was later recalled fondly by Parker:

He (Buddy Ebsen) is a gentle, talented, generous man…Buddy, being a very experienced actor, gave me a lot to bounce off of and gave me all of the support I could have possibly wanted…I think for the purposes of the story he was extremely important, because the thought process behind action should be telegraphed by Georgie's concern…or support, depending on what Davy was about to do about whatever they were going to undertake. Georgie was the Greek chorus.

When filming of the *Davy Crockett* shows began director Norman Foster found that while the relatively inexperienced Parker was an imposing figure he needed to be prodded to get a little life into his characterization as he later told Disney historian Leonard Maltin, "I found if I didn't do something to get adrenaline in his (Parker's) system, he would get slower and slower. He seemed to lack vitality. I told him to take vitamin pills."

Many of the sequences were filmed on location and the cast and crew endured less than hospitable circumstances and some dangers along the way. Parker later recalled, "That was pretty rough goin' At one time or

Fess Parker as Davy Crockett. © Walt Disney Productions.

another most of us had poison oak, fungus in our ears and lots of chigger and mosquito bites." In his autobiography Buddy Ebsen explained why he and Parker wound up doing many of their own stunts:

> The filming of the Crockett episodes were some of the most rugged location expeditions I have ever experienced...First of all, there were stunts involved. But they had sent along

only one stunt man. Now Fess is 6'5 and I am 6'3 ½. The stunt man was 5-by-5. So Fess and I wound up doing our own stunts.

Fess and I were leading a squadron of mounted soldiers across a shallow lake. No one had bothered to check the bottom of the lake. It turned out to be bottomless, quicksand-like mud, so when our horses started sinking into it, they panicked. Those of us who didn't get thrown, quickly dismounted, but we still got trampled and cut up as we tried to lead our frantic animals through the sucking mud, which was seeded with broken bottles and old tin cans.

At one point the program was going over schedule and over-budget and the big man himself, Walt Disney, decided to make an appearance on the film location—which threw the company into a bit of turmoil, especially director Norman Foster as Ebsen explains:

The *Davy Crockett* Company was three weeks over schedule on a one-week show, with probably another week to go. Director Norman Foster was sweating over the lost schedule. Then worked came that Walt was on his way to visit the set. The night before he arrived, Norman made the rounds saying goodbye to everyone. He reasoned that the boss would be introducing a new director. An electric quiver of anticipation invaded the set the following morning. When the long, black Cadillac was sighted approaching down the dusty country road, Norman was setting up the last shot before lunch. Whispers went from mouth to mouth: 'He's here…Walt's here.' Walt was accompanied by Mrs. Disney and a couple from a nearby resort town who were their hosts. A welcoming scene was played behind Norman while he was acting unconcerned…When Walt reached Norman's side, he stood for a moment and observed him busily directing…When Walt reached Norman's side, he stood for a moment and observed him busily directing. 'Hello Norm,' he said. Norman turned and greeted surprisingly, 'Oh, hello Walt.' They shook hands. 'I heard you were coming.' Then to fill a lull Norm said, 'How does the stuff look?' 'Ok,' Walt said, 'Except for one thing.' Uh-oh, Norman thought. Here it comes. 'You know that scene where Fess wrestles with the bear?...I want you to retake that scene,' Walt said, 'That bear's zipper was showing.'

When filming was completed and the three episode arc was shown on the *Disneyland* TV show—the ratings went through the roof—reaching an astronomical 40 million viewers. Equally successful was the catchy theme song ("The Ballad of Davy Crockett"). According to Bill Walsh, once shooting had been completed the studio needed to fill some gaps with regard to time, so the solution was to create a song which would be played against a backdrop showing drawings and sketches of Davy Crockett. The song was quickly written by Tom Blackburn, who had written the 'Crockett' script, and studio composer George Bruns. "I thought it was pretty awful," Walsh later said, "but we didn't have time for anything else." It caught on with viewers. There were various recordings of the Crockett theme song (by Bill Hayes, Eddie Arnold, Tennessee Ernie Ford, Mitch Miller—and even Parker himself) which in all sold over seven million copies. That was only the beginning—soon Crockett merchandise (T-shirts, coon-skin caps, books, coloring books, toy rifles, knives, etc.) was flooding the market.

A nationwide publicity tour featuring Parker and Ebsen was a resounding success, "I shook hands with 100,000 kids, and a thing like that can get pretty wearing on a man," Parker later recalled. "It was mighty flattering, but I don't want to be doing it again. Why do you know that in Miami when Buddy and I were there, the kids pitched pup tents in front of the theater at 5:30 in the morning and waited." Parker later said that he was uncomfortable for much of the tour. "In fact, I was terrorized a lot of times," he recalled. "It was not possible to go to a restaurant and have dinner unaccosted. In fact, at the height of it I couldn't leave my room."

The shows proved so successful that there was popular demand to bring it back again, but there was just one problem—the final episode had Crockett dying at the Alamo. "We had no idea what was going to happen to 'Crockett,'" Disney recalled. "Why by the time the first show finally got on the air, we were already shooting the third one and calmly killing Davy off at the Alamo. It became one of the biggest overnight hits in TV history, and there we were with just three films and a dead hero." (*The Disney Films*, pg. 122) The solution? A second series which looks back on Crockett's exploits for the following season. Later Walt edited

A Live Coon skin cap! © Walt Disney Productions.

together three episodes of the series and released it as a motion picture—it grossed $2.5 million at the box office. Davy Crockett was money in the bank for Disney. "We went a million dollars over budget last year. *Davy Crockett* pulled us out. We made the films for $700,000, while we could only get $300,000 back from TV, but the theatrical showings will possibly gross a million and a half here, and there is considerable interest in Davy abroad. We also ended up with a star—Fess Parker."

He certainly did have a star in Fess Parker, who was at the time under exclusive contract to Walt Disney Productions. But it was an at times uneasy relationship. Disney wanted to build Parker into a star in his own films, while rejecting outside interest from other studios in Parker's services. Parker admired Disney, but felt that Walt was stifling him and hurting his career. "Walt Disney was very protective," Parker later recalled. "I wanted to do (the films) *Bus Stop* and *The Searchers* and he nixed *Bus Stop* for me and he didn't tell me that they wanted me for *The Searchers* until after it was already made. I would have played the part that my friend Jeff Hunter...played...He (Disney) had things for me to do that he thought were more important. He saw it from his perspective."

Parker did go on to do several Disney projects including playing the father in the classic *Old Yeller*, a part he really didn't want to play because he felt it was so inconsequential to the film—appearing only at the beginning and the end. In the end, Walt Disney released Parker from his contract and Parker went on for several years appearing in some films (*The Hangman, The Jayhawkers*) and TV programs (including a short lived version of *Mr. Smith Goes to Washington* in the 1962-63 season), but didn't hit it big again until 1964 when he played another frontiersman for NBC television, *Daniel Boone* (1964-1970). He later retired from acting and began operating a successful vineyard and winery in Los Olivos, California. He died in 2010 at age 85. Until his dying day Parker felt gratitude towards Disney and some resentment towards him as well, due to what he believed were missed opportunities. He once put it this way: "I think the studio has to decide whether it's just going to use players to suit its own purposes or whether it will groom and build stars. So far, it hasn't shown much tendency to look after the actor's best interests."

Fess Parker: The way I always heard it was that they (the studio) were considering Buddy Ebsen, George Montgomery or Jim Arness for Davy. Jim was in a picture called *Them!* In which I had a small part. Walt decided to screen *Them!* to evaluate Jim (he wasn't yet on TV with *Gunsmoke*), and then he came to a scene that I was in that lasted two or maybe three minutes, and Walt saw something that he liked and indicated that he felt he had found his Davy Crockett in me. It was a lucky break.

What I remember most about Walt Disney is that he was very relaxed and involved in the production of the *Davy Crockett* shows. There was an agreement between Disney and the ABC Television network, which was just in its infancy, but they were partners with Disney on the theme park and in return Disney agreed to do his TV series on ABC. *Davy Crockett* was used to kick off the ABC network. Tom Blackburn, the writer, and Bill Walsh, shaped those episodes and blended them together with a little theme song, and it was just in the dialogue. It was well done. We had a wonderful director in Norman Foster on the Crocket films—he and I didn't always see eye to eye. He was a New York trained actor and he really didn't understand some of the physical dangers we encountered out on location, but in the end he certainly proved that he was the real deal.

When the Crockett films appeared it caused such a mania that it really was an extreme experience much like The Beetles that came along later, or Elvis, it was a great response from the public.

My happiest memory of the Disney years—well, there are many—and to balance it—there were a lot of disappointments. The disappointments were because my goals and the studios were not always exactly the same, but I was under exclusive contract with Walt Disney and I had to ride that circumstance out—and that took about four years. Walt was very important in my life. I respect him and still feel grateful for the fact that he plucked me out of obscurity.

5

Recollections of a Mouseketeer—Sharon Baird

Bill Walsh had done such a good job producing the *Disneyland* television series in its first season that Walt rewarded him by giving him more work and responsibility. Walt called Walsh into his office and told him, "I'm taking you off the evening show." Walsh was elated because he was exhausted and was looking forward to a vacation. Then Walt let the other shoe drop—telling Walsh that he wanted him to produce a television show—with children—that would be aired for an hour *every single week day*. Thus *The Mickey Mouse Club* was born. By January 1955, Walsh sent Walt a memorandum outlining how he saw the series—with its different daily themes and emphasize on using the backlog of Disney cartoons along with variety entertainment and serials like *Spin and Marty* and *The Hardy Boys*. He also helped audition the youngsters who would form the core of the *Mickey Mouse Club.*

Along with the children who were selected to become "The Mouseke-teers" there were two adults who were thrown into the mix. The leader of the pack was forty-year old Jimmy Dodd, whose warmth captivated the children, not only the members of the "Club" but also viewers. He wrote many of the songs that were used on the series, including the famous "Mickey Mouse Club March" (M-I-C-K-E-Y M-O-U-S-E). All the Mouseketeers looked up to him. Bobby Burgess, one of the key Mousekeers, known for his dancing ability, later recalled that Dodd and his wife couldn't have children, "so we were his children." The other—much older gentleman— known as the "big mooseketeer" was Roy Williams, who was part of the Disney animation department. He was big and gruff and loved to have the occasional nip—but Williams was beloved by the children and he was protective of them.

45

The children themselves were presented as amateurs, but that wasn't always the case. Many of them had had previous professional experience. The key members of the club were to become Tommy Cole, Sharon Baird, Lonnie Burr, Darlene Gillespie, Doreen Tracy, Cubby O'Brien, Karen Pendleton, and then most famously a sweet, dark-haired girl with deep dark eyes who would take the nation by storm and become one of the Disney Studio's greatest creations—Annette Funicello. There were others who came and went but these eight formed the nucleus.

The show began a highly successful four-year fun—and it was revived a couple of times in later years, but without the same level of success as this initial series. Walt Disney summed up what he hoped to accomplish with *The Mickey Mouse Club:*

At our studio, we regard the child as a highly intelligent human being. He is characteristically sensitive, humorous, open-minded, eager to learn, and has a strong sense of excitement, energy, and health curiosity about the world in which he lives. Lucky indeed is the grown up who manages to carry these same characteristics over into his adult life. It usually makes for a happy and successful individual. Essentially, the real

Walt with his Mouseketeers, Sharon Baird is second from the right, second row.
© Walt Disney Productions.

difference between a child and an adult is experience. We conceive it to be our job on *The Mickey Mouse Club* show to provide some of that experience…

Sharon Baird: I started dancing at the age of three in Seattle, Washington. My dancing teacher entered me in a "Little Miss Washington Beauty Contest" when I was about six. I won the contest, and, therefore, competed in the "Little Miss USA" contest where I came in second. My parents liked the weather better in Southern California (less rain) and, so, we moved to the L.A. area. My dancing teacher in L.A. sent me to an audition for an appearance on *The Colgate Comedy Hour* with Eddie Cantor. I was too small for the part, so they wrote a special part just for me. Eddie Cantor was the star of the *Colgate Comedy Hour* once a month. After the show was aired, he signed me to a seven-year contract. I appeared on his show each time—dancing, singing and performing in sketches—until his health caused our contract to be null and void. During our years together, he had my legs insured by Lloyds of London. He was a great entertainer and I learned a lot from him.

After *The Colgate Comedy Hour*, I appeared in the movie *Bloodhounds of Broadway* acting and dancing with Mitzi Gaynor. I had several acting roles before *The Mickey Mouse Club* including on *Death Valley Days, Damon Runyon Theater, The Joan Davis Show, Burns & Allen, Shower of Stars with Red Skelton and Ethel Merman*, and several appearances on *Here Comes Donald* starring Donald O'Connor—one of my all-time favorites to work with.

At the time, none of us knew what a Mouseketeer was. I was filming *Artists and Models* with Dean Martin and Jerry Lewis. While pre-recording a song for the film at Capitol Records, I met Jimmy Dodd, who was to become the leader of the Mouseketeers and wrote most of the songs we sang on the show. He was at a recording session of his own. He recommended me to the Disney Studio. They called my agent to set up an audition. She didn't want to tie me up with long-term contracts, so she agreed to send me out for an interview for a six-week serial *When I Grow Up*. When I went to the interview, they sent me to the rehearsal hall and the *Mickey Mouse Club* auditions. I sang "I Didn't Know the Gun Was Loaded," and tap danced double-time while jumping rope in front of several executive types—I don't recall who they were now. The studio contacted my agent to say I got the job. She didn't want me to take it, but I wanted to do a job where I could sing and dance every day.

Shortly after we started working at "The Studio," we were all playing and running around in the rehearsal hall. We were giggling and squealing, like kids do, during a break when someone said, 'You'd better cool it, and Walt Disney is here.' He had just come over from the Paint Department and was covered with paint—he had been mixing paint with the guys. I remember him as quiet and soft-spoken. He never allowed the crew to swear around us and always wanted us to call him "Uncle Walt." We couldn't do that because we respected him too much. To my recollection, Mr. Disney rarely came to the set. When he did, he stayed well in the background.

The Disney Studio really looked more like a college campus than a film lot. It had grass, trees and flowers everywhere. All the streets were named after different Disney characters. The boys played baseball on the baseball diamond or ping pong on the tables near the commissary during lunch. We bonded together like most normal kids would have under the same circumstances. There were some conflicts, but nothing serious. While working at the studio we spent more time during the day with each other than we did with our own family. We would rehearse numbers together and help each other with our dances and schooling in our spare time. Some of us—especially those of us who were there for the entire run) formed some long-lasting friendships.

The California Board of Education allowed us to spend eight hours a day at the studio. Three hours of those eight were to be spent with schooling, one hour for lunch and four hours of shooting—not necessarily consecutive. Some of us would rehearse while another group was in school, and, yet, another group would then rehearse. We attended school in two red trailers on the Disney Lot. It had a row of desks on each side. Our teacher, Mrs. Jean Seaman, was only allowed to teach no more than ten children at a time. She was also accredited to teach all grades through the twelfth grade. When I returned to public school, I was way ahead of the classes there because all of our personal questions were answered.

We had no idea if the show would be a success or not. I remember when we appeared at the opening of Disneyland—nobody knew who the Mouseketeers were! We were already filming the show, but it hadn't aired yet.

On the opening day of Disneyland, we were in Walt Disney's apartment above the Main Street Fire Station when the gates of the park opened for the first time. I was standing next to him at the window, watching the guests come pouring through the gates. When I looked at him, he had his hands behind his back, a grin from ear to ear, and I could see a lump in his throat and a tear streaming down his cheek. He had realized his dream.

When the kids in my neighborhood started waiting on our fence at night and wanting to hear what we did that day, I figured it was a hit. My parents made sure I didn't get a swelled head. I still had chores to do at home and rules to follow. They kept me regulated. I guess I didn't really realize what a success the show was until we arrived in Australia at the beginning of a tour. Thousands of fans greeted us—more than greeted Frank Sinatra when he arrived! They had to carry us over the crowd to our limos which were being rocked back and forth by the fans.

My love was, is and always will be dancing. Tap was my specialty along with jitterbug, swing, jive, etc. I always did a tap number and jitterbug with Bobby (Burgess) on our live appearances. I got to dance in a lot of our production number sand was featured in a couple of numbers.

Bobby Burgess is one of the best dance partners I have ever danced with. He is always happy, positive, and easy to work with and fun to be around. He and his wife Kristie have remained lifelong friends to me.

Lonnie Burr and I first worked together on *The Colgate Comedy Hour* years before *The Mickey Mouse Club*. I've enjoyed many dance numbers with him in the past but, unfortunately we have lost contact.

Annette Funicello is my dearest friend. She was America's sweetheart—loved by boys and girls alike. We spent many hours together as teenagers and I am in contact with her and visit her on a regular basis. I am very proud of her for the courage with which she faces her debilitating disease.

Cubby O'Brien was the youngest of the boys and an outrageous drummer. He was and still is a cute, little imp. He always makes me laugh. Today he is still drumming strong.

Darlene Gillespie was talented in every area. I saw her as a great singer, actress, comedienne and dancer. She's another one I have lost contact with for many years.

Jimmie Dodd was the perfect host for *The Mickey Mouse Club*. He didn't talk down to children and he taught by example. I never heard him say a bad word about anyone.

Roy Williams (aka The Big Mooseketeer) was like your favorite uncle to us. He pretended to be a grump but we could all see he was lovable. He and his wife Ethel, had lots of pool parties at their home for us.

Tim Considine was a bit older than we were. We didn't see too much of them when they were shooting *Spin and Marty*...only occasionally at lunch time. Annette and I had a secret crush on Tim, but we were too young for him to notice. Running across him in later years, he seems friendly. Another of our heartthrobs was Guy Williams. I remember sneaking onto the *Zorro* set with Annette to see if we could catch sight of Guy Williams!

Tommy Kirk was a terrific actor. Even though he was a little older, we saw a little more of him. He and I became blood brother and sister one day at the studio!

Kevin Corcoran (Moochie) was a darling little boy. Being quite a bit younger than me, I knew his older sisters better.

David Stollery always seemed quiet and shy. Again we didn't see much of the Triple R Boys. I do recall he was quite an artist and was always drawing cars.

I remember our producer, Bill Walsh, as being very distinguished. He had a big grin, loved a cigar and loved to have a piece of pie for breakfast at the local drugstore every morning.

My favorite moments were the days we filmed "Fun With Music" numbers. We got to dress up in different ethnic costumes and perform their cultural dances. I also enjoyed appearing in the Annette serial. Another of my favorite memories was the six weeks we appeared in a circus at Disneyland while we were on hiatus from filming our show.

I don't recall exactly how I heard that our show was ending, but I do recall we were shooting reaction shots and were supposed to be laughing and clapping. All Annette and I could do was cry! We must have gone through a box of Kleenex each.

After the show I went to college and I got married. I later had a nightclub act with my ex-husband and a friend (Two Cats & A Mouse). After my divorce, I started playing characters on children's TV shows...*H.R. Pufnstuf, Bugaloos, Lidsville, Sigmund and the Sea Monsters, Bay City Rollers, Land of the Lost* and *New Zoo Revue*. I had a lot of fun on "New Zoo" and developed another great friendship with Larri Thomas and her husband Bruce Hoy. I also appeared with Gallagher on stage and video and played in the film *Ratboy* as Ratboy!

Today I'm semi-retired from the business, though I do attend and appear at Disney reunions. I live in Reno, Nevada and am working in a beauty salon. The unique experience of being a Mouseketeer has left me with a chosen family of friends that have shared part of my life since 1955 and are still a part of my life. As the song says, "Through the years we'll all be friends."

Annette Funicello: I started one of the most enduring friendships of my life with Mouseketeer Sharon Baird. Like me, Sharon was on the red team all three seasons. I always thought she and Karen Pendleton were the two best dancers among the girls. Unlike most of us Mouseketeers, Sharon was a professional, having begun as a dancer at age three…Sharon's dancing was, in a word, stunning. In both her solo and our ensemble numbers, she brought a combination of grace and show-stopping preci-

Annette Funicello circa 1956. © Walt Disney Productions.

sion seen in few dancers of any age. When performed by Sharon, even the most athletic, complex tap maneuvers looked simple—until you tried them yourself.

6

A Boy and His Dog: The Making of *Old Yeller* (1957)

Old Yeller (1957) is one of Walt Disney's all-time classic live-action films. Based on a popular novel by Fred Gibson (1908-1973) it is a coming of age film as well as the tried and true "boy and his dog" saga.

Set in Texas in 1869, Papa Coates (Fess Parker, complete with glued-on mustache) is going to be separated from his family for three months so he can earn some extra money on a cattle drive. Mom (Dorothy McGuire) and their two sons, Travis (Tommy Kirk), 14, and Arliss (Kevin Corcoran), 7, will tend to the family farm in his absence.

Dad explains to Travis that he will have to be the man of the house while he is gone and Travis doesn't intend to let him down. Enter into the story a big yellow mongrel dog who at first—in Travis's estimate—is nothing but trouble. The dog chases a rabbit and destroys the garden. He frightens the pack mule which causes the mule to dart into and destroy a fence. If Travis had his way he'd get his rifle right then and there and do away with this no account 'old yeller' dog.' But little brother Arliss is attached to the dog as refers to him as 'my dog.' Mom encourages Arliss, explaining to Travis that the boy has no playmates and is lonely.

Soon, however, Yeller shows his worth to Travis. For instance, Travis is ready to shoot the dog if he touches the meat that is put out overnight to cure. Yeller must realize he is being tested (the dog is almost human in his ability to understand what his humans are thinking or feeling) because while he looks longingly (and hungrily) at the meat he doesn't touch it. Travis is impressed. But he's even more impressed when Yeller saves Arliss from a protective mother bear.

Lobby Card for *Old Yeller*.

Three other pivotal characters soon enter the story. A neighboring rancher (Chuck Connors) who recognizes Yeller as his missing dog, but soon realizes that the Coates family could use the dog more than he can; and a father and daughter—the Searcy's (Jeff York & Beverly Washburn). Mr. Searcy is a no-account—fat and lazy and calls on the Coates' on the pretext of looking out for them while Pa is gone, but what he's really after is one of Ma's home cooked dinners. Lisbeth Searcy is a sweet girl of twelve who does all the heavy lifting and she is left behind by her father to help out. She also has a noticeable crush on Travis. Lisbeth also has a dog of her own, Miss Priss, that she would like to have mate with Yeller (of course as the picture evolves in its own innocent way we come to understand that one day Lisbeth will marry Travis and they'll probably have a slew of kids of their own).

The film is episodic and leads inevitably to its emotional climax where Travis must prove himself a man and put Yeller out of his misery—caused by the rabies Yeller caught defending the family. It is that scene that has led some critics to find *Old Yeller* too disturbing for younger viewers. In an article in the journal *Bright Lights Film* author Jerry Kutner calls *Old Yeller* "one of the most disturbing children's movies in cinema history." According to Beverly Washburn she, too, felt the movie was too traumatic for younger viewers to see, but then her friend Tommy Kirk convinced her otherwise Of course this is nothing new for a Disney film. In many of Disney's animated classics there are a number of scenes which are emotional and troubling to younger viewers. As Richard Hoffer wrote in *Via* magazine in 2005, "Disney, for all his pining for a perfect world…did not entirely ignore the authentic. He did kill Bambi's mom, remember. He did permit, perhaps encourage, the occasional sense of danger."

Walt Disney optioned *Old Yeller* shortly after the novel was published. He brought the novel's writer, Fred Gipson, to the Burbank studio to help write the screenplay (in association with William Tunberg). Gipson later explained that he based the novel on the experiences of his maternal grandfather whose family had a much loved dog that had to be put down when it, like Old Yeller, got rabies. The only real difference between the film and the novel is when Yeller becomes infected with the rabies—Travis shoots the dog soon afterward, while in the movie he wants to wait to see if Yeller develops symptoms. Gipson was also less than secure about how he would handle writing a screenplay. He later explained:

I called in my friend, Bill Tunberg, to help me (on the movie script) for a couple of reasons. One, that I'd had too little experience in the technical side of writing. Two, that I had just left a hospital and was too weak and jittery to tackle any piece of work that I didn't feel perfectly confident in handling. To some extent it was like writing the book all over again. In many places I felt our movie script improved upon it.

Chosen to direct the film was a quiet Englishman named Robert Stevenson (1905-1986), whose second Disney film this would be. He had previously helmed the feature *Johnny Tremain*, a film set during the Revolutionary War. Walt had admired a TV program that Stevenson had directed and chose him for *Tremain*. Stevenson, who directed such 1940's films as *Jane Eyre, Forever and a Day,* and *Dishonored Lady,* would go on to be the Disney Studio's most prolific director over the next twenty years with seventeen more films including *Mary Poppins,* which would be nominated for Best Picture and Stevenson nominated as Best Director by the Academy of Motion Picture Arts and Sciences. Bill Walsh, who wrote and produced many of the films that Stevenson directed once said, "With Bob, you were always sure when the film finished that you had everything you needed; he covered it from all angles, so it was a cinch to cut together."

The film was shot over three months in the spring of 1957. Most of the shooting was in the rugged 700-acre Golden Oak Ranch in the Santa Clarita Valley, with interiors done at the Disney Studio in Burbank. Given the small cast (seven featured players—two of whom, Fess Parker and Chuck Connors, have very small parts) the cast and crew bonded together like a family, according to many recollections. Fess Parker, cast as the father, really didn't want to do the film, "I didn't want to do the picture. I thought the role was pretty small for the billing I got—second only to Dorothy McGuire…People have written me to say that they enjoyed the picture, but wished they had seen more of me in it!"

This would be the first of six films that would feature Tommy Kirk and Kevin Corcoran. Kirk would later refer to Corcoran as being like a little brother to him. In fact, in five of the films they made together (*Old Yeller, The Shaggy Dog, Swiss Family Robinson, Bon Voyage!, Savage Sam*) they would be cast as brothers—it is probable that some fans may have even thought they really were in 'real life.' McGuire would portray their mother again in the film *Swiss Family Robinson* (1960). Yeller himself was played by a very trainable dog named Spike, who was rescued from a shelter in Van Nuys, California. He would go on to appear in the film *A Dog of Flanders* (1960-Twentieth Century Fox) and played Brian Keith's dog on the TV series, *The Westerner.* Spike was trained by the noted film animal trainer Frank Weatherwax, who also trained the dog who became the original Lassie in *Lassie Come Home* (1943) and the original Asta from *The Thin Man* (1934). Robert Stevenson later explained how they taught Spike some of his on-screen tricks:

Most of the emotion is read by the audience. After all, a dog can only do three things: turn his head in the right direction, cock his head, and bark. The dog in *Old Yeller* had the remarkable gift of putting his dead to one side and looking quizzical. He was trained according to a particular note on a whistle. Whenever we wanted a quizzical close-up, we simply found that note on the whistle and played it.

When the film was released on Christmas Day, 1957, it was an immediate hit and also well-received by most critics. The *New York Times* critic, Bosley Crowthers, called it "a lean and sensible" adaptation of Gipson's novel, and "sentimental-yes—but also as sturdy as a hickory stick." Crowther's did warn his readers that the climax is "frightening" and that the dog has to be shot. Here is what Walt Disney had to say about the climax:

This is a Texas farm in 1869 and the dog has rabies; there's no way he can be saved. You gotta shoot him. It'll give the picture a touch of realism. The kids'll cry, but it's important for them to know that life isn't all happy endings.

Tommy Kirk has continued to be proud of this film. "*Old Yeller* will be played a thousand years from now," he once said. "And Dorothy, Fess and Kevin and I will be watched…because of Walt Disney."

Tommy Kirk: One day at the studio I got a note with a copy of the book *Old Yeller* by Fred Gipson. The note said that I will be playing Travis in the movie. I was under contract and in those days you did what they told you to do. Not that I regret that one at all. I took the accent I used in *Old Yeller* from my mother who was born in Kentucky. Can't became Cain't and Yeller became Yella.

Beverly Washburn: I read for the casting people along with Robert Stevenson, who was going to be directing the film. I was then asked to meet with Walt Disney himself. I was a little nervous as he was an incredibly important man. I was in awe, of course of meeting Walt Disney. He was very quiet and soft-spoken. He turned out to be wonderful and shortly after the meeting and reading for the part, I got a call that I had been cast. I was beyond thrilled, and of course surprised and incredibly thankful.

Fess Parker: Of course, one of the most successful and beloved movies I ever made at Disney was *Old Yeller*. It was a very successful picture, and the public loved it, but I didn't have a whole lot to do with it. My character is in the beginning and the end of the picture—kind of like a book end, so the movie captured the lives and adventures of the other characters—which it certainly did very well.

Beverly Washburn: Tommy Kirk was wonderful! He was such an amazing child actor—one of the best ever—and it came from his heart. He's so

Beverly Washburn with Yeller, photo courtesy of Miss Washburn.

adorable. Our situation off the set was the same as Lisbeth and Travis in the film. In 'real-life' I had a crush on Tommy. He asked me to go steady with him and gave me a ring—I remember it was a very romantic—a skull and cross bones ring! He was 13 or 14 and I was 12. We went steady for a while. He was my first crush and the first boy who kissed me.

Fess Parker: Tommy Kirk was my son in the film and he was a very nice young man. We shared two good scenes together. It is hard to think of him as a senior citizen, but we have all become that! He was very good in that picture.

Tommy Kirk: I looked up to Robert Stevenson immeasurably. He was very easy to work with. I never saw him in a hurry. He was always patient and always relaxed. He said everything with a smile. I never had a cross word with him and he always treated me with kindness and respect, which I didn't always get from others at the studio.

Beverly Washburn: Robert Stevenson fully explained to me who Lisbeth was—she was simply a nice, sweet, soft-spoken little girl who lived with her lazy father and has a crush on Travis. I thought that Mr. Stevenson was top-notch, truly an excellent director. He, too, was soft-spoken, but he knew exactly what he wanted and he was always prepared when we came on the set.

Fess Parker: Our director was Robert Stevenson, and we both became residents (later) of Santa Barbara. As a director, I would say he had a way of directing you without your ever being able to quite put your finger on the fact that he had something to do with the scenes you had just done—and I mean that as a compliment.

Beverly Washburn, Dorothy McGuire and taking aim is Tommy Kirk.
© Walt Disney Productions.

(*Old Yeller, Swiss Family Robinson*), was a beautiful person. She was very gentle and nice to me. She was what she appeared to be on the screen—a very sweet and cultured lady.

Beverly Washburn: Dorothy McGuire was very motherly. She was so soft-spoken and gentle. She never got flustered—just a very lovely person.

Fess Parker: Dorothy McGuire was my wife and she was a real professional, and could deliver on screen beautifully.

Tommy Kirk: Kevin Corcoran played my brother in so many films that people began to assume we were really brothers in real life. I loved him. I still love him. He was very dear to me. We had a couple of quarrels and clashes. We did have a falling out where he said something to me and I said something back, but happily we got over it.

Beverly Washburn: Kevin Corcoran was as cute as could be. On the set he was a typical 7 or 8 year old kid—getting into everything. In later years

Dorothy McGuire also played Tommy Kirk's mother in *Swiss Family Robinson*.
© Walt Disney Productions

Kevin decided he no longer wanted to be in front of the camera and he became an assistant director. He even got in touch with me and hired me to do a few lines on *Murder She Wrote* with Angela Lansbury.

Jeff York, who played my father, was wonderful! He was so hilarious—this big, jovial, fun character.

The dog—Spike was his name—was fabulous. He was found at a shelter, so he was a rescue dog. Unlike other film dogs such as Rin Tin Tin or Lassie, which had multiple dogs for different actions or emotions, there was only one Spike—he did everything! It was a dream come true for me as working with dogs is my favorite thing. The little puppy they brought in who was supposed to be Old Yeller's puppy with my dog named Miss Prissy needed to be the same color as Old Yeller, and I remember walking into the make-up room one morning and seeing him sitting in the make-up chair getting powdered down so he would be the same color! It was such a cute sight to see…a puppy in a make-up chair!

Tommy Kirk: Disney visited the set a lot. He was there a lot. But he didn't really speak with the actors. When he did come on the set it was basically to talk with the director. Disney was a soft-spoken man who was not a glad-hander. It was shut up and do your job when he was around.

Beverly Washburn: Walt Disney, of course, would visit the set, but he was very unobtrusive. He never interfered with anything. He greeted people and then kind of stood back and observed a scene or two. He was quite unlike, say, Loretta Young, on the set of her show who was involved in everything! With cameras, lighting, directing. Of course Mr. Disney always had the final say, but on the set he deferred to the director and just stood back as if he was a visitor—at his own studio. He let people do the jobs they were hired to do.

I remember when Tommy had to shoot Old Yeller. It was a very emotional scene. I was in the moment and was able to cry actual tears—it really came very easily—especially given my love for animals in real life. There was a time when I thought that maybe little kids shouldn't see it because of the dog dying and the impact that has. But Tommy told me that he felt it was better for kids to see it because in life you

I had no idea at the time that it would become such a classic film— one which would make grown men cry. The fans have been wonderful over the years, and I truly enjoy meeting them. They can be funny too! One time Tommy and I were in New Jersey doing a convention and we were sitting together with our pictures from *Old Yeller* in front of us when a woman walked up and looked at both of us, then looked at the pictures, then looked at us again and said, 'I can't believe this…Tommy Kirk and Beverly Washburn…You were both in *Old Yeller*…that was my favorite film…I must have seen it 20 times and it's so amazing that you're both still alive!!

7

The Fred MacMurray Films
1959–1967

Fred MacMurray (1908-1991) was born in the small town of Beaver Dam, WI. He began his career as a saxophone player and band singer. He was appearing on Broadway in *Roberta* opposite Bob Hope when, borrowing Hope's top hat and cane, he made a screen test for Paramount Pictures. His first film, *The Gilded Lily*, which cast him opposite Claudette Colbert, was an immediate hit and the personable, handsome MacMurray became a bankable leading man for Paramount Pictures. His bread and butter genre over the next decade would be comedies which cast him opposite some of the great leading ladies of the era including Carole Lombard in *Hands Across the Table* and *True Confession* and Jean Arthur in *Too Many Husbands*. Other notable films of this era include *Alice Adams* (opposite Katharine Hepburn) and *Remember the Night*, the first of four films with Barbara Stanwyck. It would be opposite Stanwyck that MacMurray would star in his most famous film and greatest performance, as Walter Neff, insurance man turned killer in Billy Wilder's classic film noir, *Double Indemnity*. He proved he could play against type in other films including *Pushover*, *The Caine Mutiny* and *The Apartment*, again directed by Wilder. In 1958, MacMurray returned to screen comedy in *The Shaggy Dog*. It became one of most successful films of 1959. Walt Disney liked and respected MacMurray (one reason may have been, according to one source, MacMurray's willingness to make business investments on the spot!) and cast him in five more films during the 60's—all of which made money at the box office. With his new family friendly image, MacMurray also became a huge star on TV as Steve Douglas on the popular *My Three*

Sons (1960-1972). In 1973 he starred in one more Disney film, *Charley and the Angel,* and then went into comfortable semi-retirement. In 1988, the Disney Studio honored him as the first Disney Legend recipient.

Walt Disney: He's (Fred MacMurray) a down-to-earth, practical actor. He had no temperament. He's considerate of everybody's problems and comes on understanding his lines. He has a way of handling comedy that nobody else can compare with. I've got a lot of respect for Fred and, besides, he's a wonderful fellow, I dunno, I just like him.

Annette Funicello: I'm sorry to say I never really got to know Mr. Mac-Murray well, although I admired him greatly. Also a quiet person, he was friendly but mainly kept to himself. On the last day of shooting (The Shaggy Dog) I mustered the courage to request his autograph, and he kindly consented, writing: 'I worked with Kim Novak in her first movie, and look what happened. I have no doubt the same will happen with you.'

Tommy Kirk: Disney liked Fred enormously. For one thing, Fred's movies were money in the bank.

Fred MacMurray in the comedy classic *The Absent Minded Professor.*
© Walt Disney Productions.

Fred MacMurray: Nowadays everybody gets percentage deals, Disney doesn't go for percentages. But he does make successful movies and what is good about owning 100 percent of a movie that's a flop? However, I must admit that I would like to have a few percent of *The Professor* or *The Shaggy Dog.*

The Shaggy Dog (1959)

The Shaggy Dog is a significant film in the history of the Walt Disney Studio. It is the first live-action Disney comedy—and introduced a formula that the studio would utilize for more than twenty years. It is also the first Disney film to star Fred MacMurray, who would become the top leading man of the studio and, in many ways, the alter-ego of Walt the next decade. Its premise is simple: A misfit teen (Tommy Kirk) visits a museum and inadvertently takes from it a magical ring that transforms him into a large sheep dog. Fred plays his father, and turns in a very funny performance, a postman who has come up against many a dog in his career and has developed an allergy to them. Why is he suddenly sneezing and getting itchy-red eyes around his oldest son? Add to the cast Jean Hagen as MacMurray's wife, Kevin Corcoran (as MacMurray's youngest son, who forever is pestering him about wanting a dog!), Annette Funicello, Roberta Shore, Tim Considine (as Tommy Kirk's rival for either Funicello or Shore), and Cecil Kellaway. Roy Disney, Jr, later told how Walt described the film at a family meal and the unexpected reaction it had:

"Walt was still preparing the script for *The Shaggy Dog.* It was one of the early 'Let's do a black-and-white comedy with some special effects and not much money' approach to the question, 'What else do you do besides animation?' There must have been ten-twelve people sitting around the table enjoying fried chicken and corn on the cob. Walt began his I'll-take-over-this-meeting thing, so he started: 'We're working on this wonderful story about a kid who turns into a dog.' He usually could keep people enthralled with his storytelling. He got a little bit into it, and Mother says, 'That sounds kinda dumb.' He went further on, and mother says, 'That really sounds like an awful stupid picture, Walt.' Every time she said something, Walt's distraction got a little bit worse. He got to the halfway point in the story and just gave up on it."

The film is directed by Charles Barton (1902-1981). Barton began his career as an extra in silent pictures when he was fifteen years old. He eventually became an Assistant Director at Paramount, and won an Academy Award as "Best Assistant Director" in 1933 (an award category eventually dropped by the Academy). In 1934 he made his directorial debut in a Western called *Wagon Wheel*. Most of his pictures were in the so-called "B" category. He eventually left Paramount—first for Columbia and then Universal—where he became associated with directing several Abbott and Costello films, most notably, *The Time of Their Lives, Buck Privates Come Home, Abbott & Costello Meet Frankenstein* (probably his best and most famous film), *Africa Screams* and *Abbott & Costello Meet the Killer-Boris Karloff*. He also began to direct many episodes of episodic TV including *Amos & Andy, The Gale Storm Show,* and *The Ray Milland Show*. In 1958 he was signed by Walt Disney to direct *The Shaggy Dog*. His success enhanced his reputation at the studio and so he also directed episodes of the TV series *Zorro* and *The Adventures of Spin and Marty*. In 1960 he directed his second and final Disney film, the under-appreciated *Toby Tyler: or Ten Weeks with the Circus*. Afterward he continued to direct hundreds of episodic TV shows during the 1960s including *Dennis the Menace, Hazel* and *Petticoat Junction*. *The Shaggy Dog* was actually Barton's second film with star Fred MacMurray. Way back in 1935 he directed MacMurray in a programmer for Paramount titled *Car 99*.

Newspaper ad for
The Shaggy Dog.

Production began in early August 1958 and would be completed near the end of October. The film was released in New York on March 19, 1959, and was an immediate smash hit—becoming the third highest-grossing film of the year (with $12.3 million in rentals) and beating out such other releases as *North by Northwest, Pillow Talk* and *Some Like It Hot* at the box office. As Fred MacMurray later said, "*The Shaggy Dog* was instant box office. In it I played the father of a teen-age son who changed into a

huge, floppy, hairy dog at embarrassing moments. My part wasn't much—
the dog had the biggest role—but it was comedy, and I yenned to do comedy again. I think I do that best. For one thing there's less competition. Not too many people do comedy."

Tommy Kirk: I thought it was stupid! And embarrassing. I hated having to call Fred MacMurray 'pop.' I never had to call my own dad 'pop.' But then I thought, too, that it was so crazy it might be entertaining.

I recall meeting Fred MacMurray (with whom Kirk would work with in four films) for the first time on the set. Of course, I knew who he was

Tommy Kirk, Tim Considine and Roberta Shore in *The Shaggy Dog*.
© Walt Disney Productions.

because I had seen *The Caine Mutiny* and a film called *Pushover* and I was very excited and liked him as an actor. I thought he was a wonderful and extremely sensitive actor. I perceived that he was an extremely sensitive person, too. He was not a glad hander or a back slapper. We didn't have a lot in common because he was fifty years old and I was still a teenager, but I did try to open lines of communications with him. He was polite and somewhat reserved. In between scenes he would sit in a chair and smoke his pipe and be reading a newspaper. Disney liked Fred enormously. For one thing the films that Fred would make for Disney were money in the bank. I think that Fred could express the things which Disney felt and in doing so he was a surrogate for Disney on film. Fred had a very natural human element and was easy to like, though he could be volatile, too.

The mother in *The Shaggy Dog* was Jean Hagen (best known for her brilliant performance as Lena Lamont in the film *Singin' in the Rain*) who I found to be kind of mean. Kind of tough. Not lady-like at all. I didn't really like her.

Tim Considine was kind of hard to get to know as far as I was concerned. His thing was racing cars, which didn't interest me in the least. I liked to read books. But he was a consummate professional and as smart as they come.

Our director was a gentleman named Charles Barton. I loved him! He was a little man, a pudgy little man, probably about five feet tall, but he was the kindest, nicest man and his forte was directing child actors. He later went on to direct a lot of *Dennis the Menace*.

The film was supposed to be just a TV show, but they decided to make it into a feature—and to my surprise it became a big hit—one of the biggest hits they had for a live-action film. I think it was something like number three at the box office that year.

The Absent-Minded Professor (1961)

It was near the end of filming on *The Shaggy Dog* that Walt Disney approached Fred MacMurray with the idea of making another comedy for the studio—the result was equally popular—*The Absent Minded Professor*. Bill Walsh later recalled the how the studio acquired this wacky story:

> "Somebody had written some short stories for the old *Liberty* Magazine, and Walt bought them. One was about rubber and one about flying cars and one about milk, and we combined them. A Professor Sumner Miller from El Camino College

was brought in to supervise the laboratory sequences and he helped to develop the idea of Flubber, a sort of substance with the resilience of rubber and malleability of plasticine."

Associate Producer Winston Hibler (1910-1976) adds a bit more to the story:

> "We had a technical adviser on *The Absent-Minded Professor* and after a while, Walt half-seriously thought it might be possible to actually develop something like Flubber. In other words, to Walt, there had to be credibility. The audience had to be able to say, 'Yes, even in a wild, crazy way that could be true.'"

The film opens with Fred as Professor Ned Brainard conducting an experiment in his classroom which goes array—and blows up the room—leading into the opening credits. It immediately defines Fred's character—a well intentioned scientist who is a bit absent-minded, or perhaps in his case a lot absent-minded. Later that night, he suddenly recalls that he is to be married that day to his long-time fiancée, Betsy (Nancy Olson), a wedding he had missed twice before due to his being caught up in some experiment. Well, he gets engrossed in another experiment and misses yet another wedding ceremony, leading to Betsy breaking off with him and giving confidence to his rival stuffy Professor Shelby Ashton (Elliott Reid) that he could now win the hand of the lovely Betsy. But this time Ned's experimenting pays off as he has discovered a substance he names 'Flubber'—or flying rubber. This later leads corrupt businessman Alonzo P. Hawk (Keenan Wynn, in his first of many Disney appearances) and his basketball playing son, Biff (Tommy Kirk) to try and steal the formula for there own purposes. This film was directed by Robert Stevenson.

It was on this film that Richard and Robert Sherman received their first screen credit for a song written for a Disney film (they were already, however, working on the score for *Mary Poppins*):

> Across the hall from our office was the suite of writer/producer Bill Walsh. Bill was a mainstay at the studio—he had written many screenplays and was the producer of *The Mickey Mouse Club* and *Davy Crockett* television shows. In 1960, as he was putting the finishing touches on *The Absent-Mind-*

ed Professor, it occurred to him that a bright, upbeat fight song played over the opening credits might really kick off this comedy. So late one afternoon he popped his head into our office and asked, "Can you guys write me a college fight song…something real collegiate?" "Of course we can!" was our immediate—and standard—response. "The Medfield Fight Song" was our first screen credit together.

When the film was released on March 16, 1961 (just over two years after *The Shaggy Dog*) it went on to gross an extraordinary $11.4 million at the box office, out grossing other 1961 hits as *Lover Come Back, King*

Fred MacMurray and Nancy Olson in *The Absent Minded Professor*.
© Walt Disney Productions.

of Kings, Breakfast at Tiffany's and Walt's own *The Parent Trap*. The film was so successful that it spawned a sequel in 1963, *Son of Flubber*, which reunited the same cast and basically retold the same story, and to an awesome $10.4 million take at the box office, making it the 7th biggest grossing film of that year. Bill Walsh, the writer-producer of *Absent-Minded Professor*, later made this very telling comment:

> I always stuck a little bit of Walt in the main character, so he could recognize himself. He would say, "Now this kid's got it here. It's true, real, the character is real"… the father in *The Shaggy Dog* or the professor in *The Absent-Minded Professor*, I'd give him some of Walt's own personal characteristics.

Elliott Reid: I was very fond of both of the Flubber films (*The Absent Minded Professor, Son of Flubber*) though; I think the second one, *Son of Flubber*, was the most enjoyable of the pictures. I greatly enjoyed the character of Professor Shelby Ashcroft who was the foil of Fred MacMurray's Professor Ned Brainard in those films. Shelby was a miserable, condescending person. The man you love to hate—convinced that he will get

A classic shot from *The Absent Minded Professor*. © Walt Disney Productions.

the girl and that Fred was a nothing. He was a fun character to play and I had such a great time playing Shelby. And, of course, in the end he gets his comeuppance. I remember that my character used to look condescendingly at Fred and Fred got so used to it that when I did that he would say to me, 'Oh, I know that look so well.'

Tommy Kirk: I actually like the character I played in the 'flubber' pictures very much. I thought that Biff was more realistic than and not nearly as irritating as some of the characters—especially the one I played in *Bon Voyage!*

Elliott Reid: Our director was Robert Stevenson, who was a wonderful man to work with. He didn't really direct an actor in the sense that he gave us a blow by blow description of what we should be doing. He more or less guided us and allowed us certain flexibility.

Tommy Kirk: I loved Robert Stevenson. I truly wanted Fred MacMurray's friendship and approval, but I wanted Robert Stevenson's even more.

Elliott Reid: Fred was a very reticent man of Scottish background and I think I have a good understanding of the Scottish people. I never loped up to him. I let him be on the set without drawing my chair up to his and drawing him into conversation. I let him be alone. Fred wasn't the type of man to make conversation with a stranger. I saw the pain on his face when somebody he didn't know well would try to sit with him and engage him in conversation. He was not a public man so he suffered. But by the second picture he was comfortable with me—we gradually became friends. I would say we became fond of each other.

Fred was very definitely a good actor. The thing about his acting was that you weren't conscious that he was acting. You just believed him. He had a believability factor which many of the great actors had—Cooper had it, Stewart had it. Fred radiated integrity on the screen, and so when he played a villain, such as in Double Indemnity it made it all the more effective.

Our friendship certainly never extended away from the set. He invited me to dinner at his house once and for some reason it was cancelled and it was never rescheduled.

Tommy Kirk: As a light comedian he (Fred MacMurray) was as good as it gets, like Cary Grant at his best, but in his personal life he had a wall around him.

Elliott Reid: The girl in both of the "Flubber" films was Nancy Olson. I recall she was going with Alan J. Lerner at the time we were making the picture and she had a very busy social life. I recall she was on the phone quite a bit. But she was very charming and very nice to work with.

Tommy Kirk: Keenan Wynn, who played my father in the Flubber films, was a very nice guy. He went out of his way to be nice to me, very respectful and treated me as an equal. That was something I truly appreciated.

Elliott Reid: Keenan Wynn was the villain of the films and I knew him from the very earliest radio days. I was very fond of Keenan, but he was

The Professor finally gets married. © Walt Disney Productions.

also a very unpredictable man and a bit of an eccentric. He had a slightly storm tossed life.

Bon Voyage! (1962)

The next MacMurray outing, *Bon Voyage!* is the least of the films he made at Disney. It tells the story of a family from Ohio, dad (Fred MacMurray), mom (Jane Wyman), daughter (Deborah Walley), older son (Tommy Kirk) and youngest son (Kevin Corcoran), and their adventures on a European vacation. While the film was critically lambasted in most circles it did well enough to make around $5 million at the box office when it was released

Keenan Wynn as Alonzo Hawk. © Walt Disney Productions.

in June 1962. While that seems like a healthy box office take, its location filming helped make it a very expensive film and so it only made a modest profit by Disney standards. The film also had a rare bit of risqué material, which by most standards is very mild, but at the time quite a departure for Disney. The scene featured Fred MacMurray bantering with a French prostitute. "That was a disaster," Walt later told columnist Bob Thomas. "You should have seen the mail I got over it. I'll never do that again."

The film was directed by James Neilsen (1909-1979), who had helmed the moderately successful Tom Tyron-Tommy Kirk *Moon Pilot* the same year. Neilson was another Disney director with an extensive background directing episodic TV shows. He helmed many episodes of such shows as *Wagon Train, The Rifleman, Playhouse 90, Alfred Hitchcock Presents,* and *Adventures in Paradise,* before coming to Disney to direct some of the *Zorro* TV show. He had one break in films prior to coming to Disney, replacing Anthony Mann as director of the James Stewart Western *Night Passage.* It didn't do well, and so he was back to TV until he Walt Disney gave him the opportunity to direct *Moon Pilot.* While not a big hit, it did well enough to lead to three other Disney films: *Bon Voyage!, Summer Magic* and *The Moon-Spinners,* the final two with Hayley Mills. He later came back to direct *The Adventures of Bullwhip Griffith* with Roddy McDowell, but the film was a box office disappointment. He returned to TV and an occasional film such as *Where Angels Go—Trouble Follows* and the very Disney-like *Tom Sawyer* in 1973, his final film. Disney historian and critic Leonard Maltin later said of *Bon Voyage!:*

> *Bon Voyage!* sounds like a good idea for a Disney film: the adventures of a typical American family on their first trip abroad. Any possibilities that may have been inherent in the idea were dissolved in the transition to film, however. *Bon Voyage!* is a dull, hackneyed, and tremendously overlong film. What is more (and this is especially odd for a Disney movie) it is aimed at the wrong audience.

The *New York Times* thought the film "corny" and compared it to the old "Hardy Family" series presented by MGM from the late thirties to mid forties:

> "People who fondly remember the old Hardy Family films notice a slight resemblance in this one to some of them.

Tommy Kirk, Jane Wyman, Fred and Kevin Corcoran in *Bon Voyage!*
© Walt Disney Productions.

Tommy Kirk's callow performance of the older son may not be quite as bright as Mickey Rooney's of Andy, but it is in that same brash and bumptious vein. And while Mr. MacMurray's father is not as dignified as Lewis Stone's, it is a whole lot livelier and cornier. That, indeed, is the characteristic of the whole film."

Tommy Kirk: I have very bad memories of that film. It's the film I dislike the most from my Disney years. For one thing I hated the character I played in the film—the son of Fred MacMurray and Jane Wyman, Elliot. I thought the character was an asshole—really the butt of the movie. I also couldn't stand the director, James Neilson. I had no rapport with him. I thought he was a pipe-smoking stiff shirt who acted like it as all rather distasteful. And then there was Jane Wyman—initially I was excited to be working with her, but I came away disillusioned. She was very mean to me. She went out of her way to be shitty…I thought she was a total bitch.

Then I had a run-in with Fred MacMurray that was one of the worst of my professional life. There is an actor named Elliott Reid who was always doing an impersonation of Groucho Marx. You know, 'Say the secret word and the duck will fly down.' I thought it was hilarious and started to do it too. One day on the set of *Bon Voyage!* I was getting ready to shoot a scene with Fred and the director was about to start shooting and suddenly Fred turned to the director and said, 'You know, I kinda feel funny standing here. Can I face that way instead?' and for some stupid reason I said, in my Groucho Marx voice, 'Oh, so now you get the close-up?' Of course I was just kidding around, but Fred certainly didn't take it that way. Well, he just began to tremble, he was shaking and turning red, he was bristling mad; I really thought he was going to hit me. Nobody said anything, not the director, not anybody. It scared me. He was a big guy and built like a boxer. He thought I was trying to accuse him of upstaging me. He called out, 'Did you hear that?' to no one in particular and he said, 'Did you hear that?' And he waved his finger at me, it was as if I had accused him of being a pick pocket, and he said, 'When you've been in the business as long as I have, thirty-years, to say something like that to me! You're full of shit.' It was a terrible experience.

Well, I couldn't sleep that night. I decided to write him a letter of apology. I explained I was trying to be funny but instead it came out as a really stupid thing to say. The next morning I went to the studio messenger and asked to have it delivered to Fred. A couple of days later I arrived

Tommy Kirk, Deborah Walley, Fred, Kevin Corcoran and Jane Wyman in *Bon Voyage!* © Walt Disney Productions.

Fred and Kevin Corcoran in *Bon Voyage!* © Walt Disney Productions.

on the set to shoot a scene with Fred. He greeted me with a 'Good Morning, Tom' and I replied with a 'Good Morning, Mr. MacMurray.' And we went on like nothing ever happened.

Jane Wyman: The film (*Bon Voyage!*) was no great shakes, but it was clean. I always liked Fred. He was a master of underplaying and just an absolute joy to work with. Many people assume that the prima-donnas of films are actresses, but, honey, the truth is that he prima donnas are the men, Fred was one of the exceptions!

Follow Me, Boys! (1966)

Follow Me, Boys! is a well-crafted, if somewhat overlong piece of Americana. Many critics, perhaps correctly, labeled it as corn, but it's well-done corn and gave Fred MacMurray a good role as Lemuel (Lem) Siddons, who arrives in the quaint MidWestern town of Hickory as a trumpet player in a jazz band. He has always been looking for a place to set down roots and believes he has found it in Hickory. He quits the band and soon gets a job as an assistant store keeper to Charley Ruggles. He also finds himself attracted to pretty Vida (Vera Miles) who is the girlfriend of a stuffy banker, played by Elliott Reid, with whom he will now compete in a third film for the lady. In the meantime, he takes over a rag-tag bunch of boys and forms a Boy Scout troop. One boy in the troop who needs help,

Whitey (Kurt Russell), is eventually adopted by Lem. Also cast in the picture is Lillian Gish, playing Reid's Aunt. This was Kurt Russell's first film for Disney and he later recalled in the book *Remembering Walt*:

> The script lady pulled me aside one day and said, 'I think they're going to offer you a contact. Do you know why Walt likes you? Because you're not intimidated by him. I never could figure out why anybody would be intimidated by him.
>
> Some of the things Walt and I laughed about where if you could create movies in a way so people think they're looking through a window and seeing something they aren't necessarily supposed to see. If you could create that kind of feeling with an audience, then you've done your job. We used to talk about ways we could create that illusion. It was kind of an impish thing between us. I always felt he was chuckling in his mind.

The director was Norman Tokar (1919-1979), another TV veteran who helmed nearly a hundred episodes of *Leave it to Beaver* and did directorial chores on such other shows as *The Bob Cummings Show* and *The Donna Reed Show*. His first Disney film was *Big Red* back in 1962, and thereafter he handled the *Old Yeller* sequel *Savage Sam* (1963) and the superb family drama *Those Callaways* (1965). He would be one of the most consistently successful and utilized Disney directors until the time of his untimely death at age 59 in 1979.

The film opened at Radio City Music Hall as the big attraction of the Hall for the Christmas season. The reviews were mixed—many thought it was pure corn. The *New York Times* called the film a, "splashy, sprawling picture, which is as artificial as its brightly colored sets and every bit as superficial as its lump-in-the-throat sentiments. That said, it's only fair to inform you that the first audience yesterday morning at the Music Hall (made up largely, it appeared, of older people) was chuckling and sniffling all through the film." *Variety* applauded the film and considered MacMurray's performance one of the best of his long career. The public responded with $7.3 million in ticket sales, the second highest grossing Disney film of 1966 (after *Lt. Robin Crusoe, USN).*

Elliott Reid: After the "Flubber" films we made another one called *Follow Me, Boys*! This was Disney's tribute to the boy scouts. Originally there was no real villain in the piece and Disney said, 'We need a villain' and, of

Walt with Fred on the set of *Follow Me, Boys!* © Walt Disney Productions.

course, he thought of me because of the chemistry that Fred and I had in the other pictures. So Disney said, 'Get Reid!' and they had to rewrite it. When I got the picture and found that Lillian Gish was in it I was tremendously excited to work with her—and I told her so. She was marvelous. Charlie Ruggles also was in this film and I had admired him for years and when I met him and told him so he seemed quite pleased. Our director on this one was Norman Tokar. I knew him as an actor in New York many years earlier. Norman was a very nice man and quite serious and organized. A very good director.

The Happiest Millionaire (1967)

The Happiest Millionaire tells the story of a nonconformist named Anthony J. Drexel Biddle (Fred MacMurray), and his prominent (and wealthy) Boston family, as seen through the eyes of his newly imported from Ireland butler, played by Tommy Steele. We meet his wife (Greer Garson), daughter (Lesley Ann Warren, in her film debut) and her beau, played by John Davidson. Also in the cast as the Biddle's younger sons are Paul Petersen and Eddie Hodges. The distinguished cast also includes Geraldine Page and Gladys Cooper. The film was based on a Broadway comedy (without music) which starred Walter Pidgeon. Pidgeon very much wanted to recreate the role in the film, but was passed over in favor of Walt Disney's perennial favorite—Fred MacMurray (though apparently Brian Keith, Burt Lancaster and Rex Harrison were at some point along the way considered for the part as well). This would be the last live-action film that Walt Disney would personally supervise, and he very much wanted it to be his most successful picture since *Mary Poppins*. He spared no expense and recruited the Sherman Brothers to, once again, write the songs—as they recall in their autobiography:

> "We got a call from Walt asking, 'Are you guys busy?' I've got an idea!' WE told him we were already working on five projects, and he said, 'Unless you're juggling ten, you're not working!' Of course he was right—he was juggling twenty or thirty. Walt's idea revolved around a new comedy to be called The Happiest Millionaire. Screenwriter AJ Carothers had written a bright and witty script for it, based on a play and book by Cordelia Drexel Biddle and Kyle Crichton. The more Walt looked at the script, the more he kept seeing the possibilities it would have as a musical. He had just finished Mary Poppins, and his enthusiasm for musical films was at an all-time high. Al joined us in Walt's office, and when Walt told us his idea we wholeheartedly agreed—The Happiest Millionaire would be perfect as a musical. "

Marc Breaux and Dee Dee Wood were again recruited to work out the choreography. The film cost a reported $5 million, a very high budget for that time. When the film was released in late November 1967, at New York's Radio City Music Hall, it was nearly a year since the death of Walt Disney. His final film clocked in at some 159 minutes in its wide-screen road-show format. Many reviewers felt it was over-long, and exhibitors wanted more showings and eventually the film was cut to 118 minutes (the film was restored to its original length when it was released on home video in 1984). Overall the film failed to live up to the *Poppins* standard, either commercially or critically, and as Disney's final film is considered a disappointment. Co-writer A.J. Carothers would recall the film this way:

> "It's good Disney, and like all Disney pictures it will appeal to the best people, whatever age or background. It's wholesome and optimistic and fun. The villains get it in the end and people fall in love to stay. Some self-impressed sophisticates

like to put Disney down as square or childish. But great numbers of people all over the world will enjoy it and appreciate a
breath of clean air in a heavily polluted atmosphere."

Later the Sherman Brothers, in their autobiography, added their recollections as to why they believed the film failed to live up to expectations:

"Everybody at the studio hoped that *The Happiest Millionaire*
would be the next *Mary Poppins*, and after its premiere many
of the early reviewers agreed. But it didn't go on to be the hit
that we had all hoped for. It could have come down to something as simple as a question of timing. *The Happiest Millionaire* came out around the time we were getting into the Vietnam War in a big way, and people had no interest in seeing a
film about a man who's very patriotic and flag-waving."

The reviews for it were less than resounding. Bosley Crowther's *Times*
review was pretty disdainful. "The whole picture is vulgar," he wrote. "It
is an over-decorated, over-fluffed, over-sentimentalized endeavor to pretend the lace-curtain millionaires are—or were—every bit as folksy as the
old prize-fighters and the Irish brawlers in the saloon. The biggest howls
in it (and there aren't many) are when the alligators start to roam the
house and frighten a new and uninstructed Irish maid out of her skin."
Roger Ebert in his review contrasted the feeling of the film with that of the
earlier *Mary Poppins*. "You had the feeling, however, that the people who
were making *Mary Poppins* didn't exactly know what they had," he wrote.
"They knew they were having fun, but they didn't know they were strik-
ing some sort of chord millions of people would respond to. In *The Happiest Millionaire*, on the other hand, you get the definite feeling that the
movie was put together with every piece pretested for audience appeal."
That's not to say the film didn't receive any good reviews. The *Cleveland
Press* critic wrote, "*The Happiest Millionaire* is a pleasant, tuneful, tasteful
musical that is also over-long and uneven. The overall effect, however, is
one of pleasure and the movie is ideal family entertainment," and *Variety*
also tossed the film a bouquet. "*The Happiest Millionaire*, last major live-
action production of Walt Disney, is a family comedy, blending creative
and technical elements, scripting, excellent casting, direction, scoring,
choreography and handsome, plush production."   Leonard Maltin later
said, "My personal theory about *The Happiest Millionaire* is that the av-

erage movie-goer didn't really want to see a movie about a millionaire, happy or otherwise."

The film didn't meet box office expectations (especially at road show prices) so the film's length was cut so it could be shown more often at neighbourhood theatres.

Eddie Hodges: I remember being told that my friend Paul Petersen and I would play brothers. They said we would be singing and dancing. I knew it would be fun, since Paul is a terrific dancer and singer and it would be great to see him and work with him again. I had never worked with or met Fred MacMurray, Tommy Steele, Lesley Ann Warren or any of the

Fred teaches Tommy Steele how to box. © Walt Disney Productions.

The Happiest Millionaire (1967). © Walt Disney Productions.

other actors, so I looked forward to that. They were all really friendly and so talented. Paul and I started rehearsals well before it was time to shoot our dance number. We did a scene with another actor in which we sang the song "Watch Your Footwork" as a duet. Paul was so professional and so good at choreography—and his timing is impeccable—so it was really easy to learn the movements together. We pre-recorded the vocals over a track and lip synched it when the scene was shot. Fortunately, we both had experience and needed very few takes to finish it. When we were filming it I had the feeling that I was doing vaudeville, for some reason. I guess, because it was a period piece, as were the costumes and the vernacular of the lyric. It kind of reminded me of doing Broadway. I was just really conscious about not over-playing it. WE were both kind of animated, but the scene seemed to call for that—two macho, in shape brothers toying with their sister's suitor as they had likely done before. Then, we participated in another scene and a song with many others that was also choreographed. Working with the Sherman Brothers again was really fun.

Tommy Steele was a heck of a nice guy—very friendly—a real performer, as well as a skilled and energetic dancer. You could tell he was a seasoned performer and had done stage work.

I recall Fred MacMurray as kind, quiet, smoothly professional and subtle actor. He said very little—just enough to do the job. But, nice to me. I didn't see much of Greer Garson, we had worked together years before, but I'm not sure she remembered that. Lesley Ann Warren was a lovely, beautiful young woman and a really good actress. She can do it all: drama, comedy, song, dance, TV, film, stage—you name it. I also didn't see a lot of John Davidson, but he was a really personable guy. Very friendly and warm. Easy to be around and down to earth.

Walt Disney did visit the set. I don't remember him being much different than he was during the filming of *Summer Magic*, except he seemed a lot older than I had remembered him.

The film ran very long—longer than most films. And, it was not a modern setting with modern music—more like a Broadway show. I think Fred was not really a stage actor and would have been overshadowed by

Lesley Ann Warren and John Davidson as the young lovers.
© Walt Disney Productions

Harry Morgan, Cloris Leachman and Fred in Fred's final Disney film, *Charlie and the Angel.* © Walt Disney Productions.

Tommy, a powerhouse, charismatic showman. But, Tommy was not that well-known in the United States. Also, I think the timing was not right. *The Happiest Millionaire* was not a *Music Man*: it didn't have that Mid-Western, small-town, Americana charm going for it that would pull in audiences almost anywhere it played. It may just have been a bit too sophisticated to project that kind of a warm feeling. That's just my humble opinion. I think it was a good film, but not the great film I thought it might be. It dragged in spots and could have been cut a bit.

8

A Potpourri of Disney Titles and Recollections

The Great Locomotive Chase (1956)

The Great Locomotive Chase is based on a true story, set during the Civil War. Andrews (Fess Parker) is ordered to lead a band of Union soldiers into the South to destroy the railway system. A complication arises when the conductor of the train Andrews and his men are on finds out about their mission and tries to stop them. Along with Parker the cast includes Jeffrey Hunter, Jeff York, Claude Jarman, Jr., Harry Carey, Jr., and Slim Pickens. Parker was delighted to be given this role in large part because, "At least I'll get out of these buckskins!"

Disney chose Francis D. Lyon (1905-1996) to direct. Lyon had begun his career as a film editor in his native England for the Rank Studios. He came to the United States in the late thirties and eventually won an Oscar (shared with Robert Parrish) for editing the terrific boxing film *Body and Soul* (1947). He turned to directing, mostly for TV, in the mid-1950s. After *The Great Locomotive Chase,* Lyon directed more films, usually minor but well-done Westerns like *The Oklahoman* and *Escort West* before drifting back into television direction on shows like *Perry Mason* and *Laramie.* Lyon later told Leonard Maltin that Disney was enthused about the picture because, "he was a train enthusiast, which is evidenced by the fact that he once had a miniature narrow-gauge in his huge garden at home."

Bosley Cowther gave the film a warm review in the *New York Times*: "Walt Disney's personal affection for antique railroad trains is indulged with delightful extravagance in *The Great Locomotive Chase*, the latest of his real-life color features, which came to the Mayfair yesterday. A boy turned loose in a roundhouse could not have more obvious fun. And a viewer equipped with a juvenile's fancy can get in on same from watching this film."

Fess Parker and Jeff Hunter in *The Great Locomotive Chase.*
@ Walt Disney Productions

Harry Carey, Jr.: After I got *Spin and Marty*, I was cast in another Disney picture, *The Great Locomotive Chase*. To me it was boring because I was nothing but a glorified extra, just standing still on that train. I went out of my mind! We all did. We had nothing better to do than drink. We were just a bunch of drunks running around. Not Fess Parker, though. Fess didn't do too much drinking. But Jeff York was a hell of a boozer and he had an old car and he had to go across the state line to get booze and bring it back. We were shooting in Georgia some place and it was a dry state at the time. So York would bring back the booze and we would get gassed every night. We were just so bored!—it was a boring movie, too. Fess Parker, of course, went on to big success in *Davy Crockett*—Fess was a good actor—and a great guy. I wasn't a bit surprised. Jeff Hunter was also in *Locomotive*. I didn't really get to know him well on that picture, but I did get to know him very well on *The Searchers*, which we made shortly afterward. He was a wonderful guy and a hard working actor. John Ford was very fond of him too. It's a damn shame he died so young.

Fess Parker: In between the *Crockett* shows I did other projects for the Disney Studios. I was under personal contract to Walt Disney, and pretty much had to do what he wanted. While it wasn't the best film for me in my career at that time, *The Great Locomotive Chase* was fun—we had a good time shooting it on location down in Georgia. Disney loved anything that had a tack and locomotive. He was a train nut—I don't think he would mind me saying that.

Westward Ho! The Wagons (1956)

Wagon master James Stephen (George Reeves, TV's *Superman*) leads a wagon train of settlers, including his wife and children, across the vast plains. Prominent among the settlers is Doc Grayson (Fess Parker) who, though not really a doctor, he provides what medical care he can to the travelers. The wagon train is beset by Pawnees, determined to make off with the horses. A later encounter with presumably friendly Sioux takes a dark turn when the son of the chief appears to be dying, and only Doc Grayson can help. This was Disney's first live-action Western film and along with Fess Parker and George Reeves are Disney stalwarts Jeff York, David Stollery (of *Spin and Marty*) and from *The Mickey Mouse Club* Doreen Tracey and Cubby O'Brien. Kathleen Crowley is cast as Parker's love interest. The film was directed by William Beaudine (more about Beaudine in the *Ten Who Dared* synopsis).

Walt Disney pointed out that the film would have, "no Cavalry—and the Indian fight comes in the middle, not at the end. But the settlers don't form a circle to fight the Indians off. They race toward a gay, where safety lies. The Indians aren't just killers: they want something. So Fess stampedes a herd of horse's right into their charge. Each Indian scrambles to get a horse for himself and the attack is broken. We'll have to wound a few of them, but we aren't going to go overboard. Yakima Canutt our action adviser wanted to explode one of the wagons for a spectacular scene, but I told him the settlers wouldn't be carrying that much powder."

Fess Parker: I also did *Westward the Wagons*, with George Reeves—here were Davy Crockett and Superman working together—two of the biggest cultural heroes of that era! I did enjoy getting to know George, who was a very friendly guy—and I was very sorry about his early demise.

Harry Carey, Jr: Bill Beaudine was one of those old-time directors who liked to get the job done quickly and efficiently. He rarely shot more than one take. I liked him, but felt maybe he could have done a little more.

Toby Tyler: Or Ten Weeks with the Circus (1960)

Here is Walt Disney's version of the James Otis Kaler novel about a young boy who runs away and joins the circus and the various people and adventures he encounters. Also highlighted is his relationship with the chimpanzee, Mr. Tubbs. Bill Walsh produces with Charles Barton directing a cast which includes Kevin Corcoran, finally given his own starring role in a Disney film (after supporting roles in *Old Yeller, The Shaggy Dog* and *Pollyanna*). Corcoran would be one of the busiest child actors at the studio during this time. Also included were two supporting players from the *Zorro* TV show, Gene Shelton and Henry Calvin. James Drury (later TV's *The Virginian*) also has a notable part in one of his three 1960 Disney films. This would also be the first film at Disney for Michael McGreevey who would go on to make another ten films for the studio over the next fifteen years.

The *New York Times* called the film a "friendly little yarn" and lauded the cast: "*Toby Tyler* can boast some of the most engaging, unstrained performers in many a Disney moon. Among them are Richard Eastham, Bob Sweeney, Gene Sheldon and little Barbara Beaird (Toby's eventual partner). Best of all is Henry Calvin, as the strong man with a soft heart. Mr. Stubbs? He's terrific, that's all."

Michael McGreevey: My first Disney film was *Toby Tyler: Or Ten Weeks with the Circus*. I went in for an interview, first with just the casting director, because it was a small part. After the interview, I returned to be approved by the director and producer. I remember a discussion with my agent concerning whether or not to take such a small role because I had just co-starred in a film with Alan Ladd. It was decided that I should do it because Disney was a studio that provided lots of roles for kids and you wanted to become an actor they liked. Obviously, the agent was right because I continued to work at Disney for two more decades.

It was a lot of fun because of the circus atmosphere (exotic animals, clowns, etc), but I only worked on the movie for one day. The most memorable thing about that day was that I got to see Barbara Beaird again. We had done a movie together (*The Man in the Net*) the year before and I had a major crush on her. Who wouldn't!? She was this total cutie, a terrific

Ad for *Toby Tyler*.

young actress and a really sweet girl. But this time we were no longer co-stars. Barbara was one of the stars of the film and I was just a day player. I was disappointed that I didn't get to spend much time with her because she and Kevin Corcoran were with their own teacher and I was with the teacher in charge of the child extras.

I was also excited to meet Gene Shelton and Henry Calvin who were both actors in one of my favorite Disney T.V. shows, *Zorro*. Gene and Henry didn't disappoint; they were charming and funny. I was thrilled to actually hear Gene Sheldon's voice because he played the mute butler in *Zorro* and never spoke. Throughout my career, I was fortunate to work with many great character actors and I truly adored them all. They were not only talented actors, but usually wonderful people as well.

Speaking of great character actors, I actually did my scene with one of the best—Bob Sweeney. He was so professional and actually helped me quite a lot with my performance. Bob later became a successful director (*The Andy Griffith Show*). That didn't surprise me at all. He possessed all the qualities necessary to be a really good 'actor's director'—patience, understanding and marvelous communication skills.

I didn't actually meet Kevin Corcoran on this film, but I would later get to know him as an adult when he returned to the studio in the mid 70's and worked as a production executive. He's a great guy, but as a child star I would tag him as a bit of a spoiled brat. I told Kevin what happened on the day I worked on *Toby Tyler* and even though he didn't remember the incident, Kevin confirmed that it sounded like his behavior pattern during that period. After lunch that day, I went to play softball on the field next to the commissary with Kevin and about 12 of the kid extras. As I joined the other kids in the outfield I quickly realized that we were not playing a typical game of softball or baseball or even a game of rotation. It was a game called "Moochie gets to bat the whole time and the lowly extras just play the field." I went along with it for about ten minutes then my sense of fairness forced me to confront Kevin and suggest we play a rotation game so that everybody got a chance to bat. Kevin looked at me like I was insane and ordered me to go back in the field. Just as I tried to yank the bat out of his little prima-donna's hands, the Assistant Director stepped between us and announced that lunch was over and everybody had to return to the set immediately. When I think back on the incident, I thank God for that A.D. showing up when he did. I was about to punch the star of the film. If I had followed through with my intent, I never would have had a career at Disney Studios. Funny how little things have such a huge impact on your life!

Our director was Charles Barton who, talent-wise, was just an average director. But when it came to working with kid actors, he was one of the best. He was very kind and completely unthreatening. You felt safe with him. I had just worked for the famous director Michael Curtiz (*Casablanca, Adventures of Robin Hood*), who had been a terrifying and intimidating presence, so the friendly and sweet personality of Charles Barton was a refreshing and welcomed change for me. I never worked with him again, but my father wrote dozens of *Family Affair* episodes and Charlie was the main director on that series. I visited the *Family Affair* set several times and it was always a pleasure to hang out with Mr. Barton—the gentleman director.

As a child actor at the Disney Studio it was Fun! LOTS OF FUN! Unlike the other studios in town, the Disney lot catered to the needs of child actors because they used so many young people in their productions. There was a special "Little Red Schoolhouse" trailer outside of the makeup/wardrobe department and sometimes it would be filled with kids from different shows shooting simultaneously. As I already stated, there was a softball field, ping-pong tables and a basketball court, all for the sole entertainment of the young actors on the lot. Because so many children were involved in the productions, the adult crews were more experienced working with kids and there definitely was a relaxed, family-like atmosphere on the sets. I always felt comfortable working at Disney than I did at the other studios. As a kid, it never felt like work at Disney, it was like going to a really cool and fun summer camp.

James Drury: *Toby Tyler* was a fun film. It was based on those classic children's stories and Disney brought them to life in a spectacular fashion. I'll say one thing, though; I should never have shot that chimpanzee in *Toby Tyler*! I've heard about it ever since from kids and parents alike. They didn't like me at all! Lucky I only winged him—I don't know what would have happened had I killed him.

Ten Who Dared (1960)

Ten Who Dared is Walt Disney again exploring historical Americana with this film about the adventures of John Wesley Powell and his team who were the first people to explore and chart the Colorado River through the Grand Canyon in 1869. The film was not very well received by critics upon its release, but it's a very beautifully photographed film, directed by William Beaudine (1892-1970).

Beaudine directed hundreds of films during a career which began in silent pictures in 1915 (he also worked on occasion as an actor, most notably in many Mack Sennett comedies from 1912-1915). Beaudine had a distinguished career in silent films. He served as an Assistant to D.W. Griffith on his classics *The Birth of a Nation* and *Intolerance*. He directed Mary Pickford in several films including *Little Annie Rooney* and *Sparrows*. At the advent of sound films he was considered one of the best directors in the industry. His first few years in sound films bore this out. Among his early sound pictures include *The Mad Parade, Penrod & Sam, Three Wise Girls, The Crime of the Century* and the W.C. Fields classic *The Old Fashioned Way*. However, by the late 1930s he was increasingly making B-films and by the 1940s was turning out films for poverty row companies like Monogram and PRC. In the 1950s he directed the cult film, *Bela Lugosi Meets the Brooklyn Gorilla*. His final pictures, in 1966, bore the titles *Billy the Kid Versus Dracula* and *Jesse James Meets Frankenstein's Daughter*. By this time Beaudine had acquired the nickname "One-shot Beaudine"

David Frankham: *Ten Who Dared* was an adventure film based on Major John Wesley Powell's exploration of the Colorado River. I thought that I must have spent weeks on the location but when I reviewed my diary years later I found that we spent only about ten days in the fall of 1959 shooting the film on location. I wasn't even needed until the fifth day of shooting so in the meanwhile I spent my time visiting an Indian reservation and eating, I ate a lot of hamburgers—they wanted me to fatten up a bit for my part. I was also advised to grow a mustache but when I arrived for my first day of shooting the director took one look at it and had me use a phony one instead for the film.

Our director, William Beaudine, wore a riding crop and looked and acted like one of those stereotypical silent movie directors, which is where he began. He was a man of few words. I felt in 1959 I could have used more direction. I felt insecure—I could use more reassurance. He was the kind of director who would direct you if you were going in the wrong direction and if not would let you alone—he let me alone so I guess I was doing what he wanted.

We had a good cast. Brian Keith I found unapproachable—I didn't have a lot to do with him per the script. But he was a very subtle actor and a good one—and he played this very garrulous and grouchy guy-which seemed to fit his real life personality. James Drury was playing a rather solid character and kept to himself. Most of my scenes were with that superb character actor L.Q. Jones who was easy to work with, so in character that he was already the character he was playing when we got to the set and a very subtle actor. He never got his due as an actor. We never had to do things over—we worked very well together. He was a natural actor. I'm not sure where LQ left off and the character began.

What I recall most of the location shooting along the Colorado River was the cold! We arrived the 20th of October and L.Q. and I had a fight scene in boat and we have to fall into the Colorado. There was ice on the bank of the river and I thought, 'Oh my god.' It was about 7am and we were all shivering. I didn't know anything about a wet suit. So I was outfitted with one of those and then the costume guy runs cold water down my back so that when we fall into the river it wasn't supposed to be such a shock, but it was cold, my God, it was cold.

Ten Who Dared was supposed to be a two-part Disney TV show, but when Walt Disney saw the dailies with the extraordinary location scenery he decided to make it into a feature film. Beaudine announced to us that we were extending the schedule because it was now going to be a film.

When we returned to shoot exteriors at the Disney Studios I finally got the opportunity to meet Walt Disney. I was shooting a scene with L.Q. and when it was completed I was brought over to meet Mr. Disney and I said to him, 'It's a great pleasure to meet you, Mr. Disney.' And he told me, 'around here people call me Walt.' And they did—there was none of that—'watch out here comes the boss stuff' at the studio with Walt Disney. He came by the set almost every day when we were back shooting at the studio—and stand quietly in the background and observe.

I remember I was invited to a screening of the picture and I kept sinking lower in my seat. I didn't quite enjoy watching myself on the screen, and then I just decided to leave—and it turned out I had to walk right past Walt! From that point forward I referred to *Ten Who Dared* as NINE MEN AND A COWARD. I just watched the picture for the first time in years and I thought it was O.K. It's not grade-A Disney. It's an OK adventure story with a good cast. I don't think it's as bad as some of the reviews at the time indicated.

James Drury: *Ten Who Dared* was a wonderful adventure shot with the authentic boats that the Powell Party had used and we all had a great time. It was a great American story and a wonderful cast. I call us a band of cutthroats, but we had a hell of a good time making that picture. We must have spent something like 6-8 weeks on location, I know it was over a month, and we really bonded and when you work with people for that long in rough conditions you really get to bond and we sure did—and many of those bonds lasted a life time.

The locations were breathtaking. The sad thing is that a lot of them are gone now. Lake Powell was built sometime after the picture was completed and that covered a lot of the canyons that we filmed in. We were lucky to have seen them while they were still there.

What I remember most about our director, Bill Beaudine, was that he wore a handle bar mustache and had a great calm and élan. He was the calm at the center of the storm. And believe me there were a lot of storms on that picture—what with the location shooting in sometimes dangerous situations and a bunch of guys who enjoyed a good drink now and then.

Brian Keith was just great. He was a man's man and a fine gentleman. He had gone all over the world and had a lot of stories to tell. He was just fabulous as that mountain man.

I'll never forget the memorable river fight in *Ten Who Dared*. The water was about 27 degrees and the only reason it wasn't frozen was that the current was moving at about 40 miles per hour. We went out in that cold river and spend something like 3-4 days shooting and wore wet suits under our costumes. It was just miserable.

We got sick and tired of the food, so Ben Johnson began bringing in groceries he got from some little outpost and we built our own campfire at night and began to make our own food—it was damn good.

I possibly enjoyed making *Ten Who Dared* more than any film I ever worked on. That said I would say that *Pollyanna* is the one I like to watch the most because it's a true classic.

Texas John Slaughter (1961)

Texas John Slaughter was part of the Disney TV series and ran from 1958-1961 with Tom Tryon (who also made the film *The Cardinal* for director Otto Preminger and later the film *Moon Pilot* at Disney) in the title role. Disney kept trying to keep early American pioneers alive a la Davy Crockett, and in this end, John Slaughter is based on an actual Texas Ranger. Clad in a white cowboy hat with the brim pinned up in front, Tryon made this a popular figure on the TV series. The show also included (again like Crockett) a theme song, though not quite as memorable. Later on Tryon retired from acting and became a novelist whose spooky book *The Other* was made into a motion picture in 1971.

Harry Carey, Jr.: After my stint on *Spin & Marty*, I ended up doing a couple of other things at Disney over the years—mainly for the TV show. I did a multi-part television program called *Texas John Slaughter*. It was a Western and the ones I was in dealt with a bunch of scouts on the look out for Geronimo or something like that. Tom Tryon played John Slaughter and he was terrific, but it was just another job for me. Nothing special. By the way Tom Tryon later went on to become a successful writer and wrote a book which scared the hell out of me called *The Other*. Our director was James Neilsen who was a good friend and a drinking buddy. He was a terrific director, but on our shows he would get behind schedule because he had this habit of making a lot of takes. He was a better stage director. In the early fifties he directed me in *John Loves Mary* in San Francisco—and I got some of the best notices of my career—and I didn't even have to mount a horse. Jimmy really understood actors very well.

Babes in Toyland (1961)

Tom Piper (Tommy Sand) is about to marry Mary Quite Contrary (Annette Funicello). Just before their wedding, evil Barnaby (Ray Bolger) hires two henchmen (Henry Calvin and Gene Sheldon) to drown Tom and steal Mary's sheep, cared for by Little Bo Peep (Ann Jillian), thus depriving Mary and the children she lives with of their livelihood, forcing her to marry Barnaby. Also included is the toymaker (Ed Wynn) and his assistant (Tommy Kirk).

Babes in Toyland is based on the Victor Hugo operetta and had been filmed before, most notably by Laurel and Hardy in 1933, to great acclaim. This was the first Disney live-action musical and the studio put a great deal of expense into it. For years after the L&H version would be seen under the name *March of the Wooden Soldiers*, so to differentiate it from this film. This version was the big Disney Christmas release of 1961, and was considered mildly disappointing at the box office.

Walt Disney selected Jack Donahue (1908-1984) to direct the film. Donohue began his career as a dance teacher, and among his students was Eleanor Powell. He later went to Hollywood as a choreographer. His directing career began at MGM where he directed Red Skelton in two likable films, *Watch the Birdie* and *The Yellow Cab Man*. He later directed several episodes of Skelton's popular TV series. During the 1950s he directed TV shows for Frank Sinatra, Cyd Charisse, Dinah Shore and Dean Martin. He also directed the 1954 Doris Day musical *Lucky Me*. Looking for an experienced director of musicals and dance for his own first musical motion picture, Donohue seemed a logical choice. It would be Donohue's only film for Disney. Later he would direct several television shows for Lucille Ball.

This would be the first starring motion picture that Annette Funicello would make at Disney and she had fond memories of the film as she wrote in her autobiography:

> "Of all my filmmaking experiences, *Babes in Toyland* is without question my favorite. It was one of those rare times when everything about making the film—from my director, my co-stars, the crew, the costumes, even the scenery—was perfect. Though some critics were less than overwhelming in their praise of the movie when it premiered around Christmastime in 1961, it has won a place in the hearts of families and children everywhere. I'm pleased to hear from so many people that watching *Babes in Toyland* is now part of their holiday tradition, right along with trimming the tree and drinking eggnog...It's easy to see why Mr. Disney was so enamored of this project and why so much effort and money were poured into its production. (Flawed though it may be, *Babes in Toyland* is regarded by some Disney historians as the trial balloon, so to speak, for the studio's next foray into live-action musical comedy, *Mary Poppins*."

The film was the big Christmas attraction at the Radio City Music Hall, and the *New York Times* reviewed it:

> "Mr. Disney is not setting a precedent, of course. Just about twenty-seven years ago, Stan Laurel and the late Oliver Hardy were having a joyous go at Mr. Herbert's juvenile fantasies. This time, Mr. Disney, true to himself in his own fashion, has constructed a garden of dreams to delight every child, with the aid of a few of the noted Herbert melodies, a spate of new ones, a cast of photogenic kids and willing grown-ups and sets as stylized as those of any Disney cartoon."

Ann Jillian (at this point spelled Ann Jilliann) was given the pivotal role of Little Bo Peep, and she is a wonderful addition to the cast. This would be the first film she would make under the Disney banner. She would later appear on TV in *Sammy—The Way Out Seal*. Shortly after this film she would go on to play 'Dainty' June in the film version of *Gypsy!* And grew into a three time Emmy-nominated actress and star of the TV series *It's a Living*. Here she speaks of her memories of this Christmas film perennial and how Walt Disney changed her name:

Ann Jillian: The year was 1960. I was 10 years old and I had successfully completed numerous auditions for the coveted part of Little Bo-Peep in Walt Disney's version of the classic, *Babes in Toyland*, which actually began production on my birthday. Now, I was entering not only the gates to the studio but my future, as well.

It was here that, at Walt Disney's urging, I was given my "show business" name: Ann Jillian. I was hired under my real name, Ann Nauseda. If you're having trouble getting your mouth around that name, well, that's the very reason Mr. Disney himself suggested to my mother that it ought to be changed. Now, my mother may have come from another country (Lithuania), and had an accent, but she was well educated and nobody's fool. A call came from Mr. Disney's secretary requesting that we meet with the boss, and the next thing I knew, we were sitting in front of the legendary Walt Disney, and the director of the film, Jack Donohue.

Babes in Toyland was the big Disney release of 1961. Ann Jilliann and Annette Funicello are in the center. © Walt Disney Productions.

Walt Disney ruled his kingdom with a strong and wholesome hand. Everyone in the company loved him. He was a father figure. He took the time to know every one of his employees by name. That's what I was told by so many on the lot, and what I witnessed, first-hand. From the make-up department to the cafeteria, the animation department to the "property captain," from publicity to the music department, all of them had nothing but the highest regard for their employer.

And the children who were under contract before me: Kevin and Brian Corcoran, and grown-up Annette, all ran to hug him whenever he visited the set. I was privileged to be newly included into the hug. "Mrs. Nauseda, please know that we don't think there is anything wrong with your name," he began, "However, the public, for the most part, will have difficulty pronouncing it. I know I do, and we feel that your Ann has a future in this business. A last name that could easily be read and spelled, and look good on a marquee, would be a good idea.

"Ann's first name, of course, will remain the same," he said, "I think of her as being melodious (I sang a lot as Little Bo-Peep), so her name should be the same. My own lovely daughter's name is 'Jill,' so I put the two first names together: 'Jill' and 'Ann' to make 'Jilliann.'"

We all sat there, rolling the name over our tongues to see how it felt. The decision was unanimous. From that moment on, I would be known as Ann Jilliann in film. If you ever catch the movie during the Christmas holidays, you'll see the credits with my last name spelled with two "n's". In the years that followed, I got tired of writing the second "n" and dropped it to form the "Jillian" you may be more familiar with today.

Tommy Kirk was smart, very smart. He was a gentleman on set and followed his directions courteously. Funny too! He had the set laughing with or without the script. (I thought he was cute). Tommy Sands was another gentleman. I knew he was married to Frank Sinatra's daughter, Nancy, who visited the set from time to time and was a very pretty, pretty lady. I loved his crooning (and I thought he was cute too—smile—hey, I was an 11 year old girl, I developed crushes every day!). I remember he was kind. He could have been aloof, but was kindly accessible. He liked my voice which thrilled me no end.

Annette Funicello was adorable, pretty, tiny waisted like she 'sketched.' She looked unbelievable in her costumes, delightfully graceful when she was dancing. She was preparing for her wedding while she was in production, and if I remember correctly, the wedding gown she wore in the movie is the wedding gown she was given as a gift. A Disney star, a genuinely nice young lady, and years later when I worked with her again on *Fantasy Island*, she was an equally lovely, mature woman. As the years have passed she is often in my thoughts, and prayers.

I didn't go on tour to promote the picture, perhaps Annette did and Tommy Sands. Maybe even Ray Bolger and Ed Wynn, but I was too young. Although I was part of a 'promotional' TV show on Disney's television series called *Backstage Party* for the purpose of advertising the movie. All of the characters from the movie had musical numbers and skits. I got to

Annette Funicello in *Babes in Toyland*. © Walt Disney Productions.

sing to Tommy Sands on top of a piano, and danced with Henry Calvin and Ray Bolger to special material written for us called, "I've A Flock of Sheep Named Henry..." it was great fun!

Every morning, while I was filming *Babes in Toyland*, my waist length hair was curled and carefully placed to cascade down my shoulders. Between the hair, makeup, and wardrobe, everyone was always fussing over me. I felt like a princess...and I was getting paid for it!?

We (my family and I) were invited to the 'wrap' party at the Disney ranch in Placerita Canyon for a 'ho-down.' There were staff photographers there and I believe many of those pictures were used for publicity. They must be in the archives. I have some. One is a treasured picture of Walt Disney and me. Another is with our director, Mr. Jack Donahue. Still another is with a very wet Mr. Ray Bolger who had fallen into the pond when his canoe had overturned...I had laughed as I gave him back his soaking cowboy hat, I knew it was a 'photo-op' and precociously told him so. We both had a great laugh years later when he came to visit with Mickey Rooney, Ann Miller, and myself when we were doing "Sugar Babies."

The film is now a Christmas classic and I have such fond remembrances of it: The Forest-Of-No-Return, where we danced and sang with

Ed Wynn, Tommy Kirk, Annette Funicello and Tommy Sand in *Babes in Toyland*.
© Walt Disney Productions.

moving and singing trees. Ray Bolger, who complete with the villain's regalia, taught me, between scenes, how to dance the tango. (Later at the "wrap" party at Mr. Disney's ranch, Ray fell in the lake from an overturned canoe and I felt close enough to precociously ask him if it was a publicity stunt or the real thing?) Sidney Sheldon who, together with Henry Calvin had been a comedy duo in many Disney films, taught me to "cross" my eyes individually moving them back and forth...a noteworthy accomplishment, I know, and it's not easy. Try it!

Sammy The Way Out Seal (1962)

This fun and very popular episode of the weekly Disney TV show was about two young brothers (Michael McGreevey and Billy Mumy—who do look like brothers and act like brothers—they make a good team), who secretly bring home a seal from their summer vacation and try to hide it from their parents (Robert Culp and Patricia Berry). Also in the cast are pretty Ann Jilliann and Jack Carson, in one of his last performances prior to his untimely death in 1963.

Billy Mumy: I got a chance to meet Walt Disney and he was really nice to me. He told me to call him "Uncle Walt." I wasn't really comfy with that, though. I worked with a lot of big "stars" when I was a little kid, but because of my age—they really didn't impress me all that much. But Walt Disney was…well, he was Walt Disney! He was Disneyland. He was *The Mickey Mouse Club*. I was totally into everything he produced. He was a huge star to me. And, yet, he seemed really down to earth. He wanted to know if I was having fun making *Sammy The Way Out Seal*!

Our director on *Sammy* was Norman Tokar, who became a good friend of mine. He was probably my favorite director of all that I worked with. He stated things in a kid friendly, simple way. He understood kids. He had been an actor when he was younger, playing "Henry Aldrich" on radio, and he also directed the first 100 episodes of *Leave It to Beaver*, which still hold up brilliantly today in my mind. Norman was great. He related well with kids. Before we filmed a take he used to come over to me and whisper 'think' into my ear. Just that one word. It worked. I think. In the cast was Jack Carson, he was nice, but we didn't hang out. I was really into working with Mike McGreevy, who I still stay in touch with. I was much more into being with him as his little brother, than the adult actors on that project. And, I dug working with the seals. Pat Berry who played our mom on *Sammy*, played my mom several more times during the 60's. I also worked with Ed Wynn on that this project and on the feature film, *Dear Brigitte*. He was super nice and really fun to work with. He was one of a kind. A special talent. When each of those projects wrapped, he gave everyone on the cast and crew a wallet that was engraved, "Thanks, Ed Wynn." He was a classy, nice, gentle man. I wish I still had one of those wallets—lost in time, somewhere.

Whenever you work on a studio lot for a while, you get used to seeing the cast and crew from other shows. It's not a big deal. They're just people doing their jobs just like you. One of the things I used to do was check the vending machines on every stage, because I collected Pez dispensers, and they'd have different dispensers in different machines on different stages. Also, the Disney commissary had a gift shop, where I'd buy little figurines from time to time.

Michael McGreevey: My next project was *Sammy The Way Out Seal*—and it was a joy to make. I didn't want it to end. I got to work with one of the best director's in the business, Norman Tokar. He had also written the script and it was so true to what kids really felt and how they reacted in certain situations. Also the dialogue was excellent and easy to deliver because it captured exactly how kids talked. I think Norman's many years directing episodes of *Leave It to Beaver* (almost 100 shows) had prepared him well to create and realize a project like *Sammy*. The cast was perfect and we instantly worked together with ease and precision that continued throughout the entire production. Billy Mumy and I connected the first moment we met and he became the little brother I always wanted in real life. Patricia Barry was so kind and motherly. Robert Culp was a bit intimidating, but that actually worked well for the story and Ann Jilliann was adorable as my 'love interest.' Ann and I actually became close friends and later dated in high school, going to my Senior Prom together. The highlight of the shoot for me was the three days we spent shooting in the pool with the seal. They actually built the pool on Stage Two and we got to swim and play the whole time. Because I was the oldest (and the best swimmer) Norman let me do all the tricks and cool stuff with the seal in the water. How many kids get to do that? I would later work with a lot of animals in my career, but the seals used in *Sammy* were the most interesting and talented animal actors I ever interacted with. After the show, I went down to the San Diego Zoo several times in the ensuing years to visit with the seals and they always pretended to remember me.

Billy Mumy and I never discussed how we would play the Loomis brothers we just did it. Every once in a while, two actors have that unspoken rapport that allows them to work effortlessly together—Bill and I had that close instantaneous connection in abundance. I also think the fact that we really liked each other and became good friends definitely helped and added to our chemistry on screen. For child actors, Bill and I were both pretty 'normal.' Our parents made sure that we didn't start thinking we were 'special' and they insisted that we behave appropriately on the set. Bill and I both loved acting; we hadn't been forced into it. We wanted to be on the set and we really enjoyed working together. Off camera, we were like brothers, very close and always goofing around.

Savage Sam (1963)

Fred Gipson wrote a sequel to *Old Yeller* as a novel in 1962 (a sequel is hinted at by the ending of *Old Yeller*) called *Savage Sam*, and Walt Disney quickly optioned that book as well. Given the popularity of the original film, it isn't surprising. Savage Sam is Yeller's pup, given to Travis at the end of the original film by Lisbeth. Savage Sam is less a character study than a conventional Settler versus Indians story with much more action than the original film. When compared to the original film it may not compare favorably, but when viewed on its own merits, it's a suspenseful and entertaining outdoor saga.

Both Kirk and Corcoran return for the sequel (as does Jeff York), but gone are ma and pa—they are out of town, and Travis is still trying to prove he is in charge with the ever bratty Arliss (he was only somewhat annoying six years earlier, but is now he is downright obnoxious). Lisbeth is back too, but not with the wholesomely pretty Beverly Washburn. Washburn was unavailable for the sequel so Disney hired the stunningly beautiful Marta Kristen (who was once considered as a possible Lolita in the film version of that novel). Stalwart Brian Keith, in his fourth Disney film, is cast as Travis and Arliss' uncle. Keith gives his usual finely understated performance. While the film is called *Savage Sam* the dog actually is less a center of this film than in the original film. Gipson and William Tunberg again wrote the screenplay, but this time another Disney yeoman director, Norman Tokar helms the picture (Robert Stevenson was in pre-production on *Mary Poppins*). The film clocks in at 103 minutes (20 minutes longer than the more tightly efficient *Old Yeller*).

In its review of this film the *New York Times* critic calls *Old Yeller* "a not so well-remembered" film of a few years ago" (my! How times have changed!) and then dismisses the current film in a couple of curt paragraphs: "*Savage Sam* is a far cry from the memorabilia of John Ford." In truth, *Savage Sam* didn't review anywhere near as well as *Old Yeller*, and didn't do nearly as well at the box office. Still the film has action, excitement and wonderful outdoor color photography. Kirk and Kristen are a good team, Corcoran is a brat: but that is how they wrote the character and they still insisted after all of these years that he, essentially, play "Moochie," his alter-ego from *The Mickey Mouse Club* and his earlier films.

Marta Kristen: I auditioned for the role of Lisbeth in *Savage Sam*. The person to make the final decision about whether I was to play the part was, of course, Walt Disney. I met him at an arranged lunch along with the director, Norman Tokar, and a few of the other executives involved in the production. I was very nervous and could barely eat anything. I remember vividly, however, when I finally did put fork to mouth, Mr. Disney asked me a question and I started to choke. I was mortified! Once I had recovered, Mr. Disney was lovely, asking if I was alright, and continued talking to me as if nothing happened. I could have jumped up and given him a big hug, but then I was a polite Midwestern girl, and I would never have done such a thing.

I loved working on *Savage Sam*. I had not seen *Old Yeller* prior to working on *Savage Sam*, but I did see it years later. I thought it was very sweet. I am an outdoorsy kind of person and Savage Sam was made almost completely outdoors. Because I had to ride horses throughout the film, the Disney Studio had me training with horses for one month prior to filming. I had ridden throughout my childhood, growing up in Michigan, but I had never had the chance to ride the kind of horses they gave me to ride for this training. I thought I was riding on clouds! I also worked with a stuntman who would pick me up from the ground while trotting and throw me on the back of the horse. I was in heaven! In television there is no time to do this kind of preparation. You audition; get the script, and then show up to film. There is a kind of excitement, a living on the edge, to this approach, but I think most actors prefer to have the luxury of time spent preparing for a scene, which you have in film.

Of course another actress had played Lisbeth in the earlier film. There was never any mention of the previous film or the other girl's performance. I was pretty new to film and I just played myself. As I previously mentioned, I loved working on this film. It was exciting to work with the cowboys and wranglers and stuntmen. They were a hoot! I would hear about the weekend bar room brawls…one guy or another would come to work on Monday with a black eye or a bruised cheek…but they would all be joking and kidding each other and were the best of buddies at work. The fights were usually about women. That, I believe has never changed.

We shot the film near Calabasas and its environs. Now Calabasas is filled with subdivisions and mini-malls, but when we were there it was mostly scrub brush, oak trees, rocky hills and natural streams. I remember Raphael Compos, who played one of the Indians, screaming as he was being chased by Tommy Kirk, who had a tarantula on the end of a stick. They were buddies, but Tommy scared the you-know-what out of poor Raphael! There were many critters out there, including rattlers and spiders, which would scare most city folk out of their wits, but they never bothered me and I never bothered them.

At one point in the filming I was sitting on my horse which had a minimal saddle and stirrups to make it look like I was riding bareback. In this part of the story I had been kidnapped by Indians and the actor who

Marta Kristen and Tommy Kirk in *Savage Sam.* © Walt Disney Productions.

was leading my horse was on foot and was holding the reins in his hands. When the director yelled, 'Cut!' this actor dropped the reins and for some reason the horse that I was on spooked. There was a hill near us one huge oak tree on top. My horse headed straight for that tree on top of the hill at a very fast pace. Now, having been around horses most of my youth, I knew that those reins were in danger of being trampled on and if that happened the horse and I would go flying in the air. I also knew that if the horse and I survived the reins, I was in grave danger of being knocked off by one of the low hanging branches of the tree. None of this looked pretty. There was no way I could reach the reins, so I just leaned forward as far as I could, held onto the horse's mane and neck with all my might, gripped the horse with my legs and started laughing hysterically. Meanwhile, most of the crew was running up the hill trying to come to my rescue. As the horse and I approached the tree, I was certain he wanted to knock me off his back if he could, but just as we approached this mother oak he started to slow down and then he stopped! I don't know why, perhaps nerves or the excitement of it all, but I couldn't stop laughing. When the first of the crew members came up to me they must have thought I was crazy because of my laughter. However, they all seemed very relieved that I was safe. But I figure, if you're around horses for a while, you're bound to get hurt some way, at some point, or at least have a bit of excitement.

Norman Tokar had a lot to handle while filming *Savage Sam*. We were outside so he had to deal with the elements; there were animals…always unpredictable and sometimes ornery; stunts of all kinds; and many actors (always unpredictable and sometimes ornery). Mr. Tokar took his job very seriously, but he had a good sense of humor which helped him through the rough spots.

I developed a huge crush on Tommy Kirk. He was a bit older than I, and I thought he was a man of the world. However, I never felt out of place or uncomfortable during filming, largely, I think, due to Tommy being such a generous actor and easy to be with. Kevin Corcoran was so young, with those cute freckled Irish cheeks that I just wanted to pink all the time. There was nothing spoiled or bratty about him, which I attribute to his family, who kept his feet on the ground. I hugely admired Brian Keith. Even at the age of 16, I recognized what a great actor he was. There was nothing forced or pushed about his performance. He was always immaculately prepared and was very comfortable with the crew. I had a very few scenes with him, but I learned a great deal from watching him work. Seamless!

Show business dogs are kept on a very short leash, so to speak. These dogs are very well-trained making them very valuable. It's not like you hang with them like I do with my dogs. There were a couple of dogs who played Savage Sam, and they were remarkable in what they could do. They could herd, swim, retrieve and do all sorts of tricks. The trainers had complete control of the dogs, which, I think, performed for the love of their bosses. I never saw them mistreated, and they were always given treats and a few pats of approval after they had completed their assignments.

Marta Kristen handles her horse in *Savage Sam*. © Walt Disney Productions.

Savage Sam is an old style Settler versus Indians film. Our view of American Indians has changed so much since the film was made. We are now a more educated people about the horrible mistreatment and genocide we perpetrated on the indigenous people of the Americas that I think a film like *Savage Sam* would have to take a very different perspective if it were to be made today.

At the time I worked at Disney I think the artist was very much respected. It seemed less like a business, and more like an artist's community, which made it different from the other studios. Of course there was the hierarchy of executives who called the shots, but on the set the actor was treated kindly and politely. I was never mistreated at the other studios, but there seemed to be more of a feeling of family at Disney.

Miracle of the White Stallions (1963)

In WWII Austria, Col. Alois Podhajsky must protect his beloved Lipizzaner stallions and make sure that they are surrendered into the right hands. General Patton's something of a horse fancier and can help...if he sees the stallions perform. This is an unconventional Disney film with a cast which is not usually associated with Disney, led by screen legend Robert Taylor, then making his first major film in three years. Lili Palmer, Eddie Albert and Curt Jurgens fill out a strong cast.

Walt Disney selected Arthur Hiller (born in 1923) to direct, in his first major directing assignment for films (though he had a long list of TV credits). This film led Hiller onto a major career as a film director including such films as *The Americanization of Emily, Love Story, Plaza Suite, The Hospital, The Man from La Mancha* and *Silver Streak*. When the film was released, Bosley Crowther in the *New York Times* pretty much knocked it until the last paragraph when he wrote, "However, the youngsters should like it — those who love horses, that is — and everyone should get some pleasure from watching those white Lipizzans perform, under the guidance of red-costumed horsemen in the vast Vienna riding-hall."

Arthur Hiller (director): I was fortunate to make my film debut working for Walt Disney in a picture we shot almost totally on location, *Miracle of the White Stallions*. A.J. Carothers, who wrote the screenplay, which was based on the autobiography of Col. Alois Podhajsky, was a friend of mine and I had directed a TV show of his and he really liked my work and suggested me to Walt Disney.

Director Arthur Hiller.

Disney wasn't so sure because I was young, I was 38—so I wasn't that young, but in Disney's eyes I was young and I looked younger than my age. He had already looked over a couple of other directors and wasn't sure, so he called up Carothers and said, 'Who was that kid you wanted me to look at?' and arranged an interview. So I had my meeting with Disney at his office at the studio. I must say I was very nervous—he was a legend, after all. I had done a lot of television work, but had never helmed a major film and this would be a very expensive and ambitious project. But, the meeting went very well and within about twenty minutes I felt that I would be the one directing the picture. He said, 'you know the frame work of a Disney film—keep within that framework, but within that framework you can do different things.' He was as good as his word. When I might have a problem with the associate producer, who was with me on location, all I had to do was telegraph Disney—and he would back me up.

Robert Taylor had already been signed for the leading role when I came aboard—as a matter of fact, I think Bob was the first person Disney hired for the picture. That was fine with me because I had worked with Bob a couple of times on his television show, *The Detectives*. Bob Taylor was a total professional. He had it in his contract for that he would not film after six p.m. and he stuck to that. Well on one of the shows I did with him I needed another fifteen minutes to get the scene just right. I told the producer that I was going to ask Taylor if he could give us about fifteen more minutes. I was told he would never agree to this—that he was out at six no matter what. So I go to him and I explain to him that if we got another fifteen minutes the scene would be right and we wouldn't have to reshoot it the next day. He said, 'fine' and gave it to me. He was very cooperative and a very nice man.

It was a tremendous relationship that Taylor and I had on this film. I liked him a lot personally, too. He always wanted more direction than he really needed. He would say, 'Should I do this or that?' and I would assure him that what he was doing was fine. He as aware that he wasn't a great actor; but within his range he was quite an effective actor. He always gave me everything I wanted. He was a very intuitive actor and went a great deal by feel. It was a pleasure to work with him and that entire cast.

While Disney had cast Taylor, I cast most of the other roles including Curt Jergens, who plays the Nazi, somewhat sympathetically. I also cast Eddie Albert (Otto) and Lili Palmer, which might have been a potential problem if Bob Taylor weren't such a gentleman. Just before filming Taylor came up to me and said, 'Arthur, I would prefer it if I could be filmed on my left side—if at all possible.' I told him that Lili also wanted to be shot on her left side. He just kind of smiled at me and said, 'That's okay—Arthur, just go with her.'

We did shoot the film on location and it was remarkably problem-free, considering. The only trouble that I can recall was that we had some odd problems bringing some horses into the country, but that was resolved—probably because of Disney and his reputation which could cut through red tape. We had a terrific production head that, if something came up and we had to cut here and there to keep within the budget, would not cut key scenes which would hurt the story, but look for little things here and there.

I remember a very funny story that happened during the shooting. A circus came to town while were filming, and the circus people wanted to watch the filming and they were so thrilled that they extended their thanks by inviting us all to watch them at the circus. I had been warned by Eddie Albert, who loved circuses and clowns that he wanted to pull a little prank on Taylor. It was a Saturday night and we all went to the circus—all except Eddie, who gave some kind of excuse. But Eddie's wife, Margot, joined us—me and Bob and his family. The circus opened with a

A young Walt Disney with a young Robert Taylor, circa 1938.

Volkswagen entering and about twelve clowns falling out of it. How they all fit in there I don't know! The clowns came out and did their routine. Then they came over to the boxes and began to playing with people in the audience. Then this one clown comes over to Bob Taylor and was having fun with him and Taylor was just eating it up. After about four minutes of this tomfoolery, Bob finally took a good look in the eyes of the clown and realized that the clown was none other than Eddie Albert! Eddie had always wanted to be a clown and talked the circus into letting him do it so he could have his dream come true and have a bit of fun with Bob in the meanwhile.

I thought that the film turned out very well, and I was very pleased that Walt was happy about it. The critics didn't share our enthusiasm, but I thought it was a dramatic, colorful and highly cinematic film—and Disney agreed with me. We were both disappointed that it didn't do quite as well as we hoped, but that is how it goes.

Emil and the Detectives (1964)

Emil (Bryan Russell) travels by bus to Berlin to visit his grandmother and his cousins. Along the way his money is stolen by a crook. Emil must get his money back as it is for his grandmother. While on the trail of the thief, Emil runs into Gustav (Roger Mobley) who is street-wise and gathers up his friends, the detectives of the title, to help Emil. Also in the cast is Walter Slezak as the "Baron" a master criminal planning a huge heist. The film is based on the 1929 children's novel by Erich Kastner, which had been filmed three times before.

Chosen to direct the film was TV veteran Peter Tewksbury (1923-2003), best known for directing several seasons of *Father Knows Best* and the first season of *My Three Sons*. His only previous feature film was the 1963 comedy *Sunday in New York* with Rod Taylor and Jane Fonda. Much of the film was shot on location in Berlin, which gave it an authentic touch. When the film was released the domestic box office was somewhat soft, but it did well enough abroad to make a small profit. The *New York Times* review was positive with director Tewksbury getting a strong compliment, "for once the producer has hired a good director." The *Times* also called *Emil* one of Walt Disney's "best children's pictures."

Roger Mobley: Not long after doing *For the Love of Willadean*, I was interviewed for the role of Gustav by Ron Miller, who was Walt Disney's son-in-law, and Tom Leetch. They asked me if I had money pinned to the inside of my jacket and it was stolen could I identify it and how? Without hesitation I guessed right—the stolen bills would have pin holes in them—they sent the script to the house the next day. Our director on *Emil and the Detectives* was Peter Tewksbury. He was the first director that really took time with me and squeezed some stuff out of me—had he directed more of my stuff I might have gotten more parts. We were on location in West Berlin for about four-and-a-half months. I stayed with a family called Johnson on the Army base there and they had twins (Rick and Ron), who were also in the film. We worked all night sometimes and all the kids in the cast became very close, the German crew was great, despite the language barrier. Bryan Russell and I spent every minute off camera playing baseball with the rest of the kids. It didn't matter where we were in Berlin…we managed to get a game going—usually with a broomstick and rubber ball! I like the film—but I'm biased!

For the Love of Willadean (1964)

Sweet and nostalgic tale of two brothers (well played again by Michael McGreevey and Billy Mumy) and their new neighbor (Roger Mobley), which lead to fights over the attentions of the pretty girl (Terry Burnham) named Willadean, who lives at the farmhouse down the road.

Michael McGreevey: Working with Ed Wynn on *For the Love of Willadean* was one of the most memorable moments of my time at Disney. He had a small but pivotal role in the second hour. We had all been working together for about a month when Mr. Wynn arrived to shoot his scenes. I think he was only there for two days, but he made a lasting impression on all of us. The first scene we shot with Ed Wynn contained a difficult, two-page monologue that he proceeded to deliver perfectly—in just one take! I remember standing there in that scene, watching this old man perform, and marveling at how incredible he was. Ed Wynn taught me a big lesson that day—a professional actor always comes prepared! I later worked with Mr. Wynn's son, Keenan, and I told him about his father's incredible acting feat that day. Keenan told me that his dad was 77-years old and started to suffer from the effects of Parkinson's disease at the time. His father had actually expressed concern that he couldn't possibly remember that much dialogue, let alone deliver it convincingly. Keenan encouraged his father to study extra hard and even helped him prepare for the scene. Off camera, I never really talked to him. He pretty much kept to himself. He was always nice and friendly when we would gather together to do a scene. And he was obviously a joy to work with because he was such a talented and consummate professional.

Roger Mobley: I had a blast with McGreevey and Mumy. Mumy was much younger and even then was into drawing heroes and space travel pictures. He also stole every scene he was in and at times was a pain-in-the-ass. Terry Burham was quiet. I had worked with her previously on *Hawaiian Eye*. Ed Wynn couldn't remember his lines for shit. It was filmed on the Disney Ranch outside of Newhall,CA. I recall we were doing a scene of us eating watermelon on location and there was a wildfire getting close enough to us that smoke was drifting through the scene! That was pretty exciting.

Gallegher (1965-1968)

Gallegher is set during the 1890s and was based on a series of stories written by Richard Harding Davis about a street-wise newsboy who wants to become a reporter, and to do so he begins to investigate stories big and small and runs into all kinds of adventures. As Walt put it in his introduction on *The Wonderful World of Color*, the time period was "the Golden Age of the American newspaper in a period of our nation's history fondly remembered as the Gay Nineties." Gallegher, wearing his trademark knickers and newsboy cap became an audience favorite on *The Wonderful World of Color*. Roger Mobley, who was selected to portray the resourceful young man, recalled that *Gallegher* was not only Walt Disney's favorite mini-series of his long-running series, but also the highest rated of the Disney mini-series. Disney once pointed out, "We believe in getting more action and bigger backgrounds for our stories, not just shoot them against a wall. We can justify the expense when we use sets for three or four shows for instance, I had a whole Philadelphia street in the '90's built for *Gallegher*." So much was Disney an enthusiast for this series that on his desk at the time of his passing was a script, "Gallegher Goes to Europe." However this was never produced.

Roger Mobley: I wish I would have played it better. I was into sports, surfing and girls and didn't really give a shit about acting and I can tell I was distracted when I watch the episodes. Someone should have made me read the *Gallegher* book and they should have made me do him with an Irish dialect—as he was written—that would have put it over the top. Looking at some of the *Gallegher* work I wish that Bryon Paul (director) would have kicked my ass back then and got more out of me. I hated being away from school and sports and my friends, but did have a good time on the set. Mr. Disney did come on the *Gallegher* set quite a bit. Years later, his grandson, Chris Miller, told me that Gallegher was his Grandpa's favorite project on *The World of Color*. Mr. Disney told me once, 'your portrayal of Gallegher is just as I imagined it should be.'

We did have some wonderful people for those programs—Harvey Korman and Anne Francis were so much fun to work with—we had a ball. Edmond O'Brien always accidentally spit all over me, so I hated being in a scene with him. John McIntire and Jeanette Nolan were so fricken' sweet. I didn't know how many movies they had been in when I worked with them—they were wonderful! Bruce Dern was an unknown and was pretty bizarre…but I liked him and the quirky, un-Disney-like way he played his character. Darleen Carr—I wish I had gotten to know her better. We were minors and to save road time they had us stay out at the guesthouse on the ranch where we filmed. She was a sweet girl, but we just didn't spend any time together off camera. I had a crush on Stacey Maxwell—she was a few years older than me though, and nothing came of it. I loved Ray Teal—but hid from him because he always wanted to go over the lines! Dennis Weaver was a really nice guy and a family man—he brought his kids to the set quite a lot.

My greatest memory of working at the Disney Studio was running into Annette Funicello in the studio commissary one day. She looked so gorgeous that day and knew who I was! And was a *Gallegher* fan.

Lt. Robin Crusoe, USN (1966)

Lt. Robin Crusoe is a navy pilot who bails out of his plane after engine trouble. He reaches a deserted island paradise where he builds a house, finds an abandoned submarine with lots of gadgets that he can use, and also finds a marooned chimp from the US Space program and a native girl named Wednesday who was exiled by her father. Wednesday thinks Crusoe wants to marry her, and when her father arrives on the island to collect her and Crusoe refused to marry her, chaos ensues. Walt Disney was given, for the first time, a writing credit though his name appears on screen as Retlaw Yensid, as producer Bill Walsh later pointed out in the book *Remembering Walt*:

> "The only story Walt ever wrote was *Lt. Robin Crusoe, USN*. He wrote it on the back of an envelope or throw-up bag on an airplane. I said, 'Walt, you don't want your name on this, do you?' 'I do, too!' he said. And he did! His name appears backwards in the credits—Retlaw Yensid."

Obviously the story and film was based on *Robinson Crusoe* by Daniel Defoe. Cast as the lead is Dick Van Dyke, in his second outing for Disney and first since *Mary Poppins*. Byron Paul (1920-2004) was a veteran director of many episodic TV series (including several installments of the Disney *Gallegher* series), as well as being Dick Van Dyke's manager, was chosen to direct. This was his first and last stint as a film director. The film was critically lambasted when it was released in the summer of 1966. Toni Mastroianni wrote in the *Cleveland Press* wrote that "even Walt Disney can't win them all." But that didn't deter the film from performing well at the box office, where it earned over $9 million, in all likelihood due to Van Dyke's star power. Also decorating the film (and very nicely too) is Nancy Kwan as Wednesday.

"We were in Hawaii, and so I did get to spend some evenings with Walt at that time," Dick Van Dyke later recalled. "At the time he was not well. I think his health was beginning to fail him even then." Van Dyke recalled that Disney wanted the natives to use war canoes of his own de-

Dick Van Dyke in *Lt. Robin Crusoe, USN.* © Walt Disney Productions.

sign, "So he had some built at the Disney Studios. I think they were made of fiberglass. And there must have been eight or ten of them and they had them all floating about a half-mile offshore. And as we watched them, they all sank into the bottom of the ocean. It was not too funny to him at the time, but it was funny." Van Dyke summed up the film, "I like satirical comedy . . . but in a picture like this one we don't have to worry about realism."

Peter Renaday: I eventually began getting cast in small parts or walk-ons in Disney films. I was told that Ron Miller, Walt's son-in-law, was responsible for getting me a part in my first Disney picture, *Lt. Robin Crusoe, USN*. Ron had seen me in the Disney Players productions. I was first used to read the off-camera lines to Dick Van Dyke when he was on a raft in the water (actually he was in the studio tank on stage three, the same tank where they had shot a lot of *20,000 Leagues Under the Sea*). I was "the voice of the manual" that he referred to. In the finished film the voice was done by Richard Deacon, who was one of the regular cast members on *The Dick Van Dyke Show*. While I was feeding him lines, Dick told me that when they were shooting in Hawaii, he noticed one of the chimps looking at him aggressively. The chimp suddenly got up and started toward him. Fortunately the chimp's trainer saw the look in his eye and threw his shoe at him to distract him. You never know what might upset a chimp. He had been perfectly friendly, according to Dick, up to that point.

Willie and the Yank (1966)

Willie and the Yank focuses on the lives of a young Confederate soldier, Private Willie Prentiss (Kurt Russell) and his Union friend, Corporal Henry Jenkins (James MacArthur). The film begins with Willie accidentally shooting an officer he serves under. Of course it isn't looked upon as an accident, and Willie runs away. If captured by the confederacy he would be hung as a traitor who went AWOL—and a spy by the Union. Nick Adams also appears as an unsympathetic Union soldier.

Peter Renaday: I continued to do odd roles at the studio. My next one was a multi-part TV production which starred James MacArthur and Kurt Russell called *Willie and the Yank*. I played a nasty union soldier named Haskell who finds young Kurt hiding in a barn and while still seated on his horse forces the kid to come out of hiding. Fortunately for

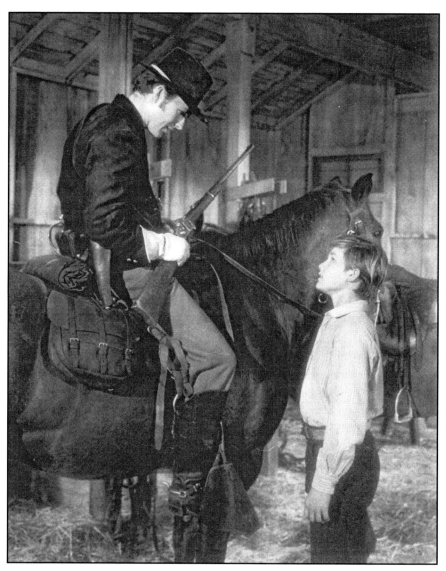

Peter Renaday with a young Kurt Russell in *Willy and the Yank*.

me, the horse was very smart and learned his blocking without having to depend on his inexperienced rider! This reminds me that I also got a chance to play James MacArthur's role in screen tests for the leading lady. They tested Barbara Hershey and Peggy Lipton!—and decided to go with the blonde (Lipton).

9

The Hayley Mills Films: The Rise of a Disney Superstar

Born Hayley Catherine Rose Vivien Mills on April 18, 1946, Hayley Mills was raised on the 400-acre dairy farm in Sussex, England owned by her parents, the famed British actor John Mills and his wife, writer Mary Hayley-Bell. She later recalled that she "read comic books on the back of a milking cow" and that her aim was not to become an actress but to "lead an equestrian life of riding and jumping horses and then to raise a lot of children."

That all changed the day that director J. Lee Thompson came to the Mill's farm to discuss a part for her father in his new film *Tiger Bay*. Thompson wanted John Mills to play the detective inspector who investigates the murder of a woman by a Polish sailor (to be played by Horst Buchholz). The murder is witnessed by a small boy who is abducted by the sailor. Thompson observed the uninhibited Hayley playing in the garden and "he just suddenly got the idea that maybe it didn't have to be a boy—maybe it could be me." Hayley did a screen test and the part was hers. She loved the idea of working with her father, whom she was devoted to. "(I) just sort of sneaked in there and started acting before I became self-conscious."

Her performance in *Tiger Bay* impressed the critics—even the notoriously fussy Bosley Crowther of the *New York Times*: "From the moment she glues her round eyes closely to a tarnished letter slot…she turns in a heart-gripping performance of a child caught by terror, dismay, morbid fascination, affection and stubborn loyalty."

Somebody else who saw Hayley in *Tiger Bay*, and was equally impressed, was Disney producer Bill Anderson. Anderson was in London doing preparation for the film *Swiss Family Robinson*, which was to star

The Mills Family, from left to right, Juliet, John, Hayley and Mary.

John Mills. Anderson had heard of Hayley's performance from his wife who, by chance, had seen the film. Anderson knew that Walt was desperate for the right young actress to star in his newest film, *Pollyanna*, and given the raves of Mrs. Anderson, he decided to check out the film himself. Upon viewing the film he was convinced that he found the right actress to play *Pollyanna*. Anderson called Walt in California—it was nine hours earlier—and trying to keep calm—he knew that Walt wasn't the type to be overwhelmed by enthusiasm—he told him about this little girl, and urged to keep from signing anybody else for the part until he saw Hayley Mills. Walt was dubious. The film was ready to begin shooting—all it lacked was the little girl to play the pivotal role. He couldn't delay the launch of the picture for another two or even three weeks until he had a chance to see Hayley Mills. Anderson told Walt to hold on for a week that he would acquire a print of the film and personally fly back to California with it. Walt was impressed by Anderson's enthusiasm for Hayley Mills.

Disney viewed the film and was persuaded. He called Anderson and told him that not only should she be in *Pollyanna*, but the studio should sign her to a long-term contract. At some point in the negotiations Walt and Lillian flew to London and were staying at the Dorchester Hotel when they invited the Mills family over. This was the first time that Hayley and Walt would meet. "I didn't find him overwhelming at all and I wasn't old enough to appreciate how remarkable it was to be shaking his hands," Hayley later recalled. "I found him very gentle and rather shy. Lilly was there, but my focus was very much on Walt Disney. Having been brought up on *Bambi, Pinocchio,* and *Snow White*—to finally meet the man who made them was riveting." That first meeting led to a five-year association with the studio which produced six films: *Pollyanna, The Parent Trap, In Search of the Castaways, Summer Magic,* and *That Darn Cat!*

John Mills: Hayley's performance in *Tiger Bay* had bowled him (Walt) over. It would, he said, be a crime if we didn't' give him the chance to build her into a big, international star. He had never seen a child like her. And how could we deprive the public of all that talent and pleasure? Walt Disney was genuinely fond of children. It didn't need Disneyland to prove that to us, Hayley adored him from the first meeting.

Walt Disney: She will become an actress more beautiful than Elizabeth Taylor and more talented than any star in motion pictures.

In my opinion, that little lady is the finest young talent to come into motion pictures in the past twenty-five years.

Karl Malden: Hayley was about to become a star, but she was totally unaffected, a little girl just like my daughters, dashing through the yard trying to get 'home' before she was tagged. I think that quality came across on the screen and helped to make her so appealing. Like Natalie Wood, Hayley was a young actress whose performance never veered into the precious or self-conscious. You believed her one hundred percent; she was never condescending toward her own childhood, a trap so many young actors fall into.

Jane Wyman: Hayley…was a joy to us all. What a person to act to. She acts right back. She'd been beautifully brought up, too. Polite. Almost curtsies when she meets you, if you know what I mean. What a grand theater family those Millses are!"

Mary Grace Canfield: I believe she was only 12 at the time and I thought she was very assured in the part and she didn't act like a 12 year old. Some child actors, I don't know what it is? But they are so self assured and know what they are doing without a great deal of training. Of course she came from a family that was quite prominent in the business, but she certainly didn't delay production due to inexperience. She acted like she had been doing it for twenty years.

Maureen O'Hara: Hayley Mills is from a wonderful theatrical family—the Mills'—and a very fine actress and she has a wonderful sister Julia, and Julia played my daughter twice and Hayley just once. So I have had the pleasure of knowing the whole family and loving them all. But look at the daddy she got her talent from, John Mills, one of the top actors in England. Hayley was witty, full of fun, charming and not spoiled one little bit.
  Hayley was a wonderful young child to work with and was at that point where she was feeling her oats and growing up—and one day Hayley came to me and said to me, "Maureen, can I ask you something— when you were my age did you resent your mother? ' "Yes, Hayley of course I did—that is normal for girls." And I told her not to worry one bit that she would get over it.

Eddie Hodges: Hayley Mills was wonderful to work with. Seeing her on TV and in the movies, I thought she might be kind of hyperactive, always moving around, etc. She was more reserved than I expected and had just a hint of cynicism in her. Nevertheless, she was fun to work with and we joked around a lot on the set. I developed a brief crush on her, though I never told her. We were friendly, but I think she just put up with me. I wasn't unlike the character I played—kind of an absent-minded nerd. But she and her brother came horseback riding with our family and I came to a swimming party she had at her home. She came out with us one night to meet Brenda Lee for dinner. The Mills' were pleasant, but rather British and reserved. I sometimes got the impression, though, that Hayley wanted to let loose more than she did around the family. After filming was over, we never really connected again.

Maurice Chevalier: I have been around longer than I have any right to be and I have seen them all. If this girl (Hayley) sails with a good wind she will pull the biggest audiences any actor has had in a score of years. She is not pretty, she is more than pretty. She has youth, which always has a shine upon it. Moreover she has vivacity, warmth and feminine wisdom. Not all English girls have warmth.

Eli Wallach: I've been a great Hayley Mills fan since I took the kids to see The Parent Trap. She's a refreshing personality, an instinctive actress and a vivacious young woman. The only way I could motivate the character so that audiences would think I wanted to kill her was to substitute the thought that Hayley was stealing all my scenes. Hey, wait a minute. Now that I think about it, she probably did.

Eli Wallach menacing Hayley in *The Moon-Spinners.* © Walt Disney Productions.

Pollyanna (1960)

Pollyanna was based on a famous novel written by Eleanor H. Porter about an orphan who comes to live with her wealthy Aunt Polly in the New England town of Harrington in 1912. The orphan, Pollyanna, sees everything through rose-colored glasses and her optimism becomes infectious with most of the towns people she encounters. She has invented "the glad game" and whenever somebody is down she can always find

Hayley as Pollyanna.

something for them to be glad about. The story had been filmed by Mary Pickford in 1920 to great success. Hayley Mills later pointed out that her "Pollyanna" was different than the one from the novel: "Our Pollyanna isn't the same as in the book. She was too sickeningly sweet. If you met any girl like that today, you'd want to kick her in the pants. This girl sees the nicer side of life, but she's a real girl, too. She can stick out her tongue when she is angry. She is much more believable."

In 1959, Walt Disney updated the story and believed he had found the perfect young actress in Hayley Mills to embody Pollyanna, and make her more palatable to 1960 audiences. Disney assigned David Swift (1919-2001) to write and direct the picture. Swift had worked for Disney back in the 1930's as an assistant animator. He left for several years and ended up writing and directing for radio and television. He created the acclaimed series *Mr. Peepers* which starred Wally Cox and Tony Randall and ran from 1952-1955. He returned to Disney to write and direct *Pollyanna*. Swift later recalled:

> "I couldn't get it right (the script treatment) and I hated it. Still, I sent it over to Walt, and a few days later I got a phone call from him. 'I read it; Bud (he always called me Bud),' he said, 'and I got a little tear there.' I was surprised because I knew from the way he said it I was to go ahead and finish the script—with him looking over my shoulder, of course. Until the final script was finished, he sat in on everything, and always had a concept of how the movie was going to be, the music, the photography, the casting, the look of it."

Disney surrounded Swift with a top-notch cast in addition to Mills. Jane Wyman, the Academy Award-winning actress from *Johnny Belinda*, was cast as wealthy and domineering Aunt Polly, Richard Egan is cast as her former beau, Dr. Chilton, Karl Malden is given the plum role as the fire and brimstone Reverend Ford, Nancy Olson is cast as Nancy, one of Aunt Polly's maids and confidant to Pollyanna, Adolphe Menjou plays the elusive child-hater Mr. Pendergast, Donald Crisp is the town's mayor, Agnes Moorehead is the grump hypochondriac, Mrs. Snow, and James Drury is George Dodds, Nancy's beau. Kevin Corcoran has one of the best of his Disney films, as the orphan befriended by Pollyanna—Jimmy Bean, Reta Shaw and Mary Grace Canfield round out the domestics and Anne Seymour and Edward Platt make good contributions as townspeople. It is one of the finest casts ever assembled for a Disney film up to that time—and would only be equaled by *Mary Poppins* four years later. Another star of the film is the town of Harrington, with its train station and Victorian homes—Santa Rosa, in California's Napa Valley, served as the fictional Harrington. The film is also lushly photographed by Oscar-winning cinematographer Russell Harlan, who had also photographed such films as *Rio Bravo, Operation Petticoat, Hatari!* and *To Kill a Mockingbird.*

The first day of shooting was a bit daunting for Hayley, as her father, John Mills, recalled in his autobiography:

> "Hayley was terribly nervous and quite ghastly in her first scene with Karl Malden on *Pollyanna*. It wasn't easy suddenly being a star in Hollywood, in a big Disney movie, with a huge star like Malden. The director David Swift, came to me, quite worried and said, 'I can't get anywhere with Hayley. Is she alright? Is she nervous?' I talked to Hayley and said, 'What's

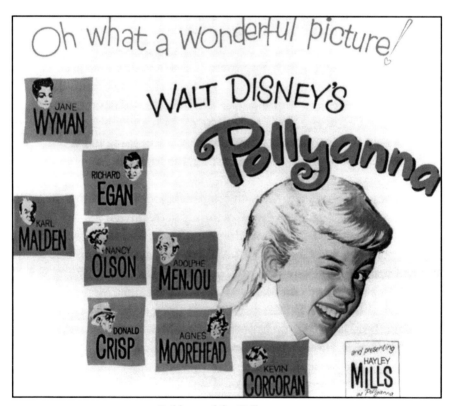

Lobby card for *Pollyanna.*

the matter? You're like a big cabbage—nothing happening!' But after lunch there was a transformation."

Malden also recalled the day in his autobiography:

"If I remember correctly, Hayley's first day of shooting was in a scene with me ... We rehearsed the scene a couple of times and I was trying to warm up things up so much that I could feel the scene turning to mush. I was trying to figure out what to do when we broke for a few minutes. I looked at her adorable little face and said, 'You know, Hayley, yours is a lot smaller, of course, but your nose is just like mine.' She burst out laughing. Whenever I felt her tensing up, I'd just point back and for the between her nose and my own. We were friends from then on."

The film has grand moments (the Bazaar, Rev. Ford practicing his sermon in the country) and warm moments (the discovery of the prisms at Mr. Pendergast's house, for instance) that are superb. *Pollyanna* is surely one of Walt Disney's all-time great live-action films, and while it clocks in at 134 minutes it doesn't seem overlong. Walt Disney had high hopes for the film, and while they didn't disappoint critically (it won nearly unanimous good reviews and Mills was especially lauded for her performance), it didn't do as well as he had hoped at the box office, where it earned $3.75 million in its initial release—which is a very respectable figure for 1960 dollars, but given the film's price tag was deemed a disappointment. Shortly after it opened Jane Wyman gave her view on the film and the reaction of fans:

"I don't know why they should come out (of the theater) crying. It is really a very funny movie in many places. Of course the ending is rather affecting. When Pollyanna wins over her Aunt Polly, the old bag I play—well, that's what she is. I think people need this movie. I think they're tired of sickness and violence. I know I am."

Despite the lackluster box office (Disney thought it had to do with the title—*Pollyanna* was based on what most people considered a book beloved by young girls—about a young girl who was sickeningly sweet.

He surmised this cut down on the number of boys who came to the movie), *Pollyanna* became one of Disney's personal favorites of the films he produced. Here is David Swift on the subject:

> "*Pollyanna* was Walt's favorite film. Because watching it made him cry. Of course, he could cry at the drop of a chord. I remember I showed him the rough cut of *Pollyanna*, which ran two hours and twenty-minutes, and I was surprised to see him crying, right there in the sweat box. I hated it. But he had his handkerchief out and he was crying. I said, 'Walt, we've got to take twenty minutes out of this,' and he said, 'No, no, no, don't touch it!'"

Mary Grace Canfield: I got the part of Angelica, the grumpy maid, in *Pollyanna* thanks to David Swift, who wrote the script and directed the picture. He had used me in some TV productions in New York, and so we had an acquaintance and he liked my work. But we had lost track of each other when we went to Hollywood. But one day, out of the blue, I got a call that David Swift wanted me for a part in a Walt Disney film, *Pollyanna*, and that he had written the part especially for me.

David Swift was very easy to work with and a very pleasant man. *Pollyanna* is probably—no, I would say it is the favorite thing I've ever done in the business. As a young actress it was such a thrill to work with people like Agnes Moorehead, Donald Crisp, Karl Malden and Jane Wyman. I think the mood on the set, which was so congenial, was due in large part to David Swift.

Jane Wyman was very pleasant to work with and the only time I was irritated with her was due to baseball! She loved baseball and when a game was on she would glue herself to the television and it would cause delays in the filming. I remember the last day of shooting was during the playoffs and she wouldn't be budged from the television! And I was getting impatient because I wanted to get it done and go home. I just wanted to get it over with. But she was wonderful in the picture.

I was thrilled to work with Agnes Moorehead because she was such a great actress, but she was also very withdrawn. She would do her scenes and then go directly to her dressing room. She spent very little time with the other players—except, occasionally Jane Wyman, because they were good friends.

Oh, I loved Reta Shaw! Everybody did. She was so much fun and so marvelous to work with. She was just the nicest lady and such a wonderful actress.

I got to meet Walt Disney, but I certainly didn't get to know him very well. He did drop in on the set quite often and I understand he was very fond of this particular film—somebody told me later that it was his favorite film. He was always very complimentary towards everybody on the film.

Pollyanna is a film that I'm just so very fond of. As I mentioned it was the most pleasant experience I had in all my years in the business. I thought it was a well done film and a very nice film for children with a great sense of nostalgia about it. It was a very pretty film, too, don't you think?

Hayley Mills with Jane Wyman. © Walt Disney Productions.

James Drury: Hayley Mills—what a sweetheart of a girl—we all adored her. Her mom and dad were on the set constantly. In between scenes I would spend a great deal of time with Sir John. We would discuss Shakespeare. Many people don't know that I had studied drama at NYU and had played twelve different Shakespearian roles (and an equal number of Shaw) while in college. So I had some very interesting and delightful conversations with him. Years later my wife and I were in London and Sir John called me to invite us to his club, 'The St. James Club.' We were treated royally. They were a wonderful family.

What a cast! Jane Wyman was a wonderful presence on the set. She was a fine, gracious lady. Nancy Olson was a sweetheart. She was the sister of my best friend in high school. She's one class act—a dear heart. David Swift was a wonderful director to work with. He was very understanding and kind and knew how to keep people on an even keel.

When we did location shooting for *Pollyanna* we stayed at a lovely hotel in Santa Rosa, California. I remember that Ed Platt and I were sitting at the bar one night and these two women came over and started talking to us. 'Are you married?' one of them asked and Ed said, 'Well, not necessarily.' We ended up partying with those girls and we raised such a ruckus that I was sure that Walt Disney, who happened to be visiting, heard it. So the next morning I came up to Mr. Disney and said, 'I hope we didn't keep you up last night,' and he just smiled and had that twinkle in his eye and said, 'No, I thought somebody just fell down the stairs.'

People still come up to me at autograph shows or wherever and tell me how much they love *Pollyanna*. It struck a chord with them because here was this girl who had such a winning personality and just wanted to make people feel happy. I'm told that the film is shown somewhere in the United States every day. I've been lucky to be in two truly classic films—*Ride the High Country* and *Pollyanna*—and I have Walt to thank for *Pollyanna*.

The Parent Trap (1962)

The Parent Trap is one of the most popular of Disney live-action films and has been beloved by kids and parents alike since its release in the summer of 1961. It is also the film where boys discovered and became infatuated with Hayley Mills. Unlike *Pollyanna*, *The Parent Trap* is a contemporary film and had a broader appeal than Mills' earlier film—especially among pre-teen and teenage boys.

The picture opens at a camp for girls, where wealthy Sharon from Boston meets her West coast lookalike, the more down to earth, Susan. They have different backgrounds and beliefs but they do look stunningly alike (obviously since Hayley Mills plays both roles, with the support of split photography and her double, Susan Hennings). They discover that they are actually sisters and Sharon lives with her mother (Maureen O'Hara) in the East, while Susan lives with her dad (Brian Keith) in the west. The two parents have been divorced since the girls were infants and decided

Hayley Mills in *The Parent Trap*. © Walt Disney Productions.

(without the story ever going into any elaboration) that they would each take one girl and apparently never have contact or allow their daughters to have contact with the other sister of the other parent. The girls decide they want to get to know their other parents—so they switch places and eventually contrive to bring the two back together and be one big happy family.

For kids going through or having been a part of a split family, *The Parent Trap* gave some of them hope that one day their own families could be reunited. The supporting cast included Charlie Ruggles, Una Merkel, Leo G. Carroll, Joanna Barnes, Ruth McDevitt and Nancy Kulp.

The cinematography, including the trick shots with a double and split screens, was done by Lucien Ballard (1908-1988), who had an eclectic career working for director Josef Von Sternberg (including *Morrocco, The Devil is a Woman*) at Paramount and The Three Stooges at Columbia. Other films he photographed include *The Lodger, Ride the High Country, The Caretakers, The Wild Bunch* and *True Grit*. Here is Ballard regarding the filming challenges of *The Parent Trap*:

> "I told them (the studio)…that I wanted a real double who really looked like Hayley. Finally I found a girl who was the same height, had the same features—everything was the same except her yes were a different color, but I was able to compensate for that. And at several figures away, you couldn't tell the difference between the girl and Hayley. So I did a lot of the over-the-shoulder shots, and threw out most of the vapor shots…But Walt made me put some of the trick shots back, because he liked technical things."

David Swift again scribes and directs the film (this would be Swift's last directorial assignment for the studio, he went on to direct such films as *Good Neighbor Sam, Under the Yum Yum Tree* and most spectacularly *How to Succeed in Business Without Really Trying*). Throw in a snappy title song written by the Sherman Brothers and performed by Tommy Sands and Annette Funicello (who recorded it while on break from filming *Babes in Toyland*) and you have a sure-fire Disney box office hit—in fact, it ranks as one of the top grossing films of 1961.

Maureen O' Hara: I was in New York when my agent called to say that there was a request from the Disney studios to do a movie, and he sent me the script, five minutes after reading it I was playing scenes from it and I called Jack Bolton, my agent, and said, "Absolutely"—so he went into the Disney Studios to see Mr. Disney or whoever makes those decisions, and they offered a ridiculous amount of money—so ridiculous because it was so low. He called me back to tell me of this dreadful offer, and I told him to say "No" because I will not belittle myself to work for that money. I would rather sell shoes at Saks Fifth Avenue. Tell them "I'm Sorry" and I was heartbroken because the script was so wonderful…Very shortly afterward he called me and said, "Yes, They will meet your price" and I said, "Fine, I'll do the movie." You have to stand up for yourself.

I don't think we could have hoped for a bitter director for the picture than David Swift. He was a comedy writer in radio and television before Walt Disney gave him his big break behind the camera. He had created the popular sitcom *Mr. Peepers* with Wally Cox, and this background gave him a great touch with comedic scenes and a sense of timing in the delivery of funny lines. His direction was significant in maintaining the rhythm of the comedy.

When we made *Parent Trap* Hayley had been in only two films before that, I didn't see the first one, *Tiger Bay*, but I did see *Pollyanna*, and when I knew I was going to make the movie I was so thrilled it was going to be Hayley and I thought, "Oh great, we're going to make music together" and I think we did.

Hayley was a wonderful young child to work with and was at that point where she was feeling her oats and growing up—and one day Hayley came to me and said to me, "Maureen can I ask you something? When you were my age did you resent your mother?" "Yes, Hayley of course I did—that is normal for girls." And I told her not to worry one bit that she would get over it.

Brian (Keith) had a lot of John Wayne's qualities—he wasn't as big a man but he had a lot of that walk…John Wayne was a better actor than anybody realized because you never said, 'Oh, my god—he's acting' he'd sneak this right over your head and Brian did the same thing—he was a fine actor and he cooperated and he would talk to you and say, "what if we did this or what if we did that."

(Brian) had always played tough and gruff characters before that, which made him my kind of leading man. He was big and strong and burly, and Swift always called him "Mr. Masculine" on the set. Brian was a natural at comedy. His delivery always came with a warm twinkle in his eye that defused his menacing size.

Maureen O'Hara with Brian Keith. © Walt Disney Productions.

Joanna Barnes told me that it was the top company she was in with that movie. She had to make the audience happy that she got her comeuppance and she did and she was wonderful.

Lucille Ball and Desi Arnaz' children used to tell me that they used to push *Parent Trap* on their parents hoping they would get back together.

When I saw it (*The Parent Trap*) for the first time I thought it was wonderful. I was proud of it and was proud that I was in it and was very thrilled.

The split screen photography was a technical trick—you have to cover up half of the screen and have the performer perform for the part of the film that is exposed in the camera and then cut and then repeat it with the other half of the camera. You have to unroll the film and go back to the beginning.

In Search of the Castaways (1962)

Hayley Mills' third Disney feature film teamed her with the legendary Maurice Chevalier in this adaptation of the Jules Verne classic story featuring earthquakes, flash floods, volcanoes, giant insects and a man-eating dog! As Mills and her younger brother search for their missing sea-captain father. Chevalier plays a French professor who aids them in their quest. The cast also includes George Sanders, Wilfred Hyde-White, Michael Anderson, Jr., and Keith Hamshere. This adventure classic was directed by Disney stalwart Robert Stevenson, and proved a box office winner when released in the summer of 1962.

Summer Magic (1963)

Summer Magic (1963) is a Walt Disney sleeper. It is one of the six films that Hayley Mills made under her contract with the studio (number four), but is not as well-known as *Pollyanna*, *The Parent Trap*—or even, for that matter, *That Darn Cat*. It's a pity because this is an extremely pleasing piece of Americana full of wonderful performances and performers. I think it's actually one of the studio's best live-action films of the early 1960s and deserves to be rediscovered.

Lobby card for *In Search of the Castaways*.

The film is based on that old chestnut "Mother Carey's Chickens," which was written by Kate Douglas Wiggin in 1911, which was, perhaps not incidentally, around the same period that *Pollyanna* was published. Wiggin was also known as the publisher of *Rebecca of Sunnybrook Farm*.

In Search of The Castaways. © Walt Disney Productions.

In Search of The Castaways. © Walt Disney Productions.

In Search of The Castaways. © Walt Disney Productions.

Wiggin had adapted her popular novel into a play in 1917 and then RKO made it as a movie in 1938. That studio wanted Katharine Hepburn to play Nancy Carey, but Hepburn balked at this and bought her way out of her RKO contract. Anne Shirley was hired and played the part in a pretty good adaptation of the film. Years later Walt Disney acquired the rights and the result is this wonderful 1963 release.

The plot deals with a Boston widow, Margaret Carey (Dorothy McGuire in her third and final Disney motherly role) and her three children, Nancy (Hayley Mills, who is top-billed), Gilly (Eddie Hodges) and Peter (Jimmy Mathers), who move to a picturesque small town in Maine. With the help of the Postmaster, with the equally picturesque name of Osh Popham (Burl Ives), they move into a large, yellow, run-down house—at no cost to the family—which is owned by the mysterious Mr. Hamilton, who Osh explains is living in Europe and wouldn't mind them occupying the house while he is away. Added to this mix of characters are Osh's wife, Maria (Una Merkel) and his son Digby (Michael J. Pollard) who has a yen to leave town and see the big city. And of course there has to be a dog—a sheepdog named Sam. There is a bit of rivalry introduced into the story when snobby Cousin Julia (Deborah Walley) comes to live with the Carey's and Julia and Nancy become rivals for a young schoolteacher

(James Stacy). Things are further complicated when the mysterious Mr. Hamilton (a younger than expected chap, played by Peter Brown) returns to claim the house.

Rather than make this a straight dramatic picture with comic undertones as the earlier one was, Disney decided to call in the Sherman Brothers who provided the bouncy score, much aided by Burl Ives and his banjo—especially "Ugly Bug Ball" which was almost not in the picture, due to Walt not understanding that beauty is in the eye of the beholder—even among bugs.

Disney selected James Neilson to direct. This would be Neilson's third of five films he would direct for Disney—and the first of two with Mills. The film is co-written by Sally Benson (1897-1972), who over the years 1929-1941 published 99 stories in *The New Yorker*. In 1941 her play *Junior Miss* opened to a very successful run on Broadway. In 1944 she went to Hollywood where she would help adapt one of her stories into the memorable MGM film *Meet Me in St. Louis* which starred Judy Garland with Margaret O'Brien playing a version of the actual Sally Benson. The movie was based on her own recollections of her childhood in turn of the century St. Louis. Certainly her selection to co-write *Summer Magic* had a great deal to do with the sense of Americana and nostalgia that she was able to evoke in many of her works. She also had a hand in the screenplay of Alfred Hitchcock's *Shadow of a Doubt* (1943), which was another film set in a typical, picturesque American small-town, but with much darker overtones.

The *Cleveland Press* liked the film: "The Walt Disney mint has coined another money maker in *Summer Magic*, a pleasant, unpretentious picture overlaid with sentiment and nostalgia an inch thick. This is neither an epic nor a milestone in cinema history but a good family picture with plenty of entertainment values." The *Pittsburgh Post-Gazette* also enthused, "Though not all Disney is good Disney—*Summer Magic* is near the top." The *Boston Globe* was more subdued writing that the film has "sugar, but no spice."

Peter Brown: I recall that during the shooting, Hayley's parents, John and Mary Mills were visiting from London. They had never seen an American baseball game, so I invited them all to one at Dodger Stadium. Dean Martin, a good buddy of mine, offered me his four dugout seats that he always had, so I had great seats for all of us. I picked them up at their hotel in my 1951 Bentley, perfect, I thought, for an English family. So we're at

Hayley Mills with Peter Brown in the underrated *Summer Magic*.
© Walt Disney Productions.

the game and I'm trying to explain what's going on. Maury Wills was our short stop at the time and a great base stealer. He was on first base after a walk, and then stole second. That broke the stolen base record of all-time so they stopped the game, pulled up the bag at second and gave it to Maury as a souvenir. Then they strapped down a new base and went on with the game. On the drive back John asked me what went on when the game stopped. I explained that out player had just broken the stolen base record so they gave it to him as a trophy. John, confused, said, 'No, no no, he didn't' steal it at all, I saw the gentleman in the little blue cap hand it to him.' All I could do was laugh; it's probably like John trying to explain a googlie in cricket to me.

Summer Magic was a lot of fun. In addition to Hayley, Burl (Ives) and Dorothy (McGuire) were both great pros and I enjoyed working with both of them. Burl gave me an autographed photo which now hangs in my library at home. It reads, 'To Peter, a swell gent—Burl.'

Things must have gone well with *Summer Magic* because I did another picture for Walt the next year, *A Tiger Walks*.

Eddie Hodges: We worked with the Sherman Brothers on the songs. They were a delightful pair! They were so much fun to work with. They taught us the songs and worked with us all the way to recording them at Sunset Sound Recorders. They really supplied the musical energy of that picture, as well as the songs. You may notice that the action didn't stop so the songs could be introduced. They were a part of the story, the characters and the action. The Sherman Brothers had a miraculous way of doing this—of weaving a song into the very fabric of the story so that you just felt it belonged there.

There was a strong scent of authenticity in that film—more than sets and costumes. There was a feeling in the characters—their attitudes and dialogue—the vernacular—so many ways that Sally (Benson, the writer of the film, who also wrote the stories which inspired the classic MGM film *Meet Me in St. Louis*, starring Judy Garland) created a place in time for the story of Nancy and the Carey's—to breathe life into them in such a way that the feeling came through the screen and into the hearts of those who were captured by it all and watched it unfold. That is a gift—you learn how to use it, but you can't buy it—it's God-given, and Sally had it.

Ron Miller (Walt Disney's son-in-law, an associate producer on this film) was present on the set a lot. I knew him, but not that well. He was a nice man—a gentleman, but didn't 'hang-out.' He seemed to be more into the production aspect of the picture—getting things done on schedule—things like that. I don't remember him being very involved in the creative part of what were doing. He was very personable—and warm.

Gilly! The Boston nerd! Gilly went through a transformation during the story and I was always mindful of what place were in the story when we were shooting a scene. At first, Gilly was angry about leaving the city and going somewhere that 'wasn't happening.' He was kind of an early 20th Century cool dude. He was a young musician who was steeped in the music of the time—rag time. He seemed set to join the ranks of all the other rag time music cats of his time—until his piano was taken away and he had to leave it all and move to rural Maine, of all places! I didn't want to play him as angry and sullen—he was not a dark characters—so I opted to make him kind of an absent-minded, nerdy kid who was frustrated, at first, but finally saw the wisdom of blooming where he was planted, taking it all in stride and making the best of the situation for the good of his family. I also wanted to fit well with Hayley's character—a vulnerable, good hearted, enthusiastic (though somewhat manipulative) teenage girl

Deborah Walley and Hayley on the set of *Summer Magic*.
© Walt Disney Productions.

who wanted only what was best for her family. You have to love that. Hayley was a glowing angel on the screen and I knew I had to, somehow, act as if I was related to her. I hope it came off as I hoped it might.

Dorothy McGuire was the sweetest lady you could ever want to know—so kind and gentle—never complained—always in a good mood and always smiling. She had a quiet wisdom that was kind of intoxicating. There was no pretense with Dorothy—she was always down to earth. I really learned to love her. A lovely, lovely lady.

Burl Ives—I had worked with him in the past—we were on the cover of a TV magazine once. He was a strong presence—quiet, but kind of awesome—he was nice to everyone, but rather quiet. He was focused on the work at work—he didn't care for any fooling around—kind of 'no nonsense' but in a really decent way. He always had a cooler by his chair full of fruit and snacks. He had his preferences—it seemed that he had learned to have things the way he wanted from the very start, just to make sure there was no confusion. He was very smart in that way. He always knew his lines, too.

Michael Pollard—I just like Michael. There was something about him that made me feel comfortable, though he seemed a little strange, at first. He was very quiet and seemed very shy. I felt he kind of under-played his role and I was told that was an Actor's Studio thing. He was a minimalist and that's what made him so interesting—his subtle presentation of the character he played. I was a bit in awe of that—I don't think I had that ability. I was always too animated for my taste.

Una Merkel was a sweetheart, like Dorothy, and very much an actress. She was always very focused and played well with the other actors. She would never upstage another actor, but I doubt any actor could ever have upstaged Una.

Peter Brown was really a friendly guy. He came to our house in Los Feliz to a poker game one night. Several people from the cast and crew were there. On the set he was always ready to shoot a scene—always prepared and professional.

I really enjoyed working with Jimmy Mathers. He was a wonderful young man—very courteous and very professional. I knew his brother, Jerry (Beaver on *Leave it to Beaver*). They were a great family. We went to their home to go swimming once. Jimmy was a really good child actor—very poised and always listened closely to the director. We got along really well.

I think the picture turned out to be a real classic. The visual effects

Eddie Hodges and Hayley in *Summer Magic*. © Walt Disney Productions.

in the long shots were a pleasant surprise when I saw the final cut. I was, as usual, highly critical of my own performance and caught myself acting too often, but I sort of believed that I was Gilly. The dedication to the story and the relationship between the characters was heart-warming. The continuity was good—I didn't see any mistakes in that regard. It was authentic, as well. I was really grateful for the editing—absolutely masterful. I can't tell you how many people of all ages tell me that *Summer Magic* is their favorite movie and they watch it over and over again.

Peter Brown: One thing which stands out in my mind is this, and I think it tells a lot about Walt Disney. We had the big barn dance sequence. We got the master, next came the two shot, and then came Hayley's close-up, which of course I had been standing off-camera for. Then came my close-up. But just before we started rolling, Hayley's tutor, who was there because Hayley was still under age, came and said, 'That's it for Hayley today, she's finished. You can have her back in the morning.' That was it. There was no discussion, she took Hayley by the hand and led her off the set. So the director, James Nielsen, and the producer, Ron Miller (who was Walt's son-in-law) asked me if we could shoot my close-up without Hayley being off-camera for me to look at and to respond to. I, of course, said, 'No, absolutely not!' They said they would put the script supervisor off camera to read Hayley's lines. I said, 'Sorry, no dice.'

Ron then took me aside and told me that I would have to talk to Mr. Disney. Damn! I thought. I had never even met him before. I reluctantly called his office, and his secretary put me straight through to him. I began to tell him the problem and he interrupted me and said for me to stay right where I was and he'd be right down. After a few minutes in walks Walt Disney, wearing a light blue cashmere golfing sweater, no tie, and a smile on his face.

After we outlined the problem, Disney looked at me and said, 'Are you aware that if we get this one last shot we can tear down this large set and begin building the next one overnight?' I told him that I wasn't aware of that, but I still didn't want to shoot my close-up without Hayley. He said he understood and that he, too, wanted the best performance out of both of us. Then he offered me a deal. He said I could accept it or not. He told me if I will shoot the shot now, he would hold the set until tomorrow, then he (Disney), me and Hayley, just the three of us would view the two shots and both close-ups in the morning and that if Hayley and I agree that it's good we'll print it. If not we will reshoot my close-up in the morning.

I couldn't turn him down so we shot my close-up, and true to his word just the three of us watched them the next morning. Hayley nodded to me and I turned to Walt and said, 'Print it.' He picked up the phone and said, 'Strike the set.' We all shook hands and he and I became more than employer and boss.

That Darn Cat (1965)

This was Hayley Mills' Disney swan song, but it also was a beginning—for a new leading man, Dean Jones, whose first Disney film this would be. The film, mild fluff directed by Robert Stevenson, was about a cat named DC (for Darn Cat) who along with her owner, Hayley, gets involved in an FBI investigation led by Jones. By this time, Miss Mills was ready to shed her Disney image and do more mature roles. She put it this

Hayley Mills with Roddy McDowell in *That Darn Cat*. © Walt Disney Productions.

Hayley Mills with a new Disney leading man, Dean Jones, *That Darn Cat*.
© Walt Disney Productions.

way in an interview with Bob Thomas of the *Los Angeles Times*, "After all, one can't go on playing young girls forever, and there are so many exciting parts for girls in their twenties nowadays." Mills' finale was a big box office hit generating nearly $9 million in revenue.

10

The Making of a Masterpiece: Mary Poppins

Walt Disney had thought of the idea of turning Pamela Lyndon (PL) Travers stories about a Nanny who comes as kind of a guardian angel to the Banks family of London, England into a film for over twenty years before the film was released. It took so long to come to completion due to one immoveable object in his path—P.L. Travers.

Mrs. Travers was an Australian who eventually moved to England. She wrote the first of her five *Poppins* books in 1935. They became worldwide best sellers and among those who enjoyed the books were Walt Disney's daughters, Sharon and Diane. They, and Disney's wife, Lilly, urged Walt to try and make a film of the books. "Years ago I saw my daughters Diane and Sharon reading this book, and they were chuckling, really enjoying it," recalled Walt later. "Then, a few nights later, my wife, Lil, was reading something and smiling and laughing. I asked her what was so amusing. She said, '*Mary Poppins*…you ought to read it." Miss Travers was highly protective of her creations and had very definite ideas of how they would be portrayed. Before Walt Disney came along other film companies were interested in buying the movie rights and she had rejected them all. Travers was a reserved lady, who never married, but later adopted a son. She believed that her books were universal and not to be relegated to children. "I have never written for children," she once said, "for who knows where childhood ends and adulthood begins."

In 1944 Walt Disney found out that Miss Travers was living in New York for the duration of the war (she came with her adopted son as a way to escape the Nazi blitz of London). Walt sent his brother Roy to sound Miss Travers out on the possibility of making an animated film of the *Pop-*

pins stories. Roy reported back to Walt, "Mrs Travers said she could not conceive of Mary Poppins as a cartoon character." But Walt wasn't one to easily give up. He then had the idea that *Poppins* could be a live-action film. At this point Disney had not yet made a live-action film, but was interested in doing so. By 1946, Walt thought that he had made a deal with Travers. He would buy the movie rights for $10,000—however, Mrs. Travers then asked for script approval—Disney wouldn't grant it and the deal fell through. Disney did, however, go on to make his first full-length live-action films around this time with *Song of the South* and *So Dear to My Heart*, and they (like *Poppins* later on) used animation in some sequences.

Fast forward to 1960 and Disney resurrects the idea of filming *Mary Poppins*. He is in London where he once again visits with Mrs. Travers, now 60 years old, and as tough-minded and opinionated as ever. Where in the 1940s the Disneys had played it cool with Travers and to make it seem that they weren't overly eager, now Mrs. Travers must have suspected that Walt very much did want the rights to her classic work and so she instructed her agent to up the ante. This time she was requesting an astronomical $750,000 for the screen rights for *Mary Poppins*. Later this was changed to 5% of the profits, with a guarantee of $100,000. Yet she still wouldn't sign the contract giving Walt the screen rights to *Mary Poppins*. Meanwhile, Walt was using his own money to come up with a presentation for Travers of story ideas and songs (Walt decided that the movie should be a musical—something else Mrs. Travers wasn't quite sure about). "The more I think about it, the more I am inclined to feel that it would be highly advantageous for all concerned if you could come to Los Angeles and spend at least a week with us here in the studio, getting acquainted with the people who will carry the picture through to completion, and giving us the benefit of your reactions to our presentation," Walt wrote Travers. The charm offensive was definitely on. Mrs. Travers later equated it with Walt, "dangling a watch, hypnotically, before the eyes of a child." Finally after two years of going back and forth, Mrs. Travers signed a contract with Walt Disney giving him the film rights but with her having final approval to the script.

The songs would be very important to the movie. The songs would enhance and advance the plot and help define characterization. He entrusted the songs to two brothers, Robert and Richard Sherman, who were best known around the studio for writing some of the songs that were used on various records that Annette Funicello (remember "Tall Paul"?)

had recorded. At the time they weren't under contract to the studio, but were writing on a song by song basis. "One day, in 1960, Walt handed us a copy of the one-volume edition of the first two *Mary Poppins* books," Richard Sherman later recalled. "He told us to read the book and let him know what we thought. We knew he was throwing down a gauntlet and we had to pick it up."

And pick it up they did. They understood that they had to make changes to make the story make cinematic sense. "We had to come up with a need for Mary Poppins to come to the Banks family," Richard Sherman recalled years later. "We had to make her a necessary person. We were going to set the thing during the Boer War and have his (Mr. Banks) regiment called up. Then you could have had a real happy ending, when he came home. And then…you could make the father emotionally absent…We made it a story about a dysfunctional family, and in comes Mary Poppins—this necessary person—to heal them." Brother Robert Sherman recalls, "The book was written in the 30's, the most depressing time in London. So we said, 'Turn it back to the turn of the century, where there was a wonderful, rollicking music-hall style. So we were just writing songs in that style, and Walt dug the idea."

Eventually Travers did come over—at studio expense, of course. Producer Bill Walsh recalled:

> "She came over for a month or so. I don't think she was too pleased with us, to tell you the truth, because she kept saying things like, 'Well, now, the rustle of Mary Poppins' skirt—there's a certain kind of sound it makes, and there's a drapery shop around the corner in Kensington and we MUST have that fabric.' Walt would interject, 'But Mrs. Travers, we're not going to spend all that time looking up draper's shops in Kensington Road.' But by this time she would be off on something else. 'And about the letter box,' she would say, 'you haven't got the right kind of red. There's a certain shade of red it has to be.' She was always getting hung up on all these details. Meanwhile, what we were trying to do was get a reasonable story out of the book. The original was a series of little fragments with no story—just a sensational character and funny little bits of episodes. We needed a story to bring the whole thing together."

Finally the brothers Sherman were given custody of Travers, as Robert Sherman later recalled:

> "One day, we were walking down to lunch—I'll never forget this—and I said, 'Pamela, you must understand something. We do not intend to even touch your books. Your books will always be there, sacrosanct. They will be there forever. More people than ever in the world are going to read your books because we're telling a story based on your books. It is not your story, no. But it is your books and your characters that we're talking about.' They were filled with delightful characters, wonderful situations, and not a single strip of a story. Nothing. There was no story line. The only thing that gives it any kind of bookends is on the east wind she flies in, on the west end she flies out, and in between she has adventures with the kids. But why she comes and why she leaves nobody knows. Well, Mrs. Travers we learned was very strange like that."

Eventually Travers approved a basic story line that Poppins flies in to bring the Bank's family together and then when her job is complete she leaves. Though she wasn't overly happy about it.

Next Walt began to look at the casting of the film. Early on somebody had the idea of Bette Davis, a more matronly Mary Poppins, but she refused to consider the film. Good thing, too, because as a musical it would not have been quite up her alley. Mrs. Travers had recommended the gifted actress Julie Harris, who followed up with a letter to Walt requesting consideration for the part. Walt politely turned her down. Mary Martin, who could sing, and might have made an appropriate middle-aged Poppins, was seriously considered, but at some point it was decided that Mary Poppins didn't have to be matronly or middle-aged as she is portrayed in Miss Travers' books. It was at this point that Walt attended a performance of *Camelot*, then playing on Broadway, and saw Julie Andrews. He went back stage that night and told her he wanted to consider her for the film. He later followed up with a letter:

> "We would so like to have you consider playing the role of 'Mary Poppins' in the Pamela Travers story, and I have just asked our casting department to contact your agent to see if some workable arrangements can be made. As it is difficult to

visualize a story of this type from a written script, I thought
you might fly out to Hollywood the early part of June and
then you could sit down with us and get a first-hand idea of
what the finished story will be. We can play the songs, lay
out the story line and I am sure after seeing this sort of presentation you will be able to make your own decision…We
definitely feel in our own minds that, with your talent, you
would create an unforgettable Mary Poppins, and we hope
you will want to portray this wonderful character after you
have seen the presentation…"

Miss Andrews wasn't at all sure she wanted to be considered since
she just lost the role of Eliza in the film version of *My Fair Lady* –the very
part she had played for over two years on Broadway to great acclaim—
to Audrey Hepburn. Her ego was a bit bruised and she didn't want to
be rebuffed again. But she did go that June to the presentation that Walt
promised and later recalled it:

"Tony (her then-husband, set designer Tony Walton) and
I went to Hollywood and Walt showed us everything to do
with *Mary Poppins* and also wined and dined us so sump-
tuously and so wonderfully. And, it was such an easy thing
to say, 'Yes, thank you, Mr. Disney. I would love to do that
movie,' because everything seemed to come full circle, because all the stuff in *Poppins* had that rum-ti-tum quality of
vaudeville. All of a sudden I thought, 'Right, I'm home because this I can embrace and perhaps bring something to.'
And again, in the kindest hands possible, I was taught how
to make a movie and that was the beginning of that. How
lucky can anybody get losing out on *My Fair Lady* and three
months later being asked to do *Mary Poppins*?"

Andrews was signed on for the part. As Robert Sherman later put it,
"The way she's created in the book, she's a very vinegary kind of woman.
She does wonderful things, but she does them with a stern attitude. Julie
made her softer than she was in the book."

After Andrews had been signed for the part, she took some time off
to prepare for the birth of her baby and on the day her daughter Emma
was born she received a call. "This strange woman's voice came on the

phone and said, 'Hello, talk to me; P.L. Travers here. I want to hear your voice.' She wanted to know if my voice was right for *Mary Poppins*. Then when we met later, she said, 'You have the perfect nose.'" Andrews did please Travers—more so than the selection of the actor to play Bert.

For the part of Bert, the chimney sweep, Walt considered casting Cary Grant, who was actually born a cockney. He enhanced the part to lure Grant, but in the end decided against it (perhaps because Travers had felt that Grant was all wrong for Bert, but right for the father!). Walt then considered Danny Kaye, who was hugely popular with British audiences, and Laurence Harvey, but Disney came around to Dick Van Dyke based on what he read in a newspaper. "I read where he wouldn't appear in a movie he couldn't take his children to see," Walt later said. "Right away I knew he was my choice, my only choice for *Mary Poppins*." Like Andrews before hand, Van Dyke got the royal studio tour. "Walt had rooms of story-boards that he showed me, and his enthusiasm for the film grew as he spoke," Van Dyke later recalled. "He was like a kid, getting so excited about it that by the time I left him I was excited about it too. He had me sold. I wanted to be part of that movie so much." Van Dyke showed that he had the charm, comedic, singing and dancing ability for the part. The only thing he lacked was the accent—which he has been chided for ever since. "It's funny," Van Dyke later reflected. "I was concentrating on the dancing, mostly, and they had given me a (voice) coach who turned out to be an Irishman (the actor J. Pat O'Malley) and his cockney wasn't much better than mine. During the making of the picture nobody kidded me about the accent, but I sure took it afterwards." Years later Andrews would say, "He's darling about it. Absolutely sweet. And he says, 'Ugh, I'm so terrible, but I tried.' It is what it is and one wouldn't change it for anything.'"

Julie Andrews, who corresponded on occasion with Mrs. Travers, later wrote, "He's (Van Dyke) extremely winning and I'd like to think that he and I look well together on the screen." But Travers was dubious. "Julie Andrews is quite satisfactory, but then she is English," Travers wrote. "But how on earth did you allow the producer to use that Dick Van Dyke to play the sweep? He's all wrong—so American."

Richard Sherman had this to say about the selection of Van Dyke:

> He had done *Bye Bye Birdie* on Broadway. He could sing very well. He was charming. He had impeccable delivery. We were looking for a long, lean character who would be perfect for Julie. Walt fell in love with Dick.

Dick Van Dyke and Julie Andrews in the classic *Mary Poppins*.
© Walt Disney Productions.

The parts of the absentee parents were also carefully cast. For the part of George Banks, the banker-father who has a difficult time relating to his children, Disney selected the British comedian David Tomlinson. Tomlinson had appeared in several British films including *The Magic Box*, *Up the Creek*, *Three Men in a Boat*, and *Tom Jones*. In his autobiography, *Luckier than Most*, Tomlinson wrote of how he got the part:

Dick Van Dyke, Julie Andrews, Karen Dotrice and Matthew Garber in
Mary Poppins. © Walt Disney Productions.

Besides making extremely successful films and constructing
marvelous parks, the Disney organization is wonderful at
cosseting its employees. I flew first of all to New York where
they had kindly arranged for me to see *Tovarich* on Broadway. It starred Vivien Leigh and I liked her performance. The
organization was perfect and the following morning I was
flown on to Los Angeles. In no time at all I was at the studio
where I met Bill Walsh, the film's producer. He had arrived
in Hollywood a considerable time before I did—1934 to be
precise. At first he had written radio shows and newspaper
columns. He'd also been an advertising writer and a PR man
before he joined Disney where he co-produced *The Mickey
Mouse Club* and the television series *Davy Crockett*. 'Now
what have we got here?' I could see him thinking as we were
introduced. He had a very good look and almost immediately called in Irwin Kostel, the musical director. Irwin carried the score under his arm. As Audrey (Tomlinson's wife)
had predicted I found myself standing by a piano. I sang a

couple of bars. 'That's fine,' Irwin said, 'let's go and see what's happening on the set.' Is that it, I thought. 'Don't you want to hear some more?' I asked. 'No.' 'You didn't give me much of a chance.' 'It's fine. You can sing.' He said laconically. They certainly make up their minds quickly, I thought. A very professional lot, these Disneyites.

For his suffragette wife the film and stage actress Glynis Johns was selected. She had already been a Disney leading lady in two excellent films shot in England in the early 1950s, *The Sword and the Rose* and *Rob Roy, the Highland Rouge*. Interestingly enough, according to Robert and Richard Sherman, when Disney called up Johns for a part in *Mary Poppins* she thought she was being offered the part of the English nanny herself! "She was under the impression that she was called to become Mary Poppins and Walt said, 'no dear, we have Julie Andrews for Mary Poppins. We want you for the mother.' Robert Sherman later recalled it. "She was kind of taken a back. She said, 'Oh, I don't know.' So he said, 'The boys are working on a song, it's almost finished. It's a great song for the mother, aren't you boys?'" The thing is, according to the Sherman's, there was no such song and they had to get on it immediately to have it ready for Johns by the following Monday. Johns recalled it a bit differently:

> "I got a call one day to have lunch with Walt to talk about *Mary Poppins*. I had been performing on stage in New York, and had just finished the pilot for my own series, *The Glynis Show*. As we were having lunch, I said, 'I'll tell you one thing, I think I'm going to get very depressed if everybody else around me is singing and I'm not. With my own series coming up now and having just finished a play on Broadway, I'm a little tired so I would need a musical incentive to see me through the project. Music lefts me up.' After our meeting, I drove to the Chateau Marmont on the Sunset Strip, where I was staying. It took about forty minutes to arrive there from the Studio. As I was coming through the door of my apartment, the telephone was ringing; it was Walt! He said, 'Hold on a minute.' During that short time, he had the Sherman Brothers write a song for me and they began singing the chorus of "Sister Suffragette" over the phone. I had no more doubts."

Interestingly enough Tomlinson and Johns had worked together twice before. "We seemed to be fated to meet up professionally every ten or fifteen years," Tomlinson later wrote. "I began to feel we had grown up together—in *Quiet Wedding,* (and) would-be lovers in *Miranda*, and now man and wife for Disney."

The children, Jane and Michael Banks, would be played by eight-year old Karen Dotrice and seven-year old Matthew Garber. They had already been well-received in the current Disney film *The Three Lives of Thomasina*, which turned out to be a kind of elaborate audition for *Mary Poppins*. They were both still relative fresh-faces and cute, but not too cute, and found to be more than acceptable in the acting department. Dotrice was the daughter of Roy Dotrice, an English actor. The Disney scouts found her as she was performing in a play, *The Caucasian Chalk Circle* for the Royal Shakespeare Company. Her godfather was none other than Charles Laughton. "The Disney people got us a wonderful home—a mansion actually—and they were very good to us," Dotrice later recalled. "Many weekends, the Disney plane was put at our disposal, and they would fly us off to various Disney retreats, ranches in Mexico and Arizona."

The "Sister Suffragete" number from *Mary Poppins*, Elsa Lanchester, Hermione Baddeley, Glynis Johns and Reta Shaw. © Walt Disney Productions.

David Tomlinson liked both the actors playing his children in the film and later wrote of his memories of them:

> At times I thought the two children who played my son and daughter were as mature as any of us. That, of course, could be expected from Karen Dotrice, who came from an acting family. Matthew Garber, however, was another matter. His father was in the rag trade and slightly mystified by the whole business. Matt was simply a natural, and highly intelligent. It didn't take him long to realise the power he wielded in this expensive production. 'My dad's coming to lunch,' he said to me one day, 'would you like to come with us?'
> 'Are you paying?' I asked.
> He thought about it for a minute. 'OK,' he decided, very seriously.
> As we went in, the lady in charge of the executive restaurant said, 'How do you do, Sir.' She wasn't addressing me, but Matt.
> His charming father was quite surprised. 'Why does that woman call you Sir?' he asked his son.
> 'Because,' Matt said, drawing himself up to his full three and a half feet, 'I'm playing a very important part in this picture.' Later I told his father that Matt was simply stating the absolute truth."

The other actors selected for key roles in the film were also selected quite carefully and each shines in their own individual moments. Ed Wynn as Uncle Albert, who when laughing, floats up in the air. Arthur Treacher—the firm, yet kindly, Constable Jones. Reginald Owen was selected to play Admiral Boom only after Sterling Halloway got confirmation that he would be recreating his role as Eliza's father in the movie version of *My Fair Lady*. Hermione Baddeley and Reta Shaw are superb (as always) as the domestics and Elsa Lanchester has a nice cameo as Katie Nanna, the disgruntled nanny prior to the arrival of Mary Poppins. Lanchester, Doltrice's Godmother, was suggested for the role to Disney by Doltrice's mother.

Chosen to direct the film was Robert Stevenson, who had already helmed eight prior Disney films including such classics as *Old Yeller*, *Kidnapped* and *The Absent-Minded Professor*. His record of success at the studio made him Disney's most prestigious director and the one given the most plum assignments. A congenial man who was well-liked by those who worked for him, he enjoyed the environment around Disney, and, like Walt himself, he loved to storyboard a film and carefully plan the shots. "When I'm directing a picture," he once said, "what I have in mind is a happy audience enjoying it in a movie house." He was also selected for *Mary Poppins* due to his British connection, himself having been a British citizen.

The songs by the Sherman Brothers are among the most memorable aspects of the film. As stated, they defined characters and moved the story along. One of the most sentimental songs on the score is "Feed the Birds" which became Walt's favorite song. The Shermans later wrote in their joint autobiography:

> "Feed the Birds" is the first song we completed for *Mary Poppins*. Taken on one level, it's a song about a woman selling bread crumbs to make pigeons fat. But that has nothing to do with what the song's story is all about—it's about giving that extra bit of kindness, a little act of love. 'Tuppence a bag' is our way of saying it doesn't take much to be kind. We thought for a long time about who could play the old bird lady. One day, Walt said 'I know the perfect person—Jane Darwell.' She was a wonderful character actress, probably best known as Ma Joad in *The Grapes of Wrath*…When she received the script, she cried, she was so thrilled. And she gave us a wonderful performance, the last of her career…On Fridays, after work, he'd (Walt) often invite us into his office and we'd talk about things that were going on at the studio. After a while, he'd wander to the north window, look out into the distance and just say, 'Play it.' And we knew exactly what he wanted, and we'd sing and play it ("Feed the Birds") for him. It was wonderful, because sometimes he could say so much just by a look or by a silence, and we knew what he was feeling."

Along with the songs, the dances required in *Mary Poppins* would be highlights. In this regard Disney went outside the studio and hired the husband/wife team of Marc Breux and Dee Dee Wood to choreograph the picture. They were known for their work choreographing *The Andy*

Williams Show and the Broadway musical *Do Re Me*. *Mary Poppins* would be their first film and they gave their dances an athleticism that was reminiscent of Gene Kelly or Michael Kidd at their best. "I stole from Michael Kidd," Marc Breaux later recalled. "He's very athletic as well. I hired people who could do flip-flops which you don't really learn in ballet schools or in modern dance, and so if they could do a somersault or a cartwheel I'd say, 'I think I can use you.'"

Dick Van Dyke especially enjoyed working with Ed Wynn, whose laughter as Uncle Albert is contagious. "Ed was a wonderful man. You know he had a, I think, Parkinson's a little bit and his head tended to shake a little. But he had such control of himself that the minute the director would say 'Action' it would stop." Dick recalled that when filming the "I Love to Laugh" number the director, Robert Stevenson, called for a lunch break. The company left the set without letting Julie Andrews and Ed Wynn down from the wires holding them up in the air. "And in quite a while, somebody finally came back and said, 'Sorry.' We thought we were going to have to eat lunch up there."

The film was shot from mid-June through September 1963. Most of the cast and crew felt they had created something marvelous. Not so, David Tomlinson, who later wrote:

Dick Van Dyke loved working with Ed Wynn. © Walt Disney Productions.

"With Walt, Bill (Walsh) and Audrey (his wife), I saw a rough cut of *Mary Poppins* before returning to England. I thought it was appallingly sentimental and that it must be a failure and very nearly said, 'Well, Walt, you can't win them all.' But I was wrong about that film…Walt very nearly did win them all. He didn't like admitting it but of course he was blessed with the common touch. What he liked and obviously that's one of the many reasons why he was so successful."

The film premiered nearly a year after principal shooting had concluded, on August 27, 1964, at Grauman's Chinese Theatre. Pamela Travers was among those present. After the film she approached Walt and told it was time to go to the cutting room. The first thing to be cut was the animated scenes—especially those featuring horses and pigs—which she detested. Disney just looked at her and said, 'Sorry Pamela, that ship has already sailed.' And that was that. The film went on to be a huge success, the highest grossing film of the year and one of the biggest-grossing of all-time. In its original run it grossed $45 million world-wide. The reviews were everything Walt Disney could have hoped for. "A charming, imaginative and technically superb movie musical, sparkling with originality, melody and magical performances," wrote Judith Crist in the *New York Herald Tribune*. Bosley Crowther's review in The *New York Times* was a rave, calling the picture, "irresistible" and praising all the performances as well as Robert Stevenson's "inventive" direction. The *Hollywood Reporter* named *Poppins* one of the four or five best films ever made and then went on to explore how the Disney brand seems to be considered an embarrassment in Hollywood:

"It is a strange fact that the entertainment public…has for some years now recognized Disney's artistic talents, while many of his cohorts in Hollywood seem somehow embarrassed by his presence—like they wish he'd go away. When an occasion arises, as it does from time to time, that the name Disney comes up in certain Hollywood circles, a rather odd disease seems to strike the conversationalists. They shuffle their feet and stare off into space like some virus carrying bug has infected them with a loss of their powers of speech."

The film was nominated for thirteen Oscars including Best Picture, Best Actress (Julie Andrews), and Best Director for Robert Stevenson. It took home five statuettes: Actress, Best Special Visual Effects, Best Score, Best Song ("Chim Chim Cher-ee"), and Best Editing. Walt didn't sit on his laurels however. "Now whenever we discuss new projects the people here say, 'it'll be another *Poppins*,' I have to keep telling them, 'don't say that, each picture has to be different.'"

Mary Poppins has enchanted audiences for almost 50 years. In 2004, on the event of its 40th anniversary, Julie Andrews had this to say about the film which made her a motion picture star:

> If you look at Mary Poppins, what they managed to do then 40 years ago, it's not at all creaky, it's not at all dated, it holds up brilliantly and I was just so staggered at how they achieved it because they didn't have the equipment they do today.

Larri Thomas: I happened to be at central casting when I was suddenly asked what my shoe size was. I told them size 7.5B and they told me to rush over to the Disney Studio. I didn't know what to expect, so when I get there they told me to act as if I'm standing on a turtle with one leg elevated—okay—and we did a shot of that. I still wasn't sure what was going on. Well eventually I found out that I was there to be evaluated for Julie Andrews's stand-in and double on the picture. The director (Robert Stevenson) didn't think it would work—he thought I looked so much different than Julie—with my hair and features and I was taller. So they put me in the same costume that Julie wore in the film including the wig—and stood us side by side and they couldn't tell the difference. They still had to convince the director and so they put me on one side of the stage and the director said, "What's Julie doing over there?' and it was, of course, me—finally he was convinced that I would work.

Walt Disney was on the lot a great deal—and he visited the set quite often. It was unusual for the studio head to do this—usually they were hidden away in their offices, but Disney liked walking around and he knew exactly what was happening on the set. When the boss came on the set it wasn't like at other studios where the crew acted as if the principal had entered the classroom—usually people would freeze, but not with Walt Disney. It was very relaxed and people enjoyed Disney and he enjoyed talking with the cast and crew. I hate to use the "F" word but the Disney Studios did have a family atmosphere. Dancers are usually at the bottom of the totem pole in Hollywood, but Walt Disney treated everybody at the studio as part of the Disney family—including us. I'll never forget in October, 1966 when my daughter was born I was sent beautiful flowers with the Disney characters (Mickey Mouse, Donald Duck, Pluto) arranged around the basket along with a note for my new baby from Walt saying , "Welcome to the family." She was my daughter but because I was part of the Disney family (I continued to do films at the studio like *The Happiest Millionaire*—after *Mary Poppins*), so too was my daughter part of the Disney family. Then— just the following month—he died.

Julie Andrews was adorable, but I think she was a little nervous, at least early on because this was only her first film. But she was great and would try anything. Basically as her stand-in I would be there on the set as they prepared the scene and wearing the costume—along with the wig—so that the camera angles and lighting would be correct. It was heavy and it was hot, but that was my job, and then Julie would come in and do the scene. Dick Van Dyke was wonderful, too, and they got along beautifully and had little jokes and asides with one another. I actually saw Dick just a couple of weeks ago. Just as warm and nice as always with his silver hair and still a twinkle in his eye. Everything on the picture was storyboarded—including the dances. Robert Stevenson, the director, worked that way.

I did a lot of the long shots on *Mary Poppins*. I was in a great deal of the "Jolly Holiday" number—riding the horse— for the long shots—and then Julie was in a lot of the medium and close-ups. I was in a lot of the shots in the "Step in Time" number, too. We rehearsed that number for a long time—outside. What happens is that we rehearse the numbers often outdoors and then do a run though from beginning to end and then when it comes to the actual filming it is blocked out and done in several takes. But prior to filming the number they did a run-through from beginning to end and they thought they would have to cut the number, but Walt was watching the run-through and he overruled that and said he wanted the number shot as rehearsed and not cut at all. It was always a blast when we would do a number with playback of that wonderful full orchestra music, because up to that time we would rehearse only using a piano! What a difference it makes. I was always happy, too, when they took the harness off of me that I had to use when I was standing in for Julie doing the flying sequences! What a pain that was. As a rule I enjoyed the rehearsing much more than the shooting—the shooting was long, tedious—and HOT!

During the making of the film I also appeared in a couple of scenes. I was made up to be one of the nannies who appears at the Banks' house to apply for the job of nanny to the children and am seen being pulled backwards from the wind that comes as Mary Poppins arrives. I also auditioned for and won the part of the pretty lady in the carriage who blows a kiss at Dick Van Dyke in one of the early scenes in the picture. When the day came for me to shoot that scene I was put in a wig and outfitted in one of the dresses that Jane Wyman wore in *Pollyanna*. Prior to filming the scene Julie and Dick sent me a telegram of congratulations along with flowers—like I said we were all family at Disney. *Mary Poppins* was just a wonderful experience all around.

Dee Dee Wood: We, my then-husband Marc Breaux and I, had been doing some TV shows in New York when Michael Kidd, my mentor, suggested us when he couldn't do a show, so the William Morris Agency called us to choreograph a number for a young, upcoming actor named Dick Van Dyke on *The Jack Benny Show*. When that aired we got a call the following Monday that Walt Disney wanted to see us. We couldn't believe that we were walking into Walt Disney's second floor office—with that great view of Burbank right outside the window. It was just so comfortable and he was so comfortable. He had mentioned how much he had liked the work we had done with Dick on *The Jack Benny Show*, and so before we knew it we were offered *Mary Poppins*—it was as simple as that.

We called him 'Uncle Walt'— he was so easy to work for and easy to talk with. We would be walking down some street at the studio and see him around quite a bit—he would be at the animation department, outdoors chatting with the animators. I recall seeing him in the commissary once. They had a gift shop attached and he showed us the Mickey Mouse watch he just bought—and was so proud of the fact that he bought it with his employee discount! He would often come by while we rehearsed the dancers in the 'Chimney Sweep' number on the back lot. He usually would swing by on his golf cart bringing along some dignitary. It was after lunch, and dancers have to eat a lot to keep up their strength and so it's hard to dance right after lunch, but when 'Uncle Walt' would come by on his golf cart we would jump up and it was…7,8,9…we just wanted to show him our best. He was more hands on than anybody else I recall working with—with the possible exception of maybe Robert Wise on *The Sound of Music*. I never saw him get angry, maybe with others but never with us, but on *Mary Poppins*, and with all the meetings with Disney—it was just a joy! I recall at those production meetings, between Walt, Bill Walsh, the Sherman's and ourselves—Walt would always ask The Sherman Brothers to play his favorite song—the one with the old bird lady played by Jane Darwell in the movie—"Feed the Birds." Bill Walsh was an unsung hero—he was very helpful and instrumental in the story conferences with Walt.

We worked very closely with the Sherman Brothers. They wrote all the music and they drove us into a frame of mind of how we would present the dances. The sound of the music and the accent and the beat would dictate the style of the whole number. I recall when we first met them they played us the entire score and by the time they sang the last song, "Let's Go Fly a Kite," I was crying! The songs so moved the story and all I could envision was Mary Poppins flying up in the air and disappearing from the Banks' family. It was emotional—which is what they hoped it would be. Robert Sherman now lives in London and Richard lives in California. Richard was the forceful one and seemed to lead everything. Robert was sweet and laid back, and when he had something to add he would say it without having to jump into the conversation like Richard. They both were very nice.

When it came to hiring the dancers, we had already heard the music so we knew what we were working with. We knew they would have to be on rooftops and balancing on chimneys and different things like that. So they had to be pretty athletic and they had to be able to do flips and somersaults and those kinds of things. The auditions were also a lot of fun! We were always looking for people with a sense of humor and a sense of fun because humor makes the work easier than it is otherwise.

When it came to the actors, every day we gave Julie and Dick a half-hour or 45-minute warm-up to get them going. We wouldn't give them anything specific until we could observe what they could do. I would give people stretching exercises, and then design what they could do. When we did that we knew how far we could go. Julie wasn't really a dancer but we never felt there were any limitations with her. It was just taking from her what she had—100 percent—she had this wonderful background in music hall and had grown up in that atmosphere and so we designed many of her routines—especially 'Jolly Holiday' around that. She was marvelous and always a hard worker.

Dick Van Dyke was something else. He always said he never was a trained dancer and yet in the Chimney Sweep routine there he is doing all those jumps, flips and somersaults with the trained dancers. There's a sequence where Dick danced as part of a trio with two other guys and Dick is in the middle. Dick did the somersaults and then jumped up on the rooftop and did the roll over's with the other two dancers. When I show this scene, at a personal appearance, people don't believe that it's really Dick because their faces have all the black chimney grease on them, but I assure them it's really Dick Van Dyke—and they are amazed! It would be

The end of the Chimney Sweep number in *Mary Poppins*.
© Walt Disney Productions.

a collaborative effort too. Sometimes Dick or Julie would say, 'When I was a kid we did this...' it was fun collaboration.

One of my favorite sequences, and my baby as I like to call it, was in "Jolly Holiday" in the sequence where Dick is dancing with the four penguins. Dick and I, along with three other dancers worked on that sequence together. We dancers were the penguins and we worked out that routine and then they filmed it and sent it to the animators to use our movements for the penguins. There was a moment in the dance where the penguins are doing a turn and I do a "whee" and then when it came time to record it I was able to do the 'Whee' on the soundtrack! Eventually the animation department made four cardboard penguins so that when Dick was working on the number they would position the cardboard penguins where he could make eye contact with them at where they would be in the scene. I still have those cardboard penguins!

I remember when we did the bank scene and Dick was playing the old banker, and nobody knew it was supposed to be him until the final credits.

Walt with Julie Andrews on the set of *Mary Poppins.* © Walt Disney Productions

Well Dick's youngest daughter was just starting to walk and Dick would come in and start to imitate his year-old daughter taking these little baby steps, and we had a good laugh and wanted 'Uncle Walt' to come by and see it because we thought it would give him a giggle. Well, Mr. Disney did come by and we said, 'Look at Dick walk up and down this step' and he did like his little daughter just beginning to walk. Well, Mr. Disney stopped the filming and had them build a step where Dick would have to walk down in the scene as the old banker when he comes out of the office. That's the way the thought. He immediately saw that was how Dick should have the old banker go down those steps—a baby just taking her first step and an old man walk the same way.

We rehearsed the chimney sweep dance outdoors. It was May and June and very hot. All the sound-stages were busy and they were building the sets for the film and so they put us out in the back lot on an open space and build slides down and a semblance of a roof top to rehearse on. It was a wonderful area to be because nobody else wanted to come back there or could unless they had a pass. But it was hot! Marc and I would usually get to the studio at 9 and then the dancers would come in by 10. Lunch lasted for about an hour—and I have to say the Disney Commissary had the best Macaroni and Cheese that they would serve every Friday! We would break at around 5 and then we would stay until around 6 planning the next day's routines. We usually worked Monday through Saturdays as I recall.

Walt with Julie Andrews and PL Travers at the premiere of *Mary Poppins.*

We didn't have a lot to do with Robert Stevenson. I felt that several of the dancers were good actors and that at the end of the chimney sweep dance when they come out of the fireplace and tip their hats at the cop and the family members that the dancers could do that. Mr. Stevenson didn't think so; he wanted to use background actors and not the dancers. I strongly felt that some of the dancers could do it just as well. In the end Bill Walsh came down to the set and mediated and in the end we used half dancers and half background actors. At another point Robert Stevenson had felt that the chimney sweep number was too long and would not hold the interest of the audience for that long—and wanted to cut it. So Walt Disney stopped over as we rehearsed on the back lot and we sent the dancers on break. We had shown this dance to Mr. Disney many times and this time he told us to film it on a 16mm camera and then he would view it. We did. The next thing we know Mr. Disney had watched it and told Robert Stevenson—'here film this' and the routine wasn't cut. Whatever Walt Disney said we would do because we admired him so much. He was with us all the way. We took great care in everything we ever did—I don't recall cutting anything short. I give all that credit to Uncle Walt and Bill Walsh.

The animators and Ariel people were very closely involved. When Dick and Julie and the children get on the horses for the merry go round, it was on a huge stage with these wires and horses, and they were in these

Mary Poppins had a combination of animation and live-action.
© Walt Disney Productions

harnesses which would scrape into their bodies…it was difficult. You saw it evolving on the story boards. When we saw it with the animators drawing in the background with the horses and the merry go round—it was like nothing I had experienced before. It was exciting and different at the same time.

I remember in the 'Jolly Holiday' number when they send the kids off, and Dick has his cane and Julie has her umbrella, we wanted the freedom of the two of them to be able to move without the cane and umbrella—especially when they got to the tea party with the penguins. So we had a production meeting and I mentioned wouldn't it be great if we could make the umbrella and cane dance like Dick and Julie, but then I said, 'That's impossible.' Well, somebody told me, 'Don't say that because at the Disney Studio—nothing is impossible!' The special effects team asked for a couple of days to work it out and asked us to give them the music, a cane and an umbrella. In the meanwhile we went on rehearsing, then three days later they said to come over to the special effects department—and they had the cane and parasol on wires and they played the music and made them dance while in the air!

I don't really remember the premiere. I think I was too numb. I just remember the making of the film as a magical time—simply magical!

Larri Thomas: A few years ago I went to the 40th Anniversary reunion of *Mary Poppins* and everyone who is still with us was there—Dick, Julie, the little girl—it was just marvelous. We all feel as if we were part of something very special—which indeed we were.

11

The Dean Jones Disney Films
1967–1977

Dean Jones was born in Decatur, Alabama in 1931. He began his career as a blues singer, but ultimately caught the acting bug. In 1956 he was signed by MGM and in the next four years made a string of films at that studio including *Gaby* (opposite Leslie Caron), *Tea and Sympathy* (with Deborah Kerr), *Jailhouse Rock* (alongside Elvis Presley), and *Never So Few* (co-starring Frank Sinatra). In 1960 he appeared in the Broadway play *There Was a Little Girl*, opposite Jane Fonda, and a few years later was cast in the sex comedy *Under the Yum, Yum Tree*. He recreated his stage role in the 1963 film. In 1964 he was invited by Walt Disney to make *That Darn Cat!* The film grossed more than $9 million. His boyish good looks made him the perfect Disney leading man, and over the next twelve years would star in ten more films for the studio, including *The Love Bug* (1969) which became the highest grossing film released by any studio in 1969. Other box office hits for Disney include *Blackbeard's Ghost, Million Dollar Duck, Snowball Express* and *The Shaggy D.A.* In addition to his work for Disney, Jones appeared in the stage productions of *Company* and *Show Boat*. In 1991 he appeared in the film *Other People's Money*. He is a born-again Christian and is active in promoting his faith.

Dean Jones: I think it was because of the success of the films I was doing there that they had me do more and more. I think if I had a big flop, that probably it would have ended the string at Disney, but I didn't.

There's a certain bubble you try to maintain carefully, so it won't pop. The roles I play in Disney pictures really don't require me to 'act,' because intensive acting wouldn't be compatible with the pictures. It would be a jarring note. None of the roles I've played (at Disney) would be 'fat parts' from an actor's point of view. But then a lot of those roles can be found in unsuccessful pictures. And I can't say I know too many performers who would rather be in unsuccessful movies.

I use Mickey Mouse, the dreams of Walt Disney, the atmosphere of the Disney image when I work. The characters I play for Disney have fewer dimensions than I do. They take things more seriously, thus providing more humor by letting the comedy play off the role. That's how I do it.

I think the studio's operation and success of its films show they are giving the movie public something they want, something that is sorely needed today. Walt had the formula and his people are just continuing it.

The late Bill Walsh, who produced *The Love Bug* and other films I've done for Disney, had a theory about these pictures: you make even the most outrageous kind of plot believable if you take the situation seriously. I found I got a lot of help from Kafka, whom I read when I was younger. Although his stories are on a different level, the approach is the same. Take something like his 'Metamorphosis,' once you accept the giant incongruities, else seems logical.

I didn't want to play Hamlet. To make people laugh was a good thing to be about.

Hank Jones: Dean Jones was one of the top Disney leading men of the day and he was easy to work with and he followed Jimmy Cagney's sage advice about how to act: 'plant your feet firmly, look the other guy in the eye, and tell the truth.' He had a natural likability that came through in his performances.

Jan Williams: Dean Jones—who you saw on film WAS Dean Jones. He was a natural and aside from remembering the words…he didn't have to act…he was the characters he played. A funny guy, a warm guy, a pro always willing to another take without carping.

Blackbeard's Ghost (1968)

Blackbeard's Ghost is an engaging slapstick/supernatural comedy. Peter Ustinov is Blackbeard, the famous pirate's ghost that returns to current times. Dean Jones plays a new track coach at a coastal North Carolina college. Inadvertently he brings back the ghost of the notorious pirate Blackbeard by saying an incantation. Blackbeard has been cursed by his last wife who was a notorious witch, so that he will never die. The only way to "break" the curse is by Blackbeard performing a good deed. This film was in production at the studio at the time of Walt Disney's death in 1966, and in one of Walt's last visits to the studio he built, he visited the set and watched a scene being shot. The film was based on a novel of the same name by Ben Stahl. Though the film went into production in the fall of 1966, it wouldn't be released until the spring of 1968. It performed well at the box office, further enhancing Dean Jones' reputation at the studio—and that of director Robert Stevenson—an old hand at handling fantasy on screen.

It was also on the set of this film that Walt Disney made one of his final visits to before he died. Suzanne Pleshette recalled in the book *Remembering Walt*:

The morning he came out of the hospital, he came onto our set. We were filming *Blackbeard's Ghost*. He looked so gray and yellow, yet still had a sparkle in his eyes. He must have been in terrible pain. I knew it was coming. If you've ever seen anybody with cancer, you know that color. He said, 'Come out from behind that desk. I wanna see if you're wearing a mini-skirt.' I said, 'You just want to see my thighs, you devil you.' Those were the last words we spoke. I gave him a big hug and went home that night and cried and cried.

Hank Jones: My first film for Walt Disney was *Blackbeard's Ghost*. One of my agents at General Artists Corporation, a gentleman named Max Arno, heard that the studio was casting this particular part in the film which was to star Peter Ustinov in the title role. Max sent over a print of my latest movie, *Young Warriors,* a World War II drama I had recently made at Universal, so that producer Bill Walsh, director Robert Stevenson and Walt Disney himself could look at it. Within a few days I heard back that I had been cast as Gudger Larkin, the nebbish head of the college track team.

Being on the Disney lot in those days reminded me of being at summer camp. Everybody smiled, really because everybody was just plain glad to be working there. There was a sense of pride in what we were doing in all of us at Disney that I never felt before or since. The boss set the tone of the team atmosphere. He would get angry if someone ever called him 'Mr. Disney' instead of 'Walt.' Everybody got into the act. On my first day on the lot, I noticed that a security guard at the gate looked familiar—kind of like a sad-faced basset hound. Later on I realized why I thought I knew him—The Disney animators had used his unique viseage as a model for one of the characters in their *Lady and the Tramp* film—and here he was making sure I had a studio pass to get on the lot!

Those two Jones boys—Dean and Hank in *Blackbeard's Ghost.*
© Walt Disney Productions.

We were fortunate to have Robert Stevenson as our director on *Blackbeard's Ghost.* He was an Englishman, very proper and somewhat reserved, but with a noticeable twinkle in his eye. Robert almost always worked from illustrated story-boards made in conjunction with the Disney sketch artists which detailed each and every shot he would eventually make. He once told me that he liked using me in his films because he told me (in his kind way), 'nobody played a goofy kid any better.' He always let me come up with my own pieces of business for the Disney characters I portrayed and would quietly chuckle off-camera as I tried to pull them off on-screen. Robert gave me lots of rope to work with and seemed pleased with the results.

Most of Robert's Disney pictures were produced by Bill Walsh, who was equally kind and wonderful. Bill once described his job as a producer as comparable to being a good chef making a tasty bouillabaisse: he told me you get the best ingredients (script, talent, crew) and mix it all together carefully with good timing so everything turns out perfectly when the meal (the final film) is finally served. I like that!

I think I've only worked with two real geniuses in my career—Robin Williams (on *Mork and Mindy*) and Peter Ustinov. He really thought himself as much a writer as an actor. I loved being around him. He was truly one of the most amazing people I've ever known. He was fluent in eight languages; he could even speak Greek and Turkish. Every morning when I came on the set I never knew what dialect he would greet me with. He was impressed that I started out at an early age with an interest in genealogy, which we would sometimes talk about. I really enjoyed his talents as a mimic. He could actually mimic the sound of a cars engine by just giving him the make and the year of the car. But was I ever honored on screen when he did an impression of me!

One stunt I had to do as "Gudger" was to fly up into the air over the stadium where the track meet was taking place. I was supposed to be propelled upward and then down by the invisible ghost of Blackbeard. To do this, I was attached to the fabled '*Mary Poppins* wires' used by Julie Andrews in her flying sequences in that film. They are nearly invisible piano wires which come down from a moving dolly on a track high up in the flys of the soundstage and were then attached to a leather harness around my waist and hidden under my tracksuit. Well, it worked fine for Julie Andrews, whose wires were cushioned by her bulky Victorian dresses; in *Blackbeard's Ghost*, I was wearing a skimpy track suit and had no protection from the sharp wires cutting into my bare shoulders and arms. So the more I flew, the more I bled. Blood was trickling right down into Ustinov's face below me. His red pirate costume was getting more crimson with each take. And then it happened! Supposedly for the first time ever on a Disney picture using this technique. The wires unraveled from my harness, and sent me crashing ten feet below and landing right on top of Peter Ustinov. Luckily neither of us was seriously hurt—we could have been killed. But typical of Ustinov, he never complained and he didn't yell. His only concern was for me—I've never forgotten that. Bill Walsh came

Peter Ustinov in *Blackbeard's Ghost.* © Walt Disney Productions.

running over and offered to postpone shooting for the day, but I said, 'No, let's try it again.' And we did—about ten more takes.

My dad and mom visited the set one day and just couldn't understand the snail's pace of shooting. But the day they showed up just happened to be a day when only Blackbeard and I were working. When my folks arrived at the studio and were shepherded onto the soundstage, all they saw amongst the clutter of cables and lights were two snazzy director's chairs sitting side by side: on the back of the first chair was written "Peter Ustinov", and on the back of the second chair—right next to it were the words "Hank Jones." I couldn't have set that scene up better if I'd scripted it myself!

The only problem we ever had with Dean Jones was that he had a terrible five o'clock shadow. We often would have to wait before a close-up so that he could go back to his dressing room and shave before a take.

Elsa Lanchester was a real piece of work. She never lost her ribald sense of humor. Her dry asides between takes continually broke all of us up and made it difficult to settle down with a straight face when it came time to shoot our own scenes.

Suzanne Pleshette was the films leading lady and she was one of Hollywood's most genuinely liked performers. She was beautiful, sexy, super-bright, says it like it is—and had the foulest mouth in town. My introduction to her sense of humor occurred on the very first day of shooting. We actors were all seated in a circle just off the busy set when the noon hour arrived. As the A.D. yelled, 'One hour everybody,' Suzanne seductively eyed all the males in the group and purred, 'Well, who wants to hump me for lunch?'

Jan Williams: After a while I began doing some small acting jobs or walk-ons. The first movie where I worked the entire schedule was when I stood in for Peter Ustinov on *Blackbeard's Ghost*. I did some of the stunts, motorcycle riding, and mast climbing and so on. Peter was a very kind man and a real pro, to play such a broad character coming from the "theater" and all was great fun. I remember at the wrap party he gave me two books, both signed. I don't remember the titles, but I do remember one was about a motorcycle trip across America and the other about sailing around the Hawaiian Islands. I remember being touched by his personal thoughtfulness and we had talked from time to time throughout the shoot about both of these dreams of mine. Never did either, but I did own a bike and I still go to Hawaii each year. It was during the filming of *Blackbeard's Ghost* that I saw Walt for the last time. Walt came by the stage and quietly pulled up a chair away from the set. I happened to be in the area and I was also working as the night watchman at his home during the remodel. I walked over and mentioned that it looked like they were doing a nice job on his house. He answered, "yes…yes, it's coming along nicely. I just hope I get to move back in.' He died a short time afterward—it was expected, so even though somber—it was a reality. I always felt the final question (after Walt's death) was 'would Walt do it that way?'

Dick Warlock (stuntman): I seem to recall doing some stunt work on *Blackbeard's Ghost*. I know I did some wire work and got hammered by a door. I would have liked to spend hours with Peter Ustinov. He was very intelligent and one can learn a lot from him.

Jonathan Daly: I worked with Peter Ustinov in another Disney picture, *Treasure of Montecumbe*, and the entire shoot was a treasure because Peter would tell stories and a more entertaining actor never lived.

Hank Jones: My favorite film hands down was *Blackbeard's Ghost*, probably because it was my first, was Walt's last, and because I had my best and biggest role in it. There was a 'family aspect' to the unity of that cast that lingers in my memory—we were all on a team together to make the BEST movie we could…and I think we did. Ten years later Suzanne Pleshette was still calling me "Gudger" whenever I would see her.

The Love Bug (1969)

The Love Bug apparently was what the American public was looking for in its entertainment buck at the movies when it was released on March 13, 1969. The film out-grossed such hip, contemporary films as *Easy Rider, Midnight Cowboy* and *Bob & Carol & Ted & Alice*. It seemed to prove that there was still a strong market for the kind of family fare that Disney films were known for. This 108-minute slapstick action-filled comedy starred Dean Jones as a down on his luck race track driver named Jim Douglas, who acquires a Volkswagen bug that seems to have real emotions and a mind of its own. "The first scene I had with him in the movie, Herbie was about to commit suicide by jumping off the Golden Gate Bridge," recalled Dean Jones. "I was supposed to save him. Right! I'm supposed to save a VW from a suicide leap? Uh-huh, Sure. I couldn't even get the lines-out—I kept breaking up. " Together Jim and the bug, nicknamed "Herbie", win many races, but ultimately Herbie "feels" unappreciated and falls into the hands of a dastardly rival—Thorndyke (David Tomlinson, in the second of his three Disney films—the final one would be *Bedknobs and Broomsticks*) and his cohort, Havershaw (Joe Flynn). Along for the ride are Tennessee (Buddy Hackett), Douglas's mechanic/friend and his girlfriend, Carole (Michele Lee).

While the film was released more than two years after Walt's passing, it was Walt who purchased the rights to the book it was based on. Dean Jones later explained on the site www.herbiemania.com:

> No. No, we had no idea (the film would become a big hit). Absolutely none. Of course Walt bought the book before he died. The book's title was 'Boy, Girl, Car," and the way they normally in those days would pick a title at Disney would be to get all the employees at the studio to suggest a title, and they'd write down the top 12 for the preview. They would let a preview audience somewhere in L.A. or someplace check the title they liked best. And 98 percent of them liked "The Love Bug." So the movie was no longer called "Boy, Girl, Car," it was The Love Bug from then on. And we had no idea it was going to bring in $58 million in the first couple of months,

Dean Jones in the #1 hit of 1969, *The Love Bug.* © Walt Disney Productions.

which was an enormous amount then. It rated under Gone with the Wind in top ten motion-pictures of all-time for several years before the ticket prices went up and big blockbusters like ET and others came in…but nobody had any idea. And I think if Walt had lived to see the release of the picture, he would not have believed it either."

Chosen to direct the film was Disney pro, Robert Stevenson, directing yet another blockbuster for the studio. Jones later summed up his director this way, "I think history will probably judge him as having been a very significant director if we just look in terms of the number of people who paid their bucks at the box office. He'd say, 'Give me one more just like that,' and I'd say, 'Why don't you just print the one you got?' and he would always say, with a sly smile, 'there was a technical problem.'

The film was made before computer generated special effects which meant that a lot of planning went into how Herbie achieved some of his stunts. Again, Dean Jones explains:

"With the first movie, there were no special effects. I mean we didn't have the computer generated stuff. If it was done, it was done for real…The scene where Herbie skips across the lake. They built two towers and they put a steel cable between them, and they started sliding a full size Volkswagen down these cables, loosen the cable, tighten the cable, and loosen the cable. Then they built a lake between the two towers, and they experimented with letting the towers go towards one another and the cable getting loose and dropping the car down to the water. Then they tightened the towers, the cable would tighten and the car would come up. So that's how they got the look that it was skipping across the water."

Peter Renaday: The next picture I was involved in was *The Love Bug* (1969). Nobody dreamed that it would be the big money-maker of the year! I was quite honored to be in the scene with Herb Vigran and Ned Glass, two of the great character actors that I had seen in movies all of my life. The director, Robert Stevenson, was as gentle as he was competent. I got the impression that he worked carefully from storyboards, as I've heard was true of Hitchcock. Most British directors seem to be extremely well organized—and polite. The star of the film was Dean Jones, who I worked with on several pictures. He was a real gentleman and a generally underrated talent. He was excellent in musical comedies on stage. MGM had him under contract in the 50's and didn't know what to do with him. He is really one of the nice guys.

Dick Warlock: I also did stunts on *The Love Bug* and other "Herbie" films. I'd like to think that I learned from the best and that was Carey Loftin. He was the epitome of the car stuntmen. He drove them before the automatic transmissions and could make a car talk. Remember *Thunder Road*? Carey drove Herbie in the first film and when they called him for the second one he had to turn it down because of an injury his wife had sustained. When Mr. Art Vitarelli asked him who he would recommend he suggested me. What a compliment from him that was. I drove the little car in the second and third films. As for the risk, if you surround yourself with good people, rehearse it and then it's minimal. Disney had some very good stunt people.

The director has a lot to say about whom the stunt coordinator is on a film but so does the producer, production manager as well as the stars. The director will get together with you in a meeting and let you know what he or she would like to see and ask for ideas and you reach a happy medium most of the time. The ultimate responsibility for the safety with the action is the coordinators. An example of hiring the coordinator, on the fourth Herbie film Vince McEveety knew a stuntman a lot better than he did me and he felt more comfortable with him than with me so he insisted on having his pick—which was Buddy Joe Hooker—by his side on that film. A good choice by the way. I've been lucky to do stunts and work with a lot of great people. Dean Jones is a real good guy—loyal to the Nth degree. A lot of fun to be around, too.

Million Dollar Duck (1971)

Million Dollar Duck is pretty minor Disney, but a hit at the box office regardless. Dean Jones plays Professor Dooley who takes a condemned-to-death duck home from his research laboratory. The duck (named Charlie) gets exposed to radiation and (naturally) begins to lay golden eggs. Jones and wife (Sandy Duncan) begin to use their new found wealth and the neighbors begin to get suspicious—and so does the government in the form of treasury agents.

A stunt from *The Love Bug*. © Walt Disney Productions.

The film is directed by Vincent McEveety (born 1929). McEveety was a prolific TV director before becoming one of the Disney Studio's most proficient and in-demand directors during the post-Walt era in the 1970s. He was well established for his work on such TV shows as *Gunsmoke, The Untouchables, Perry Mason, Star Trek,* and *Mannix.* At the Disney Studio he directed such films as *Million Dollar Duck, The Strongest Man in the World, The Biscuit Eater, The Apple Dumpling Gang Ride Again, Herbie Goes to Monte Carlo* and *Herbie Goes Bananas.* Later he directed several episodes of the 1970s TV series *Eight is Enough,* as well as Angela Lansbury in *Murder, She Wrote* and *Diagnosis: Murder* with Disney veteran Dick Van Dyke, as well as several *Columbo* TV movies of the 1990s.

The film was produced by the veteran Disney producer Bill Anderson, who later explained how they were able to find and train "Waddle" the duck and his stand-in:

> Before we had a script I decided we should find out if we could get a duck to play the role. We first contacted Hank Cowl, the animal trainer and handler, and asked him if he could find a duck who becomes the pal of a dog, a playmate for a boy, get involved in a chase and pretend he's laying eggs. Cowl came in with seven ducks and worked with them for two months. Finally he found two of them who worked with the dog. It was an interesting demonstration. The dog is a golden retriever who even picks the duck up in his mouth and brings him over to you. The duck has complete confidence in the dog and even quacks happily when he's around.
>
> The *New York Times* liked the film calling it a "delightful new live-action romp" from Disney, but Roger Ebert in the *Chicago Sun Times* was unimpressed: "Walt Disney's '$1,000,000 Duck' is one of the most profoundly stupid movies I've ever seen."

Peter Renaday: One of the pictures I had one of my biggest parts in was *Million Dollar Duck,* where I played the part of Beckert, one of the T-Men. I got three weeks work out of that one and spent a lot of time running around in a car with Joe Flynn, James Gregory, Ted Jordan and Bing Russell (Kurt's dad). One of the things that impressed me on that picture was that Tony Roberts was flying back and forth from San Francisco six nights a week. He was starring on stage in *Promises, Promises.* Now, you have got to be young to do that!

Jonathan Daly: Dean and I became very close friends. He was talented and professional and a joy to work with. In those days that meant a long career! Vince (McEveety) was another actor's director. At one point he said to me, "Do anything you want here—just have fun." And I always did with Vince. Sandy Duncan was a dream. She had a great sense of humor and was humble and always smiling. All I remember about *Million Dollar Duck* is laughing…Sandy would laugh and we'd all break up. Come to think of it I never had anything but fun working at Disney. Joe Flynn and I would run into each other and remember all the fun we had working at Disney— every time we'd see each other we'd just laugh—great guy. Both Walt and Bill (Anderson) told me they favored a stable of recognizable faces—an acting troupe—and that's what they had at Disney.

Snowball Express (1972)

John Baxter (Dean Jones) inherits a ski resort in the Rocky Mountains, and quits his job in New York and moves the family west to run it. The resort isn't exactly as he thought and what he expected—it is a broken down wreck. Baxter, his wife (Nancy Olson) and children (Johnny Whitaker and Kathleen Cody) decide to fix it up and make it operational, finding more than their share of trouble in doing so. There is a top-notch Disney supporting cast led by Harry Morgan, Michael McGreevey, Keenan Wynn, George Lindsey, Dick Van Patten and the always wonderful Mary Wickes.

Many of the film's exteriors were shot on location in and around Crested Butte, Colorado, which is some 10,000 feet up in the Rocky Mountains. It was an old mining area converted to a ski resort by the early 1970. *Snowball Express* was based on a book titled *Chateau Bon Vivant*. The *New York Times* gave the film a generally positive review, "What could be more square—or welcome—at the moment than a pleasant Disney movie, the old-fashioned, family kind? *Snowball Express* fills the bill very nicely. What it lacks in wit it has in wholesome, hearty chuckles. Add to this some nice, snowy backgrounds and slope activity in the Colorado ski country."

This is a one of the funnest and funniest of the Disney slapstick comedies of the 1970's.

Michael McGreevey: *Snowball Express* is one of the better films I made at Disney. But it was not a lot of fun to shoot because of the harsh conditions we had to endure on location. The film was shot in Crested Butte, Colorado, in January and February, the dead of winter in the Rocky Mountains. To

Dean Jones in the very funny *Snowball Express.* © Walt Disney Productions.

quote the great character actor, Harry Morgan, "Comedy and cold don't go together." If you don't believe Harry, you try to remember your lines and be funny when you're freezing your butt off. It ain't easy. My main memory of Crested Butte was that I was always shivering. Late one afternoon, my boots actually froze to the icy street while I was waiting (and shivering) for a shot to begin. The director yelled, 'Action,' and I tried to move, but I was permanently attached to the frozen concrete. With all the exposure to the cold and other hostile elements of the Rockies, it was inevitable that I would get sick—a gut-wrenching 24-hour stomach flu that brought me to the brink of death. If it wasn't for the kindness of Harry Morgan, R.N., I never would have survived the ordeal. The location was also tough for me because I missed my girlfriend. We had just fallen madly in love before I left and I was lovesick for her the whole time I was in Colorado. Once I got back to sunny and warm California (and the loving arms of my girlfriend) I really enjoyed working on this movie. The cast was great and I was being directed again by the talented Norman Tokar. I also enjoyed the character of "Wally Perkins" who was a rural or country version of "Richard Schuyler."

Harry Morgan is a terrific actor, an incredibly funny person, and a great human being. And he paid me very good money to say that. Seriously, I really enjoyed working with and getting to know Harry. We spent a lot of time together learning how to drive snowmobiles and Harry would constantly entertain me (and everybody else) during the long periods of waiting on the set. Harry and I never talked about acting, but I learned an awful lot from him—simply by being in scenes with him. The great ones make everyone else around them better too.

I didn't know Keenan Wynn as well, but I did have several conversations with him, like the aforementioned discussion about his dad. I also asked him about his son, Tracy Keenan Wynn, who was one of Hollywood's best young writers at the time. Like any proud father, Keenan bragged on his son and marveled at his talent. The weird thing with Keenan was that he was almost deaf so it was somewhat difficult to carry on a conversation with him. At first I thought he was ignoring me when I would ask him a

Dean Jones, Michael McGreevey and Harry Morgan, *Snowball Express.*
© Walt Disney Productions.

Dean Jones and Harry Morgan, *Snowball Express.* © Walt Disney Productions.

question and he wouldn't answer, but then he explained to me that he had a hearing problem and often had to read lips during a scene to know when the other actors were finished speaking. I had experienced this same 'hearing problem' with another actor, Richard Widmark, who I thought hated me for the first two days we worked together. Widmark was completely deaf in one ear and that's the side I was talking into while we sat side-by-side on mules. I was really hurt and upset that he 'ignored' me when I attempted to strike up a conversation between takes. Finally, on the third day, Widmark mentioned that he was deaf in his one ear and apologized if he seemed to be ignoring me. What a relief!!! To this day, I'm still amazed that these two magnificent actors were able to hide their hearing disability from the audience so well. But I have noticed that Keenan Wynn always spoke louder than other actors in almost all of his performances.

Mary Wickes had a remarkable career playing acid-tongued, tell-it-like-is, wise-cracking secretaries, nurses, nuns, etc. In real life, Mary was a sweet and loving person who was humble and self-effacing to a fault. In Crested Butte, there was a small tea and sandwich shop on Main Street where the actors often hung out to escape the cold. I enjoyed several conversations with Mary and we talked about everything from her longtime friendship with Lucille Ball to proper tea brewing to working with Bette Davis to what I should do to maintain my relationship with my girlfriend. I

Dean Jones and a furry friend, *Snowball Express.* © Walt Disney Productions.

really enjoyed my personal times with Mary and I still love watching all her marvelous performances that I can now discover and rediscover on TCM.

George Lindsey was best known for playing Goober Pyle on *Mayberry RFD* and being a regular on *Hee Haw*. Although he made a career playing country bumpkins, George was anything but stupid. He was a brilliant comedian and an extremely savvy businessman. He was also a damn good actor who, even though he didn't know it, helped me out with realizing my character. At first, I was a little uncertain about how to play 'Wally Perkins' but once I did my first scene with George; I picked up on his 'country' vocal rhythm and immediately decided to incorporate it into my performance. On top of helping me realize my character, George was a joy to be around on the set. He kept me laughing in spite of the cold and other horrors of the location. I will always remember George Lindsey with fondness.

The Shaggy D.A. (1976)

It only took the Disney Studio 17 years to make a sequel to the immensely popular *The Shaggy Dog*, and *The Shaggy D.A.* turned out to be a box office hit as well. Dean Jones is cast as the grown up Wilby Daniels (the role played by Tommy Kirk in the original film). Today Wilby is a lawyer and happily married (once again Jones' on-screen spouse is Suzanne Pleshette). Wilby is even running for DA against the corrupt incumbent, John Slade (the always-terrific Keenan Wynn). Naturally complications arise when the ring that had turned him into a dog when he was a teenager is stolen from a museum and the inscription is read and Wilby again turns into a dog! The veteran Robert Stevenson, in his final movie bow, was chosen to direct.

When *The Shaggy D.A.* opened nationally in December 1976 it received mixed reviews, but solid box office. It was the kind of film that the public at the time expected from Disney. It was safe, predictable—and fun. Roger Ebert in his review wrote, "The movie's not without its moments. One of them occurs in the dog pound, where Jones (as a dog) has been imprisoned with a canine supporting cast. They all talk like classic Warner Brother's gangsters and one is given to singing sad laments while the others dig tunnels to freedom. It's an original premise—a cross between a dog movie and a prison movie—and all we need is Pat O'Brien as the warden. Or dogcatcher."

Variety, the (so-called) bible of show business, called the film "brisk" (which at 91 minutes it certainly is) and lauded the cast. "Jones is a pleasant light comedian whose style is perfectly suited to the WASPish world of Disney. As his wife, Suzanne Pleshette has her first film role in five years, and her beauty and intelligence livens a part that might have been dull without her. Rounding out a large and able supporting cast are such people as Tim Conway, JoAnne Worley (in her film debut), Dick Van Patten, Hans Conreid, and in an unbilled cameo as a dogcatcher, the late Liam Dunn, who died before completing his part. Conway is particularly droll as a cloddish ice-cream salesman."

More than thirty years later the film is still fun. The only thing missing from this sequel are more references to the original picture, *The Shaggy Dog*. As I was watching it I was thinking, 'Wouldn't it have been fun to have asked Fred MacMurray to do a cameo as Wilby's dog-hating, now-retired postman dad again?' Or have a cameo with Annette Funicello as one of Wilby's old girl-friends? Who could cause a bit of jealousy with the Suzanne Pleshette character? This, I think, would have paid homage to the original film while still presenting an original story. I wonder if Walt might have thought of that.

Michael McGreevey: My final film as an actor at Disney was *The Shaggy D.A.* I came back to the studio in the 1990's as a writer and producer, but I stopped acting altogether after this movie. I think it was a film that was just a hodge-podge mixture of a lot of comedic formulas that had worked in previous Disney live-action films. But the film had no identity of its own; it had no original hook or storyline that would engage the audience. I felt it was a very episodic and disjointed movie that had no clear storyline for the audience to follow.

Hank Jones: I again worked for Walsh and Stevenson in *The Shaggy D.A.* a sequel to *The Shaggy Dog*, with Dean Jones as the grown up Wilby Daniels. I played a frustrated cop trying to corral Dean, who then turned into the huge sheepdog. Suzanne Pleshette was also cast in the film and when I showed up to film a scene with her she greeted me with a 'Where's your track suit' because the last time we had worked together had been when I was Gudger in *Blackbeard's Ghost*. A major challenge in this movie was trying not to break up at the antics of Tim Conway, whom I was attempting to arrest in one of the closing scenes. Tim is a bit nuts and his off-the-wall comic riffs make it near impossible to keep a straight face and stick to the script. Somehow I did—but it was tough!

Peter Renaday: I was reunited with director Robert Stevenson and Dean Jones for *The Shaggy DA*. I did one scene with Tim Conway in that picture and Stevenson thought I looked too young for the part (I was about 40), so the make-up people did what they could to age me up. I played a roller derby ticket player and Tim did some funny shtick getting his fingers caught in my pocket when he tried to put his ticket there, but it was cut out of the picture! I was in and out in an hour.

Jan Williams: *The Shaggy DA* was a sequel to the very popular 1959 film *The Shaggy Dog.* I think it was felt that this was a good formula and with Dean Jones, Suzanne Pleshette and Tim Conway it was a natural for an upgrade. Our director was Robert Stevenson. He had storyboards everywhere. He utilized storyboards more than any director I ever worked with…even dialogue scenes, he knew what words would be on camera from what actors. He cut the film in the camera. Very precise, exacting and with little patience. He would shoot a scene and like a machine-gun say…cut…print…over here, and he was ready for the next shot. Susanne Pleshette was a blast with a mouth like a truck driver but never offensive, only used for effect. Tim Conway was the best. What you see on camera IS Tim Conway. I did a number of projects with Tim and never, NEVER could catch him in a serious moment. Hans Conried played his pompous self on and off camera but always for a laugh—a great sense of humor.

Dick Warlock: Tim Conway is a fright! I can't say enough about his sense of humor on and off screen. What a blast to spend time with.

Jonathan Daly: *The Shaggy DA* was memorable because of my friendships with Dean and Suz Pleshette. Suz would bring me chicken or cheese every day at 4pm so that my energy would keep up. Suz was all fun and yet a total pro—fantastic gal. Dean and I would discuss religion and politics—fabulous people. It was a wonderful set. I would run into Tim Conway a lot around town. We both used to say how Disney was such a dream studio. He was maybe the world's funniest man—and nicest. Robert Stevenson was definitely old school—great respect on the set and he knew what he wanted, but made it all very simple.

Herbie Goes to Monte Carlo (1977)

Dean Jones returned to the "Herbie" franchise with this film, which was the third sequel to the immensely popular *The Love Bug* (Ken Berry, Stefanie Powers and Helen Hayes starred in the first sequel, *Herbie Rides*

Again in 1974, which did well enough to bring about this film). This time Jones is joined by a mechanic named Wheely (Don Knotts) and a new love interest (played by Julie Sommars). This time the human-like love bug competes in a road race taking place from Paris to Monte Carlo. The film-makers also took to the road with location shooting through-out France, including several locations in Paris. Dean Jones recalled one experience:

> "I know that VW backward and forward, and sometimes it really does seem almost human. There was one shot in *Herbie Goes to Monte Carlo* where we had to speed across the Place d'Alene in Paris. I thought the other cars were being driven by stunt drivers, so I stepped on the gas. Herbie flashed in and out of traffic, missing cars by inches. I found out later there wasn't a stunt driver around. We had screeched and skidded our way across three lanes of frightened Parisian motorists!"

The film did well enough to warrant yet another sequel, *Herbie Goes Bananas*, in 1980—sans Jones, who did return to do a short-lived Herbie TV-series in 1982.

Dean Jones and Don Knotts in *Herbie Goes to Monte Carlo*.
© Walt Disney Productions.

A typical slapstick scene from *Herbie Goes to Monte Carlo*.
© Walt Disney Productions.

Jan Williams: *Herbie Goes to Monte Carlo* was my first major project on my own, and I thank the lord that I had Vincent McEveety directing and Art Vitarelli on second unit—those guys were the real stars of that film. Vince was the best. He had a great sense of humor and a great communication with the actors. Art was the magic man. He was responsible for the tricks, the races, the special effects shots, the stunts, the action sequences. Art worked on all the shows and handled all the action stuff. Art also used to direct the *Wonderful World of Disney* lead-ins for Walt. Walt was comfortable around Art and felt at ease with him as director. It was Art who came up with the idea of giving Walt something to hold while he sat on the edge of his desk or moved around the set. Walt didn't know what to do with his hands so; Art came up with a book, a pen, a folder…something for Walt to hold. We shot *Herbie Goes to Monte Carlo* in France with only a few locations here, one at Laguna Seca Raceway in Monterey and another on some side roads on Mount Wilson. You just can't do better than shutting down traffic in Monte Carlo and racing 30 cars down their streets or shutting down the Chomp d Elsevier for the beginning of the race. It just doesn't get better than that.

12

The Disney Studio: Post Walt

Walt's Last Days

On November 16, 1966, Walt Disney entered St. Joseph's Hospital in Burbank. He had been putting this off for some time. But the pain from an old polo injury was getting worse. He finally was determined to have something done about it and a surgery was scheduled. When doing routine x-rays doctors noticed a spot on his left lung. They determined to go in and they found cancer—the lung was removed. However, the prognosis wasn't good. The doctors only gave Walt from six months to about a year and a half to live. Lillian (and the family) was told—but not Walt, though he may have sensed his mortality.

When Walt was released from St. Joseph's he immediately went across the street to the studio. It would be his last visit. Those who saw him then were shocked by his appearance, but noted that once he got going on a subject he truly cared about he came alive with the vigor of old. "I saw him the Monday he came back from the hospital," his friend and producer Winston Hibler later said. "He was quite weak and drawn. During the course of our conversation, however, his great vitality came back and his voice got firmer and firmer. He said, 'I had a scare, Hib. I'm okay, but I may be off my feet for a while. Now, I'm gonna be getting over this and I want to get into Florida (for Disney World). You guys gotta carry some of this load here. But if you get a real problem and you get stuck or something, why, I'm here."

He visited the set of the film *Blackbeard's Ghost,* which was then in production. "My brother and I ran into Walt in the hall," Robert Sherman recalled. "He looked ill and sort of shrunken. He was talking to director Norman Tokar and then looked at us. He saw the concern on our faces, gave us a smile and said, 'Keep up the good work, fellows.' It was the first time he said anything like that to us. He never referred to anything we did as good. He usually said, 'That'll work.'" He visited with Dean Jones who later recalled the incident in the book *Remembering Walt:*

> "While we were shooting *Blackbeard's Ghost*, I had heard that Walt had been across the street at St. Joseph's Hospital having an operation on his neck. One day, after the director yelled, 'cut,' I glanced up and right behind the camera stood Walt. He looked terrible. His cheeks were sunken and his face looked thin and extremely tired. I looked at him in shock. When I realized how I had reacted, I walked over trying to cover my feelings with a smile. "Walt, how are you? How's your neck?' He said, 'Neck, hell, they took out my left lung.' I was speechless. Normally, Walt would keep the ball rolling in a conversation. This time, he didn't—he just stood there. I was thinking cancer and 'Walt's dying'—all these thoughts were racing through my mind. Just as I was called back to the set, he said, 'I'm going to Palm Springs…'"

Walt did go to Palm Springs, along with Lillian. He expected and hoped that the desert sun would help him gain strength. He flew down in his private plane. His pilot expected not to hear back from him for several weeks, and so was surprised when Walt called him a few days later, his voice weak, and asked him to come down and pick him up. He was returning to Burbank and to the hospital. He was weak and in pain. The radiation treatments that were to retard the cancer had sapped him of his remaining strength.

When he returned to the hospital he seemed to rally at times, and tried to conduct studio affairs. He inquired into the grosses of the latest Disney film opening at Radio City Music Hall in New York, *Follow Me, Boys!* One of the last things that Disney allegedly wrote was two words— Kurt Russell—the young actor was under contract to Disney and Walt liked him a great deal. In 2007 on the *Jimmy Kimmel* talk show, Russell confirmed this. "It's true. I don't know what to make of that. I was taken into his office one time after he died and I was shown that." The day before he died he seemed to rally, and then he began to deteriorate.

When Walt Disney died of acute circulatory collapse due to complications from lung cancer on December 15, 1966, the reaction was overwhelming. Friends and colleagues were stunned and saddened. Editorials were written by papers in the United States and around the world. Ordinary people, who knew him just from his work, felt like they lost a member of the family.

His fellow studio heads were effusive in their praise. "I have lost a great friend and the world has lost a great man," his fellow independent Samuel Goldwyn said, "But in a larger sense Walt Disney hasn't died for he will live for all time through his work." Richard Zanuck, Vice President in charge of Production at Twentieth Century Fox issued a statement saying, "No eulogy will be read or monument built to equal the memorial that Walt Disney has left in the hearts and minds and imaginations of the world's people." Jack Warner of Warner Brothers stated, "Walt Disney contributed as much as any single man to the pure enjoyment of people everywhere." Producer and director Mervyn LeRoy, another good friend of Walt's said, "Walt's warmth and kindness showed in everything he did…The last time I saw him, at a party a few weeks ago, he was still talking enthusiastically about what he was planning to do."

Actors who worked at the studio and owed a great deal to Walt were equally kind in their eulogies. "The joy he brought spanned the barriers of language, customs and nationality," said Fred MacMurray. Julie Andrews, who owed her then huge Hollywood career (she was then #1 at the box office) to Walt, said in a statement, "I am greatly saddened by this loss of a wonderful man and somebody I owe a great deal to." Annette Funicello, who was connected to the Disney Studio for over a decade, was perhaps the most heartfelt: "It makes me so sad to think that my daughter will never know him. He was truly the leader of our industry and there will never be another like him." The French entertainer Maurice Chevalier said that Walt's death was "a disaster for the entire world."

Politicians also weighed in. In the 1966 Governor's race in California, Walt had backed his friend Ronald Reagan, but still maintained a cordial relationship with the defeated Democratic Governor Pat Brown. Brown issued a statement saying, "I knew Walt as a friend and a dedicated Californian…Our state, our nation and our world have lost a beloved and a great artist." Governor-elect Reagan simply stated, "There just aren't any words to express my personal grief. The world is a poorer place now."

But it wasn't only the famous names that were quoted by the newspapers in response to Walt's passing. A phone operator at Disney was quoted by the *Los Angeles Times* as saying, "He wasn't a boss to us. He was a friendly man who loved us and we loved him." Henry Strom, a screen extra for thirty-years, spoke for his group: "Whenever a call came for Disney extras—everybody jumped to go. He treated us as equals at all times."

The newspapers around the world were full of eulogies. *Le Monde* in Paris wrote, "Perhaps Walt Disney was more innocent and had more ingenuity than his success as a businessman would lead us to believe. Perhaps, all during his career, he was only selling his old dreams of childhood." The *Rheinische Post* of Germany wrote, "The father of Mickey Mouse cannot give any more joy. The movies have had big pioneers, big adventurers, big artists and big money makers…this man exceeds them all in fantasy, in ideas and in millions." Out of Belgium the *La Libre Belgigue* of Brussels wrote, "Walt Disney will remain without doubt forever the most symbolic representative of an art…enjoyed as well by purists as by the great mass of moviegoers." The *Daily Kurier* of Vienna, Austria wrote, "Movies come and go. Only a few will be remembered. But…Walt Disney set himself a monument in the hearts of children which will live forever." And in Moscow, at the height of the Cold War, the official Soviet response came from Soviet director Grigori Alexandrov who wrote, "The death of Disney is a tremendous loss for the entire art world. His creative discoveries will go down as a vivid page in the annals of art of our time…Disney wisely and gaily revealed the secrets of our lives."

And here in the United States, Bosley Crowther, the *New York Times* film critic wrote, "The popular image of Walt Disney as a shy and benign miracle man who performed varied feats of movie magic to entertain young and old does not do justice nor honor to this remarkable cinema artist and tycoon who rightly achieved an eminence as great as that of any star in Hollywood."

The Studio Post Walt

In the aftermath of Walt's death, the studio operations continued with Walt's brother, Roy O. Disney, the studio's chairman and president of Walt Disney Productions as the top man. However, Roy was uncomfortable with the idea of making the creative decisions that had always been Walt's domain. Roy was the man who provided the source of revenue to make Walt's dreams come true. He was indispensible in this regard. So the decision was made to set up a committee of six of the most talented men (yes, *men*—Walt, like the other studio heads of his generation, didn't really help bring many women up the ladder) to form a committee which would make the creative decisions. On this committee were: Bill Anderson, production vice president, Donn Tatum, assistant to the president, E. Cardon Walker, the marketing vice president, Ron Miller, Walt's son-in-law and recently elected board member as well as a producer, Roy E. Disney, Roy's son and a director at the studio and Bill Walsh, producer and board member.

Roy Disney: We will continue to operate Walt's company in the way that he had established and guided it. All of the plans for the future that Walt had begun will continue to move ahead.

My chief thought is that I should not disturb the organization that Walt built up. He established the broad policies, and now our job is to carry on. We have fine personnel, and I intend to ask the stockholders for a stock purchase plan so that we can hold onto our top men, as well as the promising young talent.

Basically we will be working by committee. That is not the best way to run an organization, because eventually someone must make the decisions. But we will have to do it that way until the new leadership develops.

I know a committee form is a lousy form in this business, but it's the best we've got until someone in the younger crowd shows he's got the stature to take over the leadership. If the chips are down, I've got the decisions. My way is to compromise, and I admit that that isn't a sound basis. But I think I would do even more damage trying to make creative decisions the way Walt did.

But one day one of the guys may grab an idea and skyrocket with it. Then we'll make him leader. That doesn't mean we will find someone to replace Walt, because no one could ever do that. But there is a whole new generation coming up, full of ideas.

We continue to get offers of merger or acquisition by big companies in steel, food, merchandizing, technical companies and conglomerates like Litton. If we accepted such an offer, it would mean dominance by outsiders. We know our operation; we've been selling entertainment for over 40 years. We don't need anyone to tell us how to do it. Why would we merge—for money? WE don't need money. Now, we're not going to turn our back on any money that's offered us. But it's not worth it at that price. He (Walt) was the damndest planner I ever saw. He loved planning things that might be three, five, even ten years in the future. That was what was so unusual about this fellow: He could take care of matters at hand while dreaming for the future. That's why we're in such good condition today. Most other film companies are in hysteria of mergers, acquisitions and diversification; that's because they didn't plan. We've got enough going to keep us busy for years.

We've never before had this much product on hand. Walt died at the pinnacle of his producing career in every way. The big thing that's bugging American industry is planning ahead. We've got the most beautiful ten-year plan we could ask for. The financial fellows think we're going to fall on our faces without Walt. Well, we're going to fool them.

Bill Anderson (producer): The system is working out well. We've had a couple of knock-down, drag-out fights, but that's healthy. We had them with Walt, too. Walt taught us how to fight and get along.

Richard Sherman: Walt was like the champion of all his people and when he Okayed a sequence or a scene it was in the picture. Nobody could cut it, nobody could screw around with it, and nobody messed with it. But then a great void happened. There was no leader anymore and there were a bunch of sergeants scrambling around wondering where the general was. They had a board of directors that was seven people that were all trying very hard to do the right thing and never quite coming together. So decisions were made to shorten pictures and to drop sequences and it was actually not very pleasant.

Bill Anderson: Walt very seldom made a policy decision without discussing it with some of us first. The difference is that now producers are getting more latitude.

Ron Miller (son-in-law/producer): We all miss the man. If any of us had a major problem, we could take it to Walt and all of a sudden we had no problem. He solved it.

Bill Walsh: Sure, we think of Walt all the time. Our decisions are influenced by the memory of what he liked and what made him mad. It's a conditioned reflex, like living in the jungle; you get so you can smell where the tiger is.

Hank Jones: Bill Walsh was the most important man at the studio after Walt's passing. It was his job to carry on the Disney tradition—and do what Walt would have wanted.

Bill Walsh: There are all kinds of producers. There are brothers-in-law, husbands of stars and sometimes a guy who has the money. One day my little boy bragged that his father was a movie producer, and the other little kids beat him up.

What I do as a producer is to find a project that contains certain elements that I suspect will appeal to a large audience. I've had the luxury of producing my own work, but I've discovered that a script is a living thing. You have to keep modifying it as you go along. Most important, you have to keep yourself open to good ideas. A good idea, I've learned, doesn't care who has it. The janitor or a grip or even, God forbid, the director or an actor may have an idea.

I'm proud to say I started as a producer and worked myself up to being a writer, but there are three reasons I'd never direct. One, I have flat feet. Two, you have to get up too early. And, three, you have to talk to actors.

Hank Jones: Walt was alive during *Blackbeard,* but then dead by my next picture *Family Band.* There *was* a difference, but to me as just a character actor it was subtle. There really was no final place for the buck to stop anymore: so sometimes it felt like the brass was looking for reinforcement for a decision that never was going to come, and other times they just plunged on ahead with kind of a braggadocio saying that THEY now were in control and forget about Walt.

I still believe that for a while most every decision made at the studio had a kind of "I wonder what Walt would do" feel to it. Then time passed, and life went on.

Robert Pine: I never felt that they went by the idea of 'what would Walt do,' I never felt it because it was just a job for me and I didn't get a feel for that. What I was aware of at the time was that the success that they enjoyed under Walt's tenure was not as strong going forward—I feel that they may have felt that. Disney by this time was coming towards the end of an era and they weren't making the best of films.

Kurt Russell: Years after Mr. Disney died, I was still at the Studio making movies and there was a common cry, 'Nothing's changed.' Everybody was trying to hold on to what Walt would have done or what Walt would have liked. I was older then, about twenty-four years old, and felt that my time was probably coming to an end at the Studio because my interests had changed. We were discussing a project and somebody said for the one hundredth time, 'The thing about this is things haven't changed. Walt would have…' I said, 'You know, that's the problem with you guys. Things would have changed if Walt were alive. Things would be very different. They would not be the same. Walt always wanted to change things. That's exactly what I don't understand, right now, is that you're trying to hold on to what you think is a mindset. Walt would never allow his mind to remain the same.'

The One and Only Genuine Original Family Band (1968)

The One and Only Genuine Original Family Band tells the story of The Bower Family Band who petitions the Democratic National Committee to sing a song in support of Grover Cleveland at the 1888 convention, but decide instead to move to the Dakota Territory on the urging of a suitor (John Davidson) to their eldest daughter (Lesley Ann Warren). There, Grandpa Bower (Walter Brennan) creates problems due to his strongly democratic ideas in the strongly Republican Dakota territories. The plan is to get the territory admitted into the union as two states in hopes of sending four Republican Senators to Washington. Cleveland (and Grandpa), of course oppose this plan, and much of the film deals (in light hearted and musical fashion) with support and opposition to this plan—naturally the young suitors played by Davidson and Warren come from families on opposite sides of the political equation. The fine cast

Lobby card from *The One and Only Original Family Band*..

also includes Buddy Ebsen, Janet Blair, Kurt Russell, Wally Cox, Richard Deacon and Disney stock company veteran Hank Jones.

Chosen to direct the film was Irish born Michael O'Herlihy (1929-1997), who had directed and would continue to direct a great deal of TV (eventually he would be nominated for two Emmy Awards). This was, however, his second film for Disney. The first was *The Fighting Prince of Donegal*. The following year he would go on to direct a third Disney film, the pro-Indian Western *Smith* which starred Glenn Ford. Unfortunately, none of the films O'Herlihy directed for the studio proved commercially successful despite their quality and interesting stories. Producer Bill Anderson recalled that, "Although it was his first musical, Michael's work was exceptional. So much a perfectionist, he re-shot some of the scenes as many as 27 times. And his professionalism is beyond compare."

Once again the Sherman Brothers were called in to write the musical numbers. Dick Sherman recalled:

> "Our toughest assignment to date was to write the title song for *The Family Band*. At best, the title was cold, impersonal and suggestive of almost nothing that could be turned into a musical number with which to kick off a big picture. Before beginning work, Bob and I did a lot of research into the Dakotas of the 1880's, where the picture takes place. We read historical accounts, the autobiographical book by Laura Bower Van Nuys, source material for the film; we listened to records, looked at old sheet music and some films made of that era. WE literally immersed ourselves into the period and decided that any song set in that time would have to be lively and big. We stuck on the idea of basing the songs on a 19th century circus barker's spiel to get people to 'come in and see The One, The Only, Genuine Family Band in existence!! That was it! It sounded right, and we wrote the lyrics to that theme.
>
> For every number used in *Family Band* we composed at least three other approaches for the same situation using different lyrics, before we came up with a tune and feeling that we considered appropriate to the story. All in all, we wrote something like 42 different approaches to songs for *Family Band*. Fourteen of which we perfected for use in the film. But because of the necessary editing and time limitations, only nine are actually on the sound track."

Brother Bob Sherman added:

> "The whole flavor of *Family Band* is strongly one of Western Americana. It's setting in the Dakota Territory of the 1880's calls for big, broad passages, dynamic dances and outdoorsy rhythms. Even the ballads, like the one by Lesley Ann, had to be alive with the rugged life of that period. Although a single song is keyed to a specific character and situation, it must also be woven of the same stuff of which the whole picture is made."

Family Band was a big, rollicking musical extravaganza with big song and dance productions and got a gala release at Radio City Music Hall in New York City—the big Easter release of the Music Hall's schedule for that year. The reviews, however, were harsh. *Family Band* "is as pepless and fizzled a musical as has ever come out of Walt Disney Productions," wrote the *New York Times*. The film ended up a disappointment at the box office as well. Perhaps it was a relic of an older age? When *Family Band* was released in the Spring 1968 the United States was bogged down in Vietnam—the Tet Offensive had shown that we were up against an enemy that wasn't going to give up easily. Martin Luther King has just recently been killed. Campuses and cities were on fire. And the assassination of Robert Kennedy was just a little more than a month away. But watched again more than forty-years later, the film is nostalgic and upbeat and fun—and, in my opinion, one of the least appreciated gems of the Disney Studio.

Hank Jones: The next picture I made for Disney was *The One and Only Genuine Original Family Band*. I played the town delivery boy, a Grover Cleveland supporter, who was the nemesis to John Davidson and his band of Benjamin Harrison loyalists. I'm convinced that one of the reasons they put me in the movie was that I didn't sue the studio after the wires broke as I was flying over the soundstage and fell so hard on Peter Ustinov when we were filming *Blackbeard's Ghost*.

The studio wanted all of the actors in *Family Band* to sing and dance in the big musical numbers. So prior to filming, for two weeks—Wally Cox, Richard Deacon and I went through basic training as dancers under the personal direction of choreographer Hugh Lambert. I gained a great appreciation for the gypsy community after that crash course—and I'm happy to say that when you see the three of us in the film we look damn good, like we actually belonged in the dance ensemble with the more seasoned pros. Wally was mild-mannered and quiet just like his character, but that belied another side of him that wasn't what you'd expect. In his 20s he was Marlon Brando's roommate in New York when they were starving actors. He was super bright, and unlike most actors, had no illusions about the trappings of stardom. Once when the crowd surrounding him seemed to be overreacting to every word and laughing at everything he said, I heard Wally mutter to himself, 'Why are they laughing? It's not funny.'

Richard Deacon, or 'Deac' as he was called, was jovial and so much fun to be around. A genuinely good guy. Deac worked so hard sweating to master those song and dance numbers in *Family Band* that sometimes I thought he was going to drop dead right there in front of us. It was Deac who introduced me to Dick Van Dyke on the lot (Van Dyke was filming *Never a Dull Moment* at the same time) and made me feel like I belonged in their company. I would see Deac every so often after *Family Band* was released, and we'd always laugh and make the claim that, between the two of us in that picture we almost sunk Disney— *Family Band* not being the mega-hit it was expected to be.

The Townspeople of *The One and Only Original Family Band.*
© Walt Disney Productions.

Walter Brennan was the star of *Family Band* but he didn't act like a star. He didn't eat lunch in the special commissary dining room reserved for 'names,' instead each morning his wife made him his midday meal and put it in his lunch-pail complete with thermos bottle, which he took to the studio almost like he was going to work in a factory. By the time we had worked together in *Family Band* I could see that age and ill health was creeping up on Walter. He had bad emphysema by then and was so short of breath that he required an oxygen tank to be hidden by his side as we filmed. On his longer speeches, Walter would say a sentence or two, the camera would keep rolling while he took a hit of oxygen, and then he would continue with the rest of his lines; the pause for air would then be cut out of the film in editing.

Walter was a character actor and, I must say, a character. It was never dull. His politics have been described as being 'a little to the right of Hitler.' Walter's specialty was to wait until the other actors were being made up, bleary-eyed and out of it at 6am, and then pouncing on them to discuss politics. You couldn't win! All you could do was nod and listen. There was no escape because you were imprisoned in your make-up chair! Oh well, I had literature from the John Birch Society to take home after work.

Buddy Ebsen was probably the most laid-back actor I've ever encountered. In between takes, Buddy would take long naps, completely oblivious to the entire hubbub going on around him. One time when he was snoring away, the still photographer got the entire cast and crew—probably one hundred people—to pose around his chair for a group shot and even then he didn't wake up.

Buddy had started out as a hoofer in a vaudeville act with his sister Velma. *Family Band* gave Buddy a chance to dance again. He glided over the floor with his smooth, yet eccentric moves, and I never tired of watching the man in our song and dance scenes together.

Kurt Russell and a very young actress named Goldie Jeanne Hawn, had parts in the film too. Who would have guessed that year's later they would become a couple and one of the most stable in Hollywood? Well, she caught my eye and most every other male eye in the cast—including Kurt Russell. She was CUTE—in capital letters. It was her first film.

From my point of view kid actors have a tough time: they're expected to act like adults in an adult world when they're still kids. It really isn't fair. The only two kid actors I ever worked with that seemed to come out A-OK were Kurt Russell and Ron(ny) Howard: both in large part I believe due to the good parenting of Bing Russell and Rance Howard, their dads. Both

Bing and Rance were marvelous character actors and had been in the acting trenches for years, so they knew how to shield their sons from some of the b.s. that goes with kid-actor territory. Ron and Kurt turned out to be savvy and sweet guys—a credit to themselves and their families.

Lesley Ann Warren was young and awfully pretty, just starting to feel her oats in her move from the Broadway stage to Hollywood.

John Davidson and I hit it off immediately. He had a self-deprecating sense of humor and loved making fun of his own leading-man 'guy with the chiseled chin looks' image. He had a beautiful home at the far end of the San Fernando Valley complete with horses and butlers and invited the *Family Band* cast to the wrap party right there at his house. One sad note was that John's brother died during production, but our director, Michael O'Herlihy, wouldn't let John off work to attend his brother's funeral, so the poor guy had to keep going in the midst of his obvious pain.

I had worked first with Michael O'Herlihy on the old *Mr. Novak* TV show at MGM with Jim Franciscus and Dean Jagger. Michael was a stereotypical Irishman in many respects. Fun-loving but at times with kind of a dark side too (he seemed to brood a bit every so often). He was very kind to me over the years and in *Family Band* was patient with this non-professional dancer as I struggled to keep up with the real dancing pros.

I've always been struck by how beautiful *Family Band* was visually whenever I've seen it again: It captures 19th Century rural America in a very vibrant and lovely way. The locales filmed at the Disney Ranch were perfect for some of those romantic settings required by the story. Also the songs by The Sherman Brothers were so well suited to the era and grew naturally out of the plot and characters as good as anything they ever wrote.

Peter Renaday: I started as the dialogue coach for *The One and Only, Genuine, Original Family Band* (1968). I was there on *Family Band* to help with the kids. They didn't need much help, so they threw me in as one of the townspeople. I spent a lot of time playing chess with John Davidson and Wally Cox. John was good—but Wally was excellent. I made friends with Jerry Marin and some of the little people who were working as stand-ins for the kids. They told me all about when they were working on the classic *Wizard of Oz*, and had children standing in for THEM. *Family Band* and *The Horse in the Gray Flannel Suit* (for which I was Dean Jones' dialogue coach) were the only features I worked on from start to finish. Speaking of *Family Band* I ran into Lesley Ann Warren the other day at a collector's show and reminded her that in the middle of shooting she took a weekend to get married to Jon Peters! She's still a very pretty lady! *Family Band* will always be associated with happy times for me.

Rascal (1969)

Rascal is a gentle Disney comedy-drama, set in rural Wisconsin, about a baby raccoon who is taken in by a lonely teenage boy whose father is frequently absent from his life. Together the boy and raccoon bond and overcome their loneliness. The film is told in the form of a "year in the life" of its protagonist, Sterling North (Billy Mumy, in an excellent performance). The film is based on the prize-winning novel *Rascal* written by Sterling North (Walter Pidgeon voices North and narrates the film). The film also stars Steve Forrest as the absent father and includes a strong supporting cast including Elsa Lanchester, Henry Jones, John Fiedler, Herbert Anderson, and in his first film for Disney, Jonathan Daly, as Rev. Thurmond. The director was Norman Tokar, one of the most durable of the Disney directors of the 1960s and 1970s. Tokar once gave his views on what it meant to be a Disney director and about the types of films that the studio made:

> You must have empathy for a Disney material to work on a picture. You bring your own attitude to the story. People in the movie industry sneer or patronize a lot of what is done at Disney. Others ponder how it's done. The term 'Disney picture" has become a cliché, but these pictures make money. People leave their television sets to go to the theatres, which is more than you can say for some other pictures. Another thing I'm aware of the pure instinct involved in making a Disney film. You know what scenes will play, what is palatable and entertaining. Taste is an important element. We realize that many of the tickets are sold to children. But we can't make a movie solely for youngsters. Our pictures—at least mine—are made for the entire family. Other studios and producers don't seem to understand that it takes more than a boy and a dog to make an appealing picture. There are other ingredients. Take *Old Yeller*. The movie was rooted in dramatic ground. It wasn't a pat situation. A good Disney picture—like any other—has a sound and feeling for its audi-

ence. I may read a script and know immediately that it isn't for Disney, but I can't explain why. If it doesn't interest me it probably won't reach the audience I'm directing for.

Billy Mumy: A few years later, after Walt had died, I made *Rascal* (1969) for the studio. I didn't' have to audition for it. I made that right after finishing up *Lost in Space*. I was pretty "happening" at the time. But I was very happy to be working with Norman again and making that film. I think it's a solid little family movie. I can still watch it and not squirm. In Sammy and then Rascal, I worked with animals (seal and raccoon). Working with animals was usually great. It certainly was on *Sammy*, and *Rascal*. It wasn't really a challenge, but with any animals, you have to be a bit careful. I had positive experiences with animals on most of the shows I did. *Rascal* ended up doing pretty good business. I liked 'em all (the Disney pictures I made), Disney was a great place to work at back in those days. At least that's how I remember it. There were indeed changes after Walt was gone. But, I can't say I was that aware of them when I was 14, making *Rascal*.

One of the most memorable things I remember about my Disney experience was filming a scene in *Rascal*, with Steve Forrest (who played my dad). It was an early scene in the script, where my character finds the orphaned raccoon pup and decides to take him home. He holds the pup up to his face and says, 'I'm gonna call you Rascal!' Well, there was a take of that, where I held the raccoon up to my face and the little pup shit all over my face. For real. And I literally said, 'I'm gonna call you…SHIT!!!' it was hysterical and very, very gross. Man, I wish I had that outtake. Totally true. That certainly has stayed with me as memorable. I also had to eat many watermelons in *Willadean*, that I couldn't stand to even LOOK at watermelon for decades. Same thing with apple pie in *Rascal*. I swear I ate 14 apples pies by myself one day on that film! Couldn't eat apple pie for about 20 years. True!

Jonathan Daly: I was interviewed at length by Bill Anderson, who was then running the studio and Norman Tokar who was directing for the role of Rev. Thurmond in *Rascal*. Norm was an actor's director…and a lousy tennis player. We all became life long friends. Bill ran things just as Walt did—hands on—caring—efficient. *Rascal* was a family drama— things eventually moved into slapstick—I preferred the older stuff.

The Computer Wore Tennis Shoes (1969)

Some college students manage to persuade the town's big business-man, A. J. Arno (Cesar Romero), to donate a computer to their college. When the problem student, Dexter Riley (Kurt Russell), tries to fix the computer, he gets an electric shock and his brain turns to a computer; now he remembers everything he reads. Unfortunately, he also remembers information which was in the computer's memory, like the illegal business Arno is involved in.

This is the first of three films featuring Kurt Russell's Dexter Riley—or as they became known, "The Medford College Trilogy." Among the supporting cast would be Michael McGreevey, who would also appear as Dexter's friend and helper, Schuyler, in each film. This film also features Jon Provost, best known as "Timmy" on the *Lassie* TV-series, now 18 years old. In his autobiography, Provost recalled the experience:

> "As usual, Disney had put together a great supporting cast of adults. I'd known Cesar Romero most of my life and always loved working with him. The out-of-step college dean was Joe Flynn, the best at playing exasperated authority figures. Patty Duke's TV Dad, William Schallert was our patient professor and Dick Bakalyan, everybody's favorite hoodlum sidekick…I hadn't met Kurt before. He was a year younger and quite an athlete. As a matter of fact, when the child star thing ended for him a year or so later, he played pro ball until an injury in '73 forced him to retire and return to the screen. I missed baseball and most sports, so we didn't have much opportunity to meet, but I sure knew his work. He'd been under contract to Disney since he was ten…It was great seeing McGreevey again. He was always fun."

The studio selected Robert Butler (born 1927) to direct. Robert Butler came to Disney with a background in directing numerous episodic TV-series such as *The Many Loves of Dobie Gillis*, *The Detectives* starring Robert Taylor, *The Dick Van Dyke Show*, *The Untouchables*, *The Fugitive*, *Batman* and *Hogan's Heroes*. He came to Disney in the early seventies and *The Computer Wore Tennis Shoes* was only his second feature film as director. He went on to direct the entire Medfield College/Kurt Russell trilogy including *The Barefoot Executive* and *Now You See Him, Now You Don't*. He has continued to be a prolific and well-regarded TV director

The Computer Wore Tennis Shoes with Kurt Russell, Debbie Paine and Jon Provost.
© Walt Disney Productions.

winning Emmy Awards for *The Blue Knight* and the premiere episode of the acclaimed police drama *Hill Street Blues*. He also co-created the popular series *Remington Steele*.

Micheal McGreevey: *The Computer Wore Tennis Shoes* was originally shot as a two-part television movie for the *World of Disney*. It turned out so well that it was decided to release it as a theatrical movie. I know that this had been done a couple of times before at Disney Studios. Both *The Shaggy Dog* and *The Absent-Minded Professor* were shot for TV, but released as features.

This film marked my return to Disney after an absence of six-years and we had a lot of fun making it. The director, Bob Butler, was probably the best I ever worked with. He later went on to win Emmy awards for directing such great T.V. series as *Hill Street Blues, Remington Steele* and *Moonlighting*. Bob was so creative and very attentive to the actors. He was also a very nice guy and created a very relaxed and fun atmosphere on the set.

Computer Wore Tennis Shoes was also my first film with Kurt Russell and the beginning of a friendship that still exists today. What can I say about Kurt Russell? I taught him everything he knows. He owes me big-time for his success…and for a restaurant bill that he agreed to go halfsies on thirty years ago. We actually were roommates for three years in the 70s and I know things about him that the tabloids would pay big bucks for. And I can be bought for the right price!! All kidding aside, it was great working with Kurt.

The character of Richard Schuyler is one of my all-time favorites. He's so different from any other character I've played. He's the ultimate innocent who is constantly amazed and surprised by what life throws at him. He's a grab-bag of contradictions: stupid one moment, brilliant the next; totally unique, but the ultimate everyman; a coward, with a hero's heart. I'm sure if Schuyler heard this description, he'd quip, 'This guy sounds a little weird. Know what I mean?'

I got to know Joe Flynn very well. I did three films and a television two-parter with Joe at Disney and we became very good friends. Until I did *The Computer Wore Tennis Shoes*, I was mostly known as a dramatic actor. I had done a little light-comedy, but never all-out, silly comedy like we were doing in the Medfield College trilogy. Joe Flynn was a comedy master and he became my 'funny' mentor on those films. I was constantly asking his opinion on how to approach my scenes, asking questions about timing, delivery, reactions, etc. I also would study Joe's work and learn tons of tricks about comedy from just watching him. Joe was also

Kurt Russell, Debbie Paine and William Schallert. © Walt Disney Productions.

extremely funny in real life and kept myself, the rest of the cast, and the entire crew laughing throughout the filming of all the movies.

Dick Warlock: Joe Flynn was another great guy. I was his double in many of his Disney films and he was loyal to me as his double. I considered him a friend.

Peter Renaday: I worked with Kurt Russell on *The Computer Wore Tennis Shoes*. Kurt, even as a kid, was a solid professional. I think I did five films with Kurt, and he was always a pleasure to be around. A truly talented guy. On *Computer* I also worked with Mike McGreevey. He and I had that one scene in *Computer* talking about the tape recorder. Oddly (director) Robert Butler neglected to cover my side of the camera, so I had to go back on the following day to shoot it. Fine with me—it was another day's pay. Mike seemed like a nice young man. I really didn't get a chance to talk much to him, but I know that he and Kurt were good friends.

Dick Warlock: My first picture as Kurt Russell's stunt man was *The Computer Wore Tennis Shoes*—and was with him off and on for about 25 years. Kurt is a very gracious individual. He supported me up until the time that I could no longer keep up ... His daddy Bing is the one who actually got us together. Kurt wasn't thinking about stunt doubles back then. Bing told me that he couldn't tell us apart on screen sometimes and that he wanted to put me in Kurt's contract so that I could stay with him when he was cast in a film. I stayed off and on for 25 years. I think there were about four pictures that I didn't do for and with him during that time. I sure would have loved dong Elvis with him. He did a great job on that film. I will be eternally grateful to him and his father for all of their help during my career. In fact I may not have had one if it hadn't been for them. Thanks Kurt

Kurt is as handy as any stuntman I know. He would always ask me whether or not he should do the stunt. I think it was mostly courtesy on his part because he could have done as well as I did. The production companies don't want the stars doing their own stunts for obvious reasons. Some actors enjoy doing their own stunts— well, I think if they feel they can do it they would like to and in some cases it is advisable for the films sake. The audience likes to think their star is doing it. I remember driving the dune buggy for Kurt in *Now You See Him-Now You Don't*—that was a blast!

Ride a Northbound Horse (1969)

Carroll O'Connor was a well established character actor at the time he made this two-part Disney TV show about an orphan (John Shea) who journeys to Texas in hopes of becoming a cattle rancher. Two years before O'Connor would find the role of a life-time as Archie Bunker on *All in the Family*, he plays a con man who gets young Shea mixed up in trouble involving a racing. Along for the ride are Ben Johnson (only two years away from winning an Oscar for *The Last Picture Show*) and Harry Carey, Jr., giving an authentic Western-John Ford stock company look to the presentation. The director was Robert Totten (1937-1995) who was also an occasional actor. He directed some twenty-seven episodes of *Gunsmoke* between 1966-1971.

Harry Carey, Jr.: I did a Disney TV program called *Ride a Northbound Horse*. That wasn't much fun. For one thing the director, Robert Totten, thought he was a combination of John Ford and Cecil B. DeMille, when in actuality he wasn't like either of them at all. I found him to be a really strange guy and kind of a rebel. He tried to act like he was a tough guy, but he wasn't. He was a bit of a ham and trying to be something he wasn't. Carroll O'Connor was in this, too. This was just a few years before he was Archie Bunker on *All in the Family*. O'Connor was wonderful to work with, but he wasn't too happy either. I never thought he would become this huge star. He was just a damn good character actor at the time. Truth be told *Ride a Northbound Horse* was just another paycheck for me—it wasn't anything special—but I liked to work—and I liked the Disney Studio.

The Barefoot Executive (1971)

Another Kurt Russell Disney slapstick comedy about a young man (Russell) who works in the mailroom of a TV network, who hopes to eventually work his way up to the top. He soon discovers a sure-fire way to move ahead when a neighbor's chimpanzee has a knack for picking TV shows that will become hits! Such as what the networks use today. In addition to Kurt Russell there are many familiar faces in the cast, including Disney stock players Hank Jones and Peter Renaday, as well as Joe Flynn, Harry Morgan, Wally Cox, John Ritter, Hayden Rourke (Dr. Bellows on *I Dream of Jeannie*), Sandra Gould (the second Gladys Kravitz on *Bewitched*) and Bill Daily (*I Dream of Jeannie* and *The Bob Newhart Show*). This satire of the television industry works pretty well and has much of the same cast, writers, director and crew as the popular Russell-Dexter Riley films—that it makes a fine companion piece to those films. *The New York Times*, however, was unimpressed calling the film "genial, but strained."

Hank Jones: I worked with Kurt Russell in *The Barefoot Executive*. How that came about was one morning I got a frantic call at home at around 9 a.m. from the head of casting asking if I could be at the studio at 10 to be in a picture. The guy they hired just didn't show up, and they really were behind the eight ball. So I took the world's fastest shower, put on my grubby jeans and sped over to the corner of Goofy Lane and Dopey Drive. They slapped some make up on me, shoved a script in my hand, and the next thing I knew I was spending the day throwing double-takes at a chimp and doing several scenes with Kurt.

Peter Renaday: Another one we did together was *The Barefoot Executive*, again with Robert Butler directing. I liked Bob. In *Barefoot* I played a cop called to the scene when Joe Flynn and Wally Cox were thought to be about to jump from a high building. Bob wanted me to drive toward the camera as I could, hit the brakes so that the car was just short of the camera, get out and do my lines. The first time I tried it, Bob thought I could come in faster and stop closer to the camera! The second time I did, and when I finished my dialogue the camera crew applauded. I don't think they thought my acting was so special; they just didn't want me to try it again! Speaking of Joe Flynn—he was a very funny guy and a nice man. I remember someone asking him why he still dyed his hair, and he said, 'There's nothing funny about an old man falling off a building!

Hank Jones: I've always felt that *The Barefoot Executive* was a serviceable, formulistic comedy that was just OK: a bit contrived, but providing some chuckles along the way. Not the best—but certainly not the worst. Robert Butler was easy to work with, a nice guy with a light touch directing his actors.

Michael O'Hara IV (1972)

Michael O'Hara the III (Dan Dailey) comes from a long line of Michael O'Hara's who have been involved in law enforcement. However, his one and only child is a girl, and despite this he decides to name her Michael O'Hara IV. She goes by the nickname "Mike" (played by Jo Ann Harris). Mike, too, wants to follow the family tradition and gets involved in police activities much to the chagrin of her loving father. She is told to keep out of it but she has a nose for police work and can't stop her amateur detective ways. Getting mixed up in her adventures is Norman (Disney veteran Michael McGreevey). Robert Totten directs this *Wonderful World of Disney* teleplay.

Michael McGreevey: I think that my performance in *Michael O'Hara IV* was the best acting I ever did at Disney Studios. It was directed by a very intense and talented young director, Bob Totten, with whom I had a love/hate relationship, but who really brought out the best in me as an actor. The script was by Joe McEveety, who also wrote the Medfield College movies. I always felt at ease with Joe's dialogue and the character of "Norman" was the most well-rounded and three-dimensional person I ever played at Disney. For the first time, I got to take on a leading man role; albeit an unusual and funny leading man. The love relationship between 'Norman' and 'Mike' (detective Dan Dailey's daughter in the show) was very easy for me to play because I was quite taken with my co-star, Jo Ann Harris. She was cute, sexy and overflowing with personality! Couple that with the fact that Jo Ann was also a terrific actress and you've got a great formula for onscreen chemistry. I didn't have many leading ladies in my acting career, but Jo Ann Harris was the best I ever worked with.

Working with Dan Dailey was a dream comes true for me. My first job in the film business was as a dancer, performing with Jane Powell in a movie musical, *The Girl Most Likely*. As a little boy I took dance classes four times a week and I had three heroes that I looked up to and admired—Fred Astaire, Gene Kelly and Dan Dailey. Dan was a consummate professional and a very giving actor, but he was a very reserved and private person. We didn't' talk much, but I did get to ask him about working with Gene Kelly and Michael Kidd in *It's Always Fair Weather*. His face lit up with a big smile as he recalled the movie as an incredible creative experience. He said the dance sequences were particularly challenging and rewarding as the three perfectionists tried to out-dance one another in take after take. I asked him who won and he replied, 'The audience!' Unfortunately, that was the only extended conversation I shared with Mr. Dailey. He was in ill health during most of the filming and spent his non-working time resting in his dressing room. I remember hearing of his death a few years later and thinking how lucky I was to meet and work with a total pro like Dan Dailey.

Now You See Him, Now You Don't (1972)

Now You See Him, Now You Don't is second in the trilogy of Medfield College films featuring Dexter Riley (Kurt Russell). This time Dexter is a chemistry student who invents a spray that makes its wearer invisible. Naturally crooked AJ Arno (Cesar Romero) finds out about it and sensing a money maker intends to steal it. Michael McGreevey also returns as Dexter's friend Schuyler and Joe Flynn as Dean Higgins. The *New York*

Now You See Him, Now You Don't.

William Windom and Joe Flynn in *Now You See Him, Now You Don't*.
© Walt Disney Productions.

Times assessed the film and came to the judgment that kids "ate it up" and "the Disney people, with their obvious gimmicks have kept the antics as merry as they are broad and clean."

Michael McGreevey: My favorite film of the Medford College trilogy was *Now You See Him, Now You Don't*. I probably feel that way because it was the film that featured me the most and contained my all-time favorite scene (the demonstration where I think I'm invisible, but I'm not). I also liked the fact that Kurt Russell was invisible throughout most of the movie. I'm kidding!! But seriously, I feel that everybody and everything improved from the first film because we were coming off a success and wanted to outdo ourselves. The writing was better, the direction sharper, the entire cast was more at ease and comfortable in their roles and with one another. All the characters were more defined and better realized than they were in *Computer Wore Tennis Shoes*. Everything just came together perfectly on this film and we had a blast making it. Even the crew had a good time on this film. I don't think I ever laughed so much during a production.

Speaking of laughs, I believe this film contains Joe Flynn's best performance in the trilogy. He's truly hilarious. And all the great character actors were also at their best—Alan Hewitt, Jim Backus, William Windom, Dick Bakalyan, Bing Russell, Frank Welker, Ed Begley, Jr., Larry Gelman, Burt Mustin, Winnie Collins and Eddie Quillan. A smile comes across my face just thinking of these wonderful performers.

Herbie Rides Again (1974)

Herbie Rides Again is the first sequel to the phenomenally popular *The Love Bug*, but with a new cast. Dean Jones indicated that he wasn't interested in doing this film as he thought the script was fairly weak. Keenan Wynn reprises Alonzo Hawk, from the *Flubber* films, and still a property developer he has bought several blocks of land to build a shopping mall. An elderly widow (Helen Hayes) will not sell the remaining lot that Hawk needs to complete his mall, so he devises a scheme to do so. Luckily the widow has the help of the Volkswagen with human emotions, Herbie, as well as a younger couple (Ken Berry and Stefanie Powers) to help her out. Like its predecessor, the film had its premiere at Radio City Music Hall. Unlike the earlier film the reviews weren't as kind. Vincent Canby in the *New York Times* called the film "witless" and said that the bad guys were "much more appealing than the good-guys." Of course this film, like many of the Disney product of this time, were critic proof and it made a profit at the box office.

Hank Jones: A few years later I was cast, again by Robert Stevenson, to play Sir Lancelot, the drag racer, in *Herbie Rides Again*, the first sequel to *The Love Bug*. When I completed my part in that film I got a call from the studio saying that Bill Walsh and Robert Stevenson wanted me back for yet another part in the same movie! They darkened my skin with full body make-up, gave me new eyebrows and a hippy-dippy brown wig, and suddenly I was transformed into the surfer dude riding the big waves in Hawaii along with Herbie the Love Bug right at my side!

Jan Williams: Acting was ok, but with only bit parts and me not being a leading man I could see no future in it really. I had always loved the idea of being a producer. They were the gods of the lot and seemed to have all the real fun, so I went after that. I was working on *Herbie Rides Again* as a stand-in and Bill Walsh was on the set one day talking about needing some footage of wrecking balls taking down buildings for the movie. He turned to me saying that I had been around the studio for a while and that he would keep me on salary if I would try and locate some stock footage. I said sure, having no idea where to start, but it was a chance to do something. Right after the conversation with Bill I was getting a cup of coffee and Walter Tyler, the art director, was at the coffee urn and I proudly mentioned to him that I had a new assignment. He wished me well. Later in the day Walter came over and said he had been thinking and he knew the owners of Controlled Demolition, they take down buildings with dynamite, he didn't know…but there may be film somewhere, he gave me a phone number. I called and it turned out that the son of the owner was a camera enthusiast and had 16mm shots of many of the buildings going down. We talked and I managed to get the film in town and had a look…DYNOMITE was right. I set up a showing for Bill Walsh…he came in and said…so you think you have something? I told him…it may work. They ran the film and I watch him sit up, slide forward in his seat and literally grab the back of the seat in front of him. After about ten minutes of building, after building, after building is being collapsed on itself he said he had seen enough. He turned to me and said 'great job!' The shots can be seen in the film to this day.

Fast forward to *Island at the Top of the World*. I had been standing in and when the principal photography was over my old friend Art Vitarelli was shooting second unit. To learn more about shooting even though I was on unemployment, I came to the set every day for almost a month… watching and learning. Then one day the guard on the set called me over and said Ron Miller, the studio head, wanted to see me in his office…now! I told Art I had to go and he said, 'I think you are in trouble for working on the lot without authorization.' I went up to Ron's office, he had a scowl on his face and said, 'I understand you've been coming on the lot and you don't have authorization.' I said yes…certain that my days at Disney were over. He then said, 'we can't have that you know…' I was doomed for sure…he went on… 'I guess I'll have to start paying you.' He went on to tell me how Bill Walsh had talked to him and what Art Vitarelli thought of me and he offered me a job as production assistant at $200 a week…and so it began. It was 1973. Ron Miller was the first studio chief to hire me as a production assistant. He was a good guy; he cared about the studio and its image.

Hank Jones: Even the smallest part was cast usually by using a character actor familiar to and often loved by the public. For example, in my scene in *Herbie Rides Again* where I'm wimpy Sir Lancelot in that car-race sequence, who starts the race off comically by blowing a huge bugle-like horn in just a three-second shot?...none other than the marvelous Huntz Hall of Bowery Boys/ Dead End Kids fame. Huntz is only on-screen for the briefest time, but to the audience it's like seeing an old friend you haven't seen in a while show up unexpectedly at a wonderful party. Every film I did and that the Studio did overflowed with actors like that, in roles big and small.

The Bears and I (1974)

The Bears and I was a surprise hit when released in the summer of 1974. *The Bears and I* (based on a novel by John Franklin Leslie) tells the story of Bob Leslie (Patrick Wayne), a Vietnam vet who is seeking out the father of a deceased buddy in the remote Canadian Rockies. While camping he comes upon a bear and her three cubs, but then the mother is killed and the cubs are too young to care for themselves—especially in the wild, so he takes them under his wing. He also helps local Indians in a dispute over land. The cast includes such veteran actors as Michael Ansara, Chief Dan George, Andrew Duggan and Robert Pine.

The film is beautifully shot on location in the Colorado Rockies. It was produced by Winston Hibler (1910-1976). Hibler was a long-time veteran of the Disney Studios and had probably been best known for narrating Disney's famous series of true-life adventure films such as *Seal Island,* *The Vanishing Prairie* and *The Living Desert,* many of which he also wrote. He later narrated, wrote and directed *Men Against the Arctic,* which won an Academy Award. He moved on to produce several live-action films including *Those Calloways* and *Island at the Top of the World.* Hibler, known to most as "Hib," was the perfect choice to produce *The Bears and I* which had so many elements of the Disney true-life adventure films.

Hibler choose Bernard McEveety (1924-2004) to direct the film. McEveety, like his brother Joe, had worked primarily in television and had a long list of credits on shows like *Rawhide, Gunsmoke, The Virginian, The Big Valley, The Fall Guy, Simon and Simon, Eight is Enough*—among others. He was also one of the primary directors of the TV series *Combat.* He directed his first feature for Disney in 1972, *Napoleon and Samantha* which featured Michael Douglas, Will Geer and a very young Jodie Foster in her feature film debut.

The film includes songs by John Denver and breathtaking scenery and is an enjoyable way to spend 90 minutes.

Patrick Wayne: The film was unusual in that it was shot over two summers and one winter. The first summer it was basically the bears and I and a menagerie of animals—wolverines, elk, deer, raccoons, etc. and we did a lot of animal action and interaction sequences. The winter was getting the bears ready for hibernation. It was so cold...the area was aptly called "Hurricane Ridge" and the wind chill kept the effective temperatures well below freezing. We were staying in cabins designed for summer fishing... not much help against the bitter cold. We would stoke the stove at night but in the morning the fire was out and the first morning my boots were frozen to the floor! I learned to hang the boots over a hook in the evenings and I put my clothes inside the bedding to keep it warm. Unfortunately, my wardrobe didn't allow me to wear proper gear for the temperature, but I did have down-filled long underwear which worked well enough.

The following summer the bears came out of hibernation and the fun began. The Indians wanted the bears to be free (a problem for me as they had become my only family). It all worked out in Disney fashion. We had an excellent cast, headed by Michael Ansara, Robert Pine, and Chief Dan George. Dan George was pretty advanced in age but still very hip. Bernie (McEveety) was a saint to work for and very easy going. Everyone got along quite well. This was good because we were in a remote part of British Columbia— on Chilko Lake. The closest town was 140 miles away and it took six hours to drive there! The first summer my dad (John Wayne) flew up in a pontoon plane to visit and he left my younger brother, Ethan, who stayed with me for the rest of the shoot. His nickname was Heathen— well-earned and I had my hands full keeping him in tow. Bob Pine and I had an unusual experience. We were taking a drive on our day off when we saw some Indians gathered by the lake. I knew one of the older Indians had died so we decided to pay our last respects. When we reached the group, we noticed that they were digging a grave and there was a body laid out nearby. They had been drinking and were in a sour mood. We told them that we had come to offer our condolences and one of them said, "dig." So we picked up the shovels and started digging. After a couple of minutes Bob says, "Hey, look." On his shovel he had a human skull. I told him to put it in the pile and I said to one of the Indians I knew, "Voyne, there is someone buried here already." He said, "oh, I know, but it is so pleasant here we thought we'd put him in the same place."

Robert Pine: I have very fond memories of *The Bears and I*. Patrick Wayne and I went back many years—and he still is one of my closest friends. I remember we made this up in British Columbia and we had to be flown in by a sea plane which landed on a lake. We were housed in modules, which had a communal dining room. It was fun—and we really bonded, the cast really bonded. I recall Disney had to cut a dirt road in between some highway, so that we could get to the modules we were housed in.

I remember, too, that it was just the beginning of the remote phone era and I remember that I wanted to call home and we would go to this high location where we could get the best reception and use this mobile phone and I'd call home and talk to my wife and tell her, 'Isn't this fantastic!' I remember that very well.

I didn't really work with any of the animals, Patrick did most of that. But I was interested and there was a mountain lion in a cage and somehow I decided I wanted to go in and see how it was—I was curious. There was a trainer there who said, 'Ok, just don't make any sudden moves' I said, 'Don't worry about that.' So in I went and the lion brushed up against my legs, just like a house cat might. Still I had my thrill and I wanted to get out of there!

I do recall that we also helped some local Indians –I'm a little vague about the reason, but we were filming in Indian country and we helped with an Indian burial ceremony. I forget the particulars but it was unique. Chief Dan George was also in that film and he was quite a character—he was a little odd. I think he may have been smoking a little grass. He was fun, though.

Bernard McEveety was a wonderful director and I had worked with him on a *Gunsmoke*, and it was the best part I had up to that time. I worked for both Bernie and his brother Vinnie. Bernie, to me was a wonderful director because of the break he had given me on *Gunsmoke*. I wouldn't say he was a great actor's director—I know this is vague, but he was certainly a very good, competent director—who delivered the goods on time to a studio (and what studio isn't) that was very cost conscious.

One of the great things about our industry is when we do a film like *The Bears and I* and are able to go to these remote and interesting locations—you have some unique experiences.

The Strongest Man in the World (1975)

The final film in the Dexter Riley-Medford College trilogy, it came three years after the second, with the characters noticeably older. A school laboratory accident mixes one student's vitamin cereal mix with Dexter Riley's chemical experiment. Upon getting rid of the messy goo by feeding it to a cow, they discover that the cow has incredible strength—and, naturally, Dexter tries it out for himself and acquires super-human strength. Once again the college is in financial trouble, and Dean Higgins (Joe Flynn) believes that the formula will be a way out for the college. However, A.J. Arno (Cesar Romero), the crooked businessman has plans of his own for the formula. Added to the mix are veterans Eve Arden and Phil Silvers. Sadly this was Joe Flynn's final film. He died in his pool shortly before the film was released in a freak accident. He had broken his leg and had a cast

Lobby card for *The Strongest Man in the World*.

put on. He went for a swim—suffered a heart attack, and drowned. Again the film was reviewed in the *New York Times* which judged the film as "nowhere near as funny as the first but a lot better than the second."

Michael McGreevey: By the time we did our third of the Medfield College trilogy, *Strongest Man in the World*, indeed we were a little too old to be playing college students again, but Disney called, made an offer and we couldn't resist playing those characters one last time. I justified my age by rationalizing that it would take 'Schuyler' at least eight years to complete college. So by my calculations he was still only in his junior year during this movie. Creatively, it was probably a mistake to return, but it was so much fun to make that movie and it was a thrill to be back at Disney Studios. All the usual suspects returned—Joe Flynn, Caesar Romero, Dick Bakalyan, William Schallert, and Dick Van Patten.

Kurt and I were rooming together at the time so we could carpool to work. There were also some new faces that made it a thrill to show up every day—two of my all-time favorite stars, Eve Arden and Phil Silvers. Although both Phil and Eve were past their prime, it was still a kick to be around 'Miss Brooks' and 'Sgt. Bilko.' These two were legendary figures in television history and I thoroughly enjoyed watching them work, remembering all the great moments they had created for television audiences over the years. I also fell in love on this movie so I have nothing but good memories about that time in my life. Too bad we didn't' make a better film.

Our director was Vincent McEveety, who was the brother of Joe McEveety, the writer of the Medfield Trilogy whose talent I greatly admired and who was a good friend. Vincent was a very good director, with a lot of credits in T.V. dramas, Vince was not really experienced doing comedy, especially the very specialized kind of comedy required for these movies. He also didn't feel comfortable criticizing our performances because we had all been playing these characters for so long. The result was a formulaic movie that didn't have any of the sparks or magic the previous two films possessed. Even though we were familiar with our characters, we cold have used direction and suggestions to embellish and improve our performances. Vince was a great guy with a lot of talent, but he was not the right director for this project.

Jonathan Daly: Kurt was level headed and warm and a great chum to all around. We all loved working with him.

No Deposit, No Return (1976)

Two would-be safe-crackers (Darren McGavin and Don Knotts) kidnap the two grandchildren (Kim Richards and Brad Savage) of millionaire J. W. Osborne (David Niven). The only problem is that the kids enjoy being with their kidnappers and Osborne isn't interested in paying a ransom. Norman Tokar is once again at the helm, of this, his 14th feature film as a Disney director. This would be the first of two films that Niven would make for Disney (*Candleshoe* opposite Helen Hayes and Jodie Foster would follow in a couple of years). "I had always wanted to do a film for Disney, but I was always in another picture or the correct script didn't show up while Walt himself was alive," Niven recalled at the time. "Finally, everything meshed and here I am. I have to be on my toes. I am working with child actors, a dog and a skunk— everything an actor should avoid!" In his review Vincent Canby of the *New York Times* legitimately criticized the film for its length, which at nearly two hours made some of the action drawn-out and repetitive.

Jan Williams: I worked as an assistant to the producer, associate producer and producer. Depending on the project you were a gofer or in charge. As an assistant to the producer you basically do anything that needs doing from finding stock footage to making sure the dailies are ready every day. As an associate producer, depending on who was producing, you had a lot more control of how the show went. The budgeting, scheduling and you made decisions on the set. As a producer, working under Ron as head of the studio, you ran the show and made all the decisions. When I was leaving for France on my first producing project I called Ron. I asked him, 'If I get in trouble—when should I call you?' He said, 'You'll know.' I didn't call him then, or on any of my films.

One of my first films in the production end was *No Deposit, No Return*—Norman Tokar, the director/producer on the film, had more to do with the concept and I worked the set more. A great cast to work with but they needed wrangling from time to time. I handled some of the second unit shooting on that one as I was just getting my feet wet. Norman had a very clear picture of what the film should look like and how the actors should work. He liked to walk into the middle of a shot and read the lines. He had lots of energy and knew what he was doing. The cast was great. Don Knotts was the best. He was friendly, funny and totally professional. David Niven loved to hide behind the 'British' thing but under it all he was a very real and nice man. Kim Richards was a little pro. She knew her words and where the camera was and she worked it. When we cast a Disney film we would have casting meeting with the casting department and discuss the characters and possible actors. We would also discuss budget and then have a casting call and read the actors. Some were returning actors and some were new.

Dick Warlock (stuntman): I didn't get to know Don Knotts very well, but he was always cheerful and friendly and made working conditions a happy time.

Hank Jones: I really don't remember much about *No Deposit, No Return*, except that I ended up in a car crash as a cop with a banana in my mouth. Ah, method acting!!

The Apple Dumpling Gang Rides Again (1979)

The Apple Dumpling Gang released in the summer of 1975 was a hugely popular Disney film. It was the third most successful live-action Disney film for the studio after *Mary Poppins* and *The Love Bug*. A major part of its success was the teaming of two comedy icons—Don Knotts and Tim Conway—to play the inept outlaws. Its success, inevitably led to this sequel, as Tim Conway explained at the time:

There's no great statement in *The Apple Dumpling Gang* films, but I think Disney threw together, if I may, the next Laurel and Hardy. We're just two guys who entertain through funny situations that may not be as far out as they would seem. The situations, of course, are amplified and you say, 'those idiots,' but in reality you probably have been there yourself. I think you've just seen the beginning of Don and I in a series of these films. It's a natural combination. I think as long as Rocky keeps on fighting, the Apple Dumpling Gang will keep shooting. Sequels are fine as long as the freshness of the storyline is maintained. We'll know when it goes stale.

Don Knotts added to the Laurel and Hardy comparison:

It's really fun to work together in another comedy with a guy who's really funny. Like, if I'm not so funny in a particular scene—he will be. It's similar to Laurel and Hardy in some ways. At first we thought we were too similar and …couldn't work together. But we found out that wasn't true because each of us has something different to bring to the character we're playing.

Don Knotts and Tim Conway made a popular team in *The Apple Dumpling Gang.*
© Walt Disney Productions.

Alas, this film didn't do as well as the original and there were no more sequels, though Knotts and Conway did continue to work together in other projects at other studios. *The Apple Dumpling Gang Rides Again* does however have another strong cast of superb character actors including Kenneth Mars (a veteran of such Mel Brooks films as *The Producers* and *Young Frankenstein*), Harry Morgan, Jack Elam and Robert Pine. Knotts and Conway are also supported by another pair of love birds, this time played by Tim Matheson and Elyssa Davalos. Vincent McEveety directs.

Robert Pine: I think I may have spent two weeks on *The Apple Dumpling Gang Rides Again*. What a blast that was. Tim Conway was great fun. I remember that we went to dinner one night at the motel we stayed at in Kanab, Utah, it was the best digs in town. It was myself, Tim, Don Knotts, Andy Duggan and a couple of others. There was a German tour group that was sitting there, too, and Tim begins talking with a German accent and it was quite hilarious. I don't think the German tour group minded, I'm not even sure that they realized what he was doing. But that was Tim. Don was great, too. But quieter. Tim and Don got on well but when the cameras were off, Don was content to sit still and let Tim take the stage.

Ken Mars and I had a day off and we decided we wanted to take a hike—it was such beautiful country. Anyway we managed to get lost. I wasn't really worried because I knew we must not be too far off the trail, but Ken got panicked. He said, 'you're going to kill me out here in the desert.' Anyway, we were lost I think for only a couple of hours and eventually found our way back, but from then on whenever we ran into each other, Ken would tell anybody who was standing by that I almost got him killed! It was a joke then, but at the time he sure was scared.

Jack Elam was another wonderful guy. We did some location work, I think in Sonora, California, with an old railroad and I remember that we went to a poker palace and I don't pay a lot of poker, but I recall I lost all of my money that I had received per diem—probably about $300 cash— in about twenty minutes just because I wanted to play poker with Jack Elam—who was a very good player.

Tim Matheson was in this picture too, and he was a great guy, too. I remember back in 1966 or 1967 I worked on an episode of *The Lucy Show* and I think it was one of the first times her daughter, little Lucie, worked with her. She played a high school student, and so did I even though I was 24 or 25 years old. Anyway, Lucy took a liking to me and she was about ready to start shooting a picture called *Yours, Mine & Ours* and she told me that she thought I'd be great as her oldest son in that film. We were

Apple Dumpling Gang Rides Again. © Walt Disney Productions.

Apple Dumpling Gang Rides Again. © Walt Disney Productions.

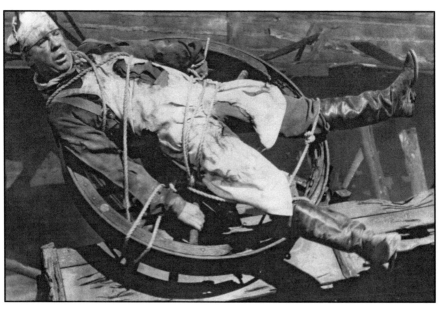

Apple Dumpling Gang Rides Again. © Walt Disney Productions.

Apple Dumpling Gang Rides Again. © Walt Disney Productions.

shooting the show on the Paramount lot at the time and her movie was going to be shot there, too, so she took me over to meet the director, Mel Shavelson, and she told Mel, "I think he would be great as my oldest son." Long story short I didn't get it—because I really was too old. The kid in the movie was supposed to be 18 and I was 25. Tim Matheson ended up getting that part.

Vinnie McEveety, our director, was more colorful than his brother Bernie (who directed me in *The Bears and I*). I remember he used to walk around with a cane, and I'm not sure he really needed it.

The Apple Dumpling Gang Rides Again I loved doing because I always enjoyed working in Westerns—even if they were of a humorous bent as this one was. It was a lot of fun.

The Cat from Outer Space (1978)

A UFO is crash lands on earth and impounded by the US Government. Its pilot, a cat with a collar that has special powers, including the ability to allow the cat to speak with humans (he is voiced by Ronnie Schell), has eluded the authorities and needs the help of a man named Frank in order to reclaim and repair his ship to get back home. The cast

The Cat from Outer Space was Disney's entry into the ET world.
© Walt Disney Productions.

includes Disney stalwarts Ken Berry, Harry Morgan, Hank Jones, Sandy Duncan, Roddy McDowell—and also features Alan Young and McLean Stevenson. With Morgan and Stevenson in the cast we have the two commanding officers of the 4077th *M*A*S*H* in the same film. This is one of the last in the long series of Disney formula comedies: from this time forward, Disney would attempt to change its image and even begin to use actors from other than the usual Disney stock company. This was Norman Tokar's 15th and final film as a director for Walt Disney Productions, in a career that went back to the Walt-era beginning with *Big Red*. The *New York Times* review was generally positive from the opening scene which parodies the (at the time) very popular *Close Encounters of the Third Kind*. The actors are all deemed "credible," but the feline actor was especially lauded, "no one could steal a scene from him."

Alan Young: As it turned out I didn't get to work at Disney again until after Walt was gone. I had worked for the director Norman Tokar on television and one day he called me up and offered me a part in a picture and said, "The part isn't much—but we'll build it up." The film was *The Cat from Outer Space*, and so I did it, and of course the part wasn't built up—after all of these years in the business I should have known better! It was a small part, so I didn't mind it. The film, however, turned out to be unsuccessful. The film did give me the opportunity, though, to work with Hans Conried. He was a real fella—and a real work man. He had worked with me on radio and on my television shows including *Mr. Ed*. If we were ever stuck for a gag we would just call up Hans and he always came through for us.

Hank Jones: My final film at Disney was *The Cat from Outer Space*. I played that completely against my usual nebbish or wimpy Disney type. Instead I'm a loud army officer whose only mission in life was to make things miserable for Ken Berry and his cat. I screamed and yelled at my troops until I was finally frozen in my tracks by the magic of the cat's supernatural powers. By the way, there were eleven cats, all dyed to look the same, that played the title role.

McLean Stevenson is also in the picture, and he was a nice guy—and very easy to be around. He loved to spin yarns between takes about some of his show business pals.

Cat from Outer Space also had Mel Carter in it. I had several good scenes with him playing a soldier under my (blustering) leadership. I remember he was anxious to spread his wings as an actor, having had immense success on the music charts in the 60's with several hits including "Hold Me, Thrill Me."

I'm always amazed at the quality of excellent character actors in most every Disney live-action film: they were the backbone of every production. It was such an honor to work with them all—and every one delivered!

Jan Williams: *The Cat from Outer Space* was a Norman Tokar film all the way (as director and producer)—I was more or less the gofer on that picture. It had a wonderful cast. Ken Berry was nice, quiet—a real pro. Sandy Duncan had energy—was fun—and great to have around. Alan Young loved to talk between setups—stories, stories and more stories. Harry Morgan had a great sense of humor, always coming up with a prank or set up.

Dick Warlock: A more down to earth guy you will never meet is Ken Berry. I liked him very much. I wish we had known each other on *F-Troop*. That would have been a blast to do stunts on that show!

Hans Conried, Ken Berry and Harry Morgan, *The Cat from Outer Space.*
© Walt Disney Productions.

Ken Berry and McLean Stevenson, *The Cat from Outer Space.*
© Walt Disney Productions.

Harry Morgan and assorted military men, *The Cat from Outer Space.*
© Walt Disney Productions.

Jonathan Daly: I worked with Hans (Conried) many years earlier on *The George Gobel Show* he was a true gentleman and an actor's actor. Hank (Jones) is one of my dearest friends. We worked together at Universal and became so close that we still stay in touch. I adore Hank. Ronnie (Schell) and I would always meet and have long chats regarding Disney and Hollywood in general. A great guy.

The Last Flight of Noah's Ark (1980)

Noah Dugan (Elliott Gould) agrees to fly a missionary (the beautiful Genevieve Bujold) and a cargo of animals to a remote island—both are unaware that two of her students (played by Ricky Schroeder and Tammy Lauren) have stowed away with the animals and that a transistor radio interferes with the plane's instruments causing the plane to go miles off course. They are forced to land on a remote island—where they soon find two Japanese soldiers who have been stranded, alone on the island since World War II. Somehow, they must make the plane seaworthy if they are going to make it home. Thus the reference to Noah's Ark—since the animals cannot be left behind.

Charles Jarrott, who had directed Disney's lovely *The Littlest Horse Thieves* in 1976, was chosen to direct. The British-born Jarrott served in the Royal Navy during the Second World War. After the war he became a stage manager and later a director. His film debut was prestigious: *Anne of the Thousand Days*, starring Richard Burton. Jarrott won a Golden Globe nomination for this film and directed Burton to an Oscar nomination. He also directed such films as *Mary, Queen of Scots* (Vanessa Redgrave was nominated for an Oscar for this film), the disastrous 1973 remake of *Lost Horizon*, and *The Dove*. In 1979 he was hired by Disney producer Jan Williams to direct two films for the studio, in a move away from the usual directors and casts and gives the studio product a newer look. Those films were *The Last Flight of Noah's Ark* and *Condorman*. He continued to direct several prestigious movies, mostly for TV, up through the 1990s including *Ike, Poor Little Rich Girl: The Barbara Hutton Story, Lucy & Desi* and *The Christmas List*.

Jan Williams: My next picture *The Last Flight of Noah's Ark* was Disney trying to change its image a bit. We got Charles Jarrott to direct and a un-Disney cast, but it still has people, elements of family, adventure and triumphs in it. That was a tough film to shoot—the water! Always the water…tough. The script worked very well, I thought. I liked to work with my writers and I would add my two cents and eventually joined the Guild so I could do it legally. It was great to have a story meeting, throw out a sequence idea and then a few days later see it in script form. The visual of the B-29 sailing at sea was something that I had never seen. Add a strong cast, Hawaii and Charles Jarrott—and I think it worked. Elliott Gould is a very funny guy and loves to laugh. He knows his words and delivers on camera. Ricky Schroeder was just a small fry then but he was terrific.

Condorman (1981)

Condorman tells the story of a comic book writer/artist named Woody (Michael Crawford) who, while performing a courier job for his friend Harry (James Hampton), a CIA operative, he gets involved with hostile agents, and yet earns respect from the beautiful Natalia (Barbara Carrera), who needs his help in her planned defection to the US. This gives Woody the idea of bringing his comic book hero, Condorman, to life. Oliver Reed also appears as the evil Krokov.

Jan Williams: My last film was *Condorman*. I thought it was a fun spoof on all the super-heroes, putting the artist into his character and making him deliver just sounded like it would lead to some great visuals. Location shooting, effects, racing cars, racing boats, escapes—it all sounded campy and fun. Again I had Charles Jarrott as the director. Charles was a pro. He knew the script better than the writers and better than that he knew the spirit of the scenes, the feel of what he was going after. He always kept a light feel on the set and communicated well with everyone from the stars to the craft service man (coffee man). Michael Crawford was our star and he was a joy! He really got into the character and 'got it' that here was this little guy who knew nothing more than his back room with a pen, ink and paper taken out of his element and forced to perform. He got it! Some of the visual effects were fuzzy but overall I think it delivered. Henry Mancini did wonders for the feel of the film; he was great to work with. I always loved post production, putting the pieces together, cutting film, dialogue, sound effects and finally the music. I was lucky to work with some of the very best composers…now there is a real genius.

Appendix
Disney Love-Action Releases, 1955–1981*

Davy Crockett, King of the Wild Frontier (1955)

The African Lion (1955)

The Littlest Outlaw (1955)

The Great Locomotive Chase (1956)

Davy Crockett and the River Pirates (1956)

Secrets of Life (1956)

Westward Ho, the Wagons! (1956)

Johnny Tremain (1957)

Perri (1957)

Old Yeller (1957)

The Light in the Forest (1958)

White Wilderness (1958)

Tonka (1958)

The Shaggy Dog (1959)

Darby O'Gill and the Little People (1959)

Third Man on the Mountain (1959)

Toby Tyler (1960)

Kidnapped (1960)

Pollyanna (1960)

* bold entries discussed in book

The Sign of Zorro (1960)

Ten Who Dared (1960)

Swiss Family Robinson (1960)

The Absent-Minded Professor (1961)

The Parent Trap (1961)

Nikki, Wild Dog of the North (1961)

Greyfriars Bobby (1961)

Babes in Toyland (1961)

Moon Pilot (1962)

Bon Voyage! (1962)

Big Red (1962)

Almost Angels (1962)

The Legend of Lobo (1962)

In Search of the Castaways (1962)

Son of Flubber (1963)

Miracle of the White Stallions (1963)

Savage Sam (1963)

Summer Magic (1963)

The Incredible Journey (1963)

A Tiger Walks (1964)

The Misadventures of Merlin Jones (1964)

The Three Lives of Thomasina (1964)

The Moon-Spinners (1964)

Mary Poppins (1964)

Emil and the Detectives (1964)

Those Calloways (1965)

The Monkey's Uncle (1965)

That Darn Cat! (1965)

The Ugly Dachshund (1966)

Lt. Robin Crusoe, USN (1966)

The Fighting Prince of Donegal (1966)

Follow Me, Boys! (1966)

Monkeys, Go Home! (1967)

The Adventures of Bullwhip Griffin (1967)

The Gnome Mobile (1967)

Charlie, The Lonesome Cougar (1967)

The Happiest Millionaire (1967)

Blackbeard's Ghost (1968)

The One and Only, Genuine, Original Family Band (1968)

Never a Dull Moment (1968)

The Horse in the Gray Flannel Suit (1968)

The Love Bug (1968)

Smith! (1969)

Rascal (1969)

The Computer Wore Tennis Shoes (1969)

King of the Grizzlies (1970)

The Boatniks (1970)

The Wild Country (1970)

The Barefoot Executive (1971)

Scandalous John (1971)

The Million Dollar Duck (1971)

Bedknobs and Broomsticks (1971)

The Biscuit Eater (1972)

Now You See Him, Now You Don't (1972)

Napoleon and Samantha (1972)

Run, Cougar, Run (1972)

Snowball Express (1972)

The World's Greatest Athlete (1973)

Charley and the Angel (1973)

One Little Indian (1973)

Mustang (1973)

Superdad (1973)

Herbie Rides Again (1974)

The Bears and I (1974)

Castaway Cowboy (1974)

***The Island at the Top of the World* (1974)**

The Strongest Man in the World (1975)

Escape to Witch Mountain (1975)

The Apple Dumpling Gang (1975)

One of Our Dinosaurs is Missing (1975)

The Boy Who Talked to Badgers (1975)

Ride a Wild Pony (1975)

No Deposit, No Return (1976)

Treasure of Matecumbe (1976)

Gus (1976)

***The Shaggy D.A.* (1976**)

Freaky Friday (1976)

Escape from the Dark (1977)

Herbie Goes to Monte Carlo (1977)

Pete's Dragon (1977)

Candleshoe (1977)

Return from Witch Mountain (1978)

The Cat from Outer Space (1978)

Hot Lead and Cold Feet (1978)

The North Avenue Irregulars (1979)

The Apple Dumpling Gang Rides Again (1979)

The Black Hole (1979)

The Watcher in the Woods (1980)

Herbie Goes Bananas (1980)

The Last Flight of Noah's Ark (1980)

The Devil and Max Devlin (1981)

Amy (1981)

Condorman (1981)

Notes

Chapter One: A Little about Walt/Walt on Walt

Disney re-issue statistics, *Film Daily,* 6/17/1964

"We're through with Caviar…," *Time,* 12/27/1954

"Nothing makes him as happy as his work…," *Woman's Day,* 10/1962

"And if Walt were still living…," *New York Times,* 12/5/2001

"I formed my work patterns early in life…," *Ocala Star Banner,* 12/22/1966

"I had to get up at 3:30…," *Los Angeles Times,* 12/1966

"I wanted to draw…," *Montreal Gazette,* 12/23/1966

"If you keep busy…," ibid

"I've always had a great deal of natural curiosity…," ibid

"A person should set his goals…," *Walt Disney Magician of the Movies,* Bob Thomas, pg. 116

"Hell, I'm Disney…," *Newsweek,* 12/31/1962

"I am just an entertainer…," *Woman's Day,* 10/1962

"Always when I finish a picture…," *Saskatoon Star-Phoenix,* 7/2/1957

"I really don't concern myself…," *Daytona Beach Morning Journal*, 4/29/1961

"There is no way of pleasing everybody…," *Today's Health*, 4/1962

"I don't like depressing pictures…," ibid

"My feeling is that picture makers…," *Parade*, 1/7/1962

"I don't make films exclusively for children…," ibid

"All we are trying to give the public…," *New York Times Magazine*, 3/6/1938

"We have an organization of young men…," ibid

"I don't go for that sloppy kissing in films…," *Ottawa Citizen*, 4/28/1961

"Our part in things is to build along the lines…," *Newsweek*, 12/31/1962

"Producers too often are afraid…," *The Robesonian*, 6/30/1960

"We like to have a point of view in our stories…," *The Gospel According to Disney: Faith, Trust and Pixie Dust*, 2004, Steven Watts, pg. 401

"I can't laugh at intellectual humor…," *How to Be Like Walt*, pg. 345

"All right, I'm corny…," *The Magic Kingdom: Walt Disney and the American Way of Life*, 2001, Steven Watts, pg. 401

"There's enough ugliness…," *McCalls*, 11/1964

"There's no magic to my formula…," *Los Angeles Times*, 12/16/1966

"I try to make happy, humorous pictures…," *New York Daily News*, 9/22/1964

"I believe in the worthwhileness…," *Today's Health*, 4/1962

"We've got to make it more comfortable…," *The Robesonian*, 6/30/1960

"I am a patient listener…," *How to be Like Walt*, pg. 357

"I don't get ulcers…," *Los Angeles Times*, 12/16/1966

"Childishness?…," http://www.disneydreamer.com/walt/quotes.htm

"One of the things I want to do...," *Reading Eagle*, 12/2/1957

"Kids are too idle nowadays...," *Ocala Star-Banner*, 12/22/1966

"The American child is a highly intelligent...," *Faith is a Star*, Ronald Gammon, EP Dutton, 1963

"I'm against censorship...," *Reading Eagle*, 11/4/1959

"I agree that the American public wants sex...," *Parade*, 1/7/1962

"I've done a lot of thinking about a model community...," *Miami News*, 11/16/1965

"People who have worked with me...," *How to be Like Walt*, pg. 8

"I've got a lot of ideas...," ibid, pg. 227

"When we do fantasy...," *McCalls*, 12/1964

"I suppose my formula might be...," *Wall Street Journal*, 2/4/1958

"I feel what's wrong...," *Walt Disney*, Neal Gabler, pg. 539

"I'm never so filled up with my work...," *New York Daily News*, 9/29/1964

"Everybody can make their dreams come true...," *How to be Like Walt*, pg. 291

"In the last ten years...," *Lakeland Ledger*, 12/25/1961

"Some of us just wouldn't be satisfied...," *Walt Disney Conversations*, 2006

"I don't even want to be president of the United States...," *Dallas Morning News*, 5/29/1966

Chapter Two: Encounters with and Thoughts about Walt

"He was a charming man...," Julie Andrews, *Playboy*, 12/1982

"Walt was a great guy to work with...," Ken Annakin, *The Hollywood Interview*

"Of all the studio chiefs...," Ken Annakin, *Disney's World*, pg. 278

"The first time I met Walt Disney...," Harry Carey, Jr, to author

"One day many years ago…," Jonathan Daly to author

"Walt Disney would come out to the studio grounds…," James Drury to author

"Mr. Disney knows what he wants…," Annette Funicello quoted in *Today's Health*

"One day my agent…," Eddie Hodges to author

"I auditioned for the role of Lizbeth…," Marta Kristen to author

"Disney didn't ask for much…," Karl Malden to Author, *I Love the Illusion*

"Every day Walt Disney visited the set…," Michael McGreevey to author

"I seem to remember…," Hayley Mills quoted in *Disney's World*, pg. 259

"Walt Disney, apart from being a genius…," Mills, John. *Up in the Clouds*, Sir John Mills Gentleman Please, Orion

"Mr. Disney was a truly wonderful gentleman…," Pola Negri , *Memoirs of a Star*, Doubleday, 1970

"I was just insane about him…," Suzanne Pleshette quoted in *Remembering Walt*, pg. 89

"I had very little contact with Walt…," Peter Renaday to author

"Walt Disney was on the lot a great deal…," Larri Thomas to author

"I think it was around 1964…," Dick Warlock to author

"I grew up in a home…," Jan Williams to author

"My first association with the Disney organization…," Alan Young to author

Chapter Three: First Impressions of the Studio

"Walt Disney requested me…," Peter Brown to author

"One thing I'll say for the Disney Studio…," Harry Carey to author

"Other studios were like concrete…," David Frankham to author

"Not too many years ago…," Annette Funicello, *A Dream is a Wish Your Heart Makes*, pg.29

""It wasn't extremely different at Disney…," Eddie Hodges to author

"The Disney Commissary was by far…," Hank Jones to author

"When Disney was alive…," Tommy Kirk to author

"Back in the 60's the Disney lot…," Roger Mobley to author

"I remember the Disney lot…," Bill Mumy to author

"I am a lucky man to have worked at Disney…," Jonathan Daly to author

"Working at the Disney Studio was like a paid vacation…," Elliott Reid to author

"The atmosphere in the Walt Disney Studios was quite different," Richard Todd, *I Shot an Arrow in the Air*, pg. 277-278

"I enjoyed working on the Disney lot…," Dick Warlock to author

Chapter Four: Fess Parker: Disney's First Live-Action Super Star

"Walt Disney's right arm," *The Magic Kingdom*, pg. 381

"clean, pleasant taste…, ibid, pg. 378

"I thought it might be a good thing…," Bill Walsh quoted in *Disney's World*, pg. 245

"The first one I happened to pick…," Los Angeles Times, 12/29/1974

"He saw me in a TV program…," Buddy Ebsen, *The Other Side of Oz*

"I was twenty-nine…," *How to be Like Walt*, pg. 196

"Norman Foster was apologetic…," Ebsen, *The Other Side of Oz*

"He (Buddy Ebsen) is a gentle, talented…," http://www.dvdtown.com

"When I'd say to Walt's secretary…," *Remembering Walt*, pg. 73

"I found if I didn't do something…," Norman Foster quoted in *The Disney Films* by Leonard Maltin

"Foster was a man who had been a Broadway star…," http://www.dvdtown.com

"We were about three or four weeks…," ibid

"Disney liked to film a story where it occurred…," ibid

"That was pretty rough goin'…" *The Pittsburgh Press*, 8/21/1955

"When Buddy and I got through with our buckskins…," http://www.locatetv.com/blog/fess-parkers

"The filming of the Crockett episodes…" Buddy Ebsen quoted in *The Other Side of Oz*, pg. 204-205

"We had no idea what was going to happen to Crockett…," Walt Disney quoted in *The Disney Films*, pg. 122

"I thought it was pretty awful…," *The Magic Kingdom*, pg. 315

"We went a million dollars over budget last year…," *Lewiston Evening Journal*, 9/14/1955

"I shook hands with 100,000 kids…," *Pittsburgh Press*, 8/21/1955

"It was an extremely emotional reaction…," Fess Parker quoted in *Walt Disney* by Neal Gabler, pg. 515

Everything happened so fast…," *Daytona Beach Morning Journal*, 10/25/1958

"Walt Disney was very protective…" http://www.dvdtown.com

"I think the studio has to decide…," *Reading Eagle*, 5/6/1958

"An actor's got to spread his wings…," *Los Angeles Times*, 3/30/1958

"I could never hate Davy Crockett…," *The Calgary Herald*, 12/7/1955

Fess Parker recollections to author

Chapter Five: Recollections of a Mouseketeer: Sharon Baird

"I'm taking you off the evening show," *The Magic Kingdom,* pg. 379

"So we were his children," ibid, pg. 337

"At our studio we regard the child…," ibid, pg. 340

"I started one of the most enduring friendships of my life…," Annette Funicello, *A Dream is a Wish Your heart Makes*, pg. 48

All subsequent quotes in this chapter are from an interview by the author with Sharon Baird.

Chapter Six: A Boy and His Dog: The Making of Old Yeller

"I called in my friend, Bill Tunberg…," quote by Fred Gipson found in *Old Yeller* press book

"One day at the studio I got a note with a copy…," Tommy Kirk to author

"I read for the casting people…," Beverly Washburn to the author

"I didn't want to do the picture…," Fess Parker quoted in *Reading Eagle*, 5/6/1958

"Of course (it's) one of the most successful…," Fess Parker to author

"Tommy Kirk was wonderful…," Beverly Washburn to author

"Tommy Kirk was my son in the film…," Fess Parker to author

"I looked up to Robert Stevenson immeasurably…," Tommy Kirk to author

"Robert Stevenson fully explained…," Beverly Washburn to author

"Our director was Robert Stevenson…," Fess Parker to author

"Dorothy McGuire…was a beautiful person…," Tommy Kirk to author

"Dorothy McGuire was very motherly…," Beverly Washburn to author

"Dorothy McGuire…was a real professional…," Fess Parker to author

"Kevin Corcoran played my brother in so many films…," Tommy Kirk to author

"Kevin Corcoran was as cute as could be…," Beverly Washburn to author

""Jeff York…was wonderful…," Beverly Washburn to author

"The dog-Spike…," ibid

"Most of the emotion is read by the audience…," Robert Stevenson quoted in *Film Crazy*, pg. 217

"Disney visited the set a lot…," Tommy Kirk to author

"Walt Disney…," Beverly Washburn to author

"I remember when Tommy had to shoot Old Yeller…," ibid

"This is a Texas farm in 1869…," Walt Disney quoted in *Walt Disney* by Bob Thomas, pg. 293

"I had no idea at the time…," Beverly Washburn to author

"Old Yeller will be played a thousand years from now…,"

Chapter Seven: The Fred MacMurray Films

"He's a down to earth, practical actor…" *Charleston (WVA) Sunday-Gazette*, 7/2/1961

"I'm sorry to say I never really got to know Mr. MacMurray well…," Funicello, Annette and Patricia Romanowski. *A Dream is a Wish Your Heart Makes*, Hyperion Press, 1994

"Disney liked Fred enormously…," Tommy Kirk to author

"Nowadays Everybody gets percentage deals…," Fred MacMurray quoted in *Saturday Evening Post*, 2/24/1962

"Walt was still preparing the script for The Shaggy Dog…" *Walt Disney* by Bob Thomas pg. 227-228

"It brought Fred MacMurray back into films…," *Disney's World*, pg. 267

"The Shaggy Dog was instant box office…," Fred MacMurray quoted in *Saturday Evening Post*, 2/24/1962

"It's an interesting role…," *New York Journal American*, 3/12/1959

"I thought it was stupid…,"Tommy Kirk to author

"We had a technical adviser on Absent Minded Professor…," Winston Hibler quoted in *Man Behind the Magic: The Story of Walt Disney*, pg. 130

"Across the hall from our office…," The Sherman Brothers, *Walt's Time*

Recollections of Elliott Reid and Tommy Kirk re: *Absent Minded Professor*, to author

"Bon Voyage! Sounds like a good idea for a Disney film…," *The Disney Films*, pg. 198

"I have very bad memories of that film…," Tommy Kirk to author

"The film…was no great shakes…," Jane Wyman to author

"The script lady pulled me aside one day…," Kurt Russell quoted in *Remembering Walt*

"After the Flubber films…," Elliott Reid to author

"We got a call from Walt asking…," The Sherman Brothers, *Walt's Time*

"It's good Disney…," A.J. Carothers quoted in *New York Daily News*, 11/19/1967

"Everybody at the studio hoped…," The Sherman Brothers, *Walt's Time*

"My personal theory about *Happiest Millionaire*…," Leonard Maltin to author

Happiest Millionaire recollections from Eddie Hodges to author

Chapter Eight: A Potpourri of Disney Titles and Recollections

"He was a train enthusiast…," Francis Lyon quoted in *The Disney Films*

"After I got Spin and Marty…," Harry Carey, Jr., to author

"No calvary—and the Indian fight comes in the middle…," Walt Disney quoted in *Saskatoon Star-Phoenix*, 1/27/1956

"In between the Crockett shows…," Fess Parker to author

"Bill Beaudine was one of those old-time directors…," Harry Carey, Jr to author

"My first Disney film was Toby Tyler…," Michael McGreevey to author

"Toby Tyler was a fun film…," James Drury to author

"Ten who Dared was an adventure film…," David Frankham to author

"Ten who Dared was a wonderful adventure…," James Drury to author

Texas Jack Slaughter recollections by Harry Carey, Jr. to author

Babes in Toyland recollections by Ann Jillian are a combination excerpts from http://www.thecolumnists.com/jillian/jillian11.html and e-mail response to interview questions to Miss Jillian from the author.

"Of all my filmmaking experiences…," Annette Funicello, *A Dream is a Wish Your Heart Makes*, pg. 125-126

"I got a chance to meet Walt Disney…," Bill Mumy to author

"My next project was SAMMY THE WAY OUT SEAL…," Michael McGreevey to author

Savage Sam recollections by Marta Kristen to author

Miracle of the White Stallions recollections by Arthur Hiller to author

Emil and the Detectives recollections by Roger Mobley to author

For the Love of Willadean recollections by Michael McGreevey and Roger Mobley to author

Gallagher recollections by Roger Mobley to author

"We believe in getting more action…," Walt Disney quoted in *Daytona Beach Morning Journal*, 8/8/1964

"The only story Walt ever wrote…," Bill Walsh quoted in *Remembering Walt*, pg. 135

"We were in Hawaii…," *Classic Images*, 12/2010

Lt. Robin Crusoe, USN recollections from Peter Renaday to author

Willie and the Yank recollections by Peter Renaday to author

Chapter Nine: The Hayley Mills Films: The Rise of a Disney Super Star

"Hayley's performance…had bowled him (Walt) over…," *Up in the Clouds, Gentlemen Please*, pg. 237

"In my opinion, that little lady…," Walt Disney quoted in *The Magic Kingdom*, pg. 332

"Hayley was about to become a star…," Karl Malden, Where Do I Start, Limelight Editions (August 1, 2004)

"Hayley was a joy to us all…," Jane Wyman quoted in *Jane Wyman: the Actress and the Woman*

"I believe she was only 12…," Mary Grace Canfield to author

"Hayley Mills is from a wonderful theatrical family…," Maureen O'Hara, *Tis' Herself*

"Hayley Mills, what a sweetheart of a girl…," James Drury to author

"Hayley Mills was wonderful to work with…," Eddie Hodges to author

"I have been around longer than I have any right…," Maurice Chevalier, *Saturday Evening Post*, 7/28/62

"I've been a great Hayley Mills fan…," Eli Wallach quoted in *Los Angeles Times, How Eli Wallach Gets in the Mood for Murder*, 1964

"Our Pollyanna isn't the same as in the book…," *Sarasota Journal*, 10/7/1959

"I couldn't get it right and I hated it…," David Swift quoted in *Disney's World*

"Hayley was terribly nervous…," *Still Memories: An Autobiography in Photographs*

"If I remember correctly…," *Where do I start?*

"I don't know why they should come out…crying…," *Jane Wyman: The Actress and the Woman*

"Pollyanna was Walt's favorite film…," *Disney's World*

Mary Grace Canfield recollections on *Pollyanna* to author

James Drury recollections on *Pollyanna* to author

"I told them…that I wanted a real double…," Lucien Ballard quoted in *Saturday Evening Post*, 7/28/1962

Maureen O'Hara recollections of *Parent Trap* from taped interview sent by her secretary and from her autobiography, *'Tis Herself.*

Summer Magic recollections by Peter Brown to author

Summer Magic recollections by Eddie Hodges to author

Chapter Ten: The Making of a Masterpiece: Mary Poppins

"Years ago I saw my daughters…," *Disney's World*, Leonard Mosley, Scarborough House, 1990

"I have never written for children…" *New York Times Magazine*, 12/25/1966

"Mrs. Travers said she could not conceive of Mary Poppins as a cartoon character," *Disney's World*

"Dangling a watch, hypnotically…," *Mary Poppins she Wrote: The Life of P.L. Travers*, Valerie Lawson, Simon & Schuster, 1999

"One day in 1960...," Playbill.com, 5/14/2007

"She came over for a month or so," *Disney's World*

"One day, we were walking down to lunch...," *Boston Gobe,* 2/6/2011

"We would so like to have you...," Walt Disney to Julie Andrews, *Disney's World*

"Tony and I went to Hollywood...," Julie Andrews interview, Academy of Achievement, 6/10/2004

"Hello, talk to me, P.L. Travers here...," *St. Joseph Gazette,* 9/10/1964

"It's funny I was concentrating on the dancing...," Dick Van Dyke interview, CNN, 1/27/2009

"He's extremely winning..." Julie Andrews to P.L. Travers, *Mary Poppins she Wrote*

"Julie Andrews is quite satisfactory...," ibid

"He had done Bye Bye Birdie...," Richard Sherman, SFGate.com, 12/26/2004

"Besides making extremely successful films...," *Luckier than Most: An Autobiography,* David Tomlinson, Hodder & Stoughton, 1990 pg. 139-140

"She was under the impression she was called to become Mary Poppins," *Walt's Time,* Richard and Robert Sherman, Camphor Tree Publishers, 1998

"I got a call one day to have lunch with Walt...," *Remembering Walt,* Amy Boothe Green & Howard Green, Disney Edition, 2002

"I began to feel we had grown up together...," *Luckier than Most,* pg. 139

"The Disney People got us a wonderful home...," *Sarasota Journal,* 7/1/1980

"At times I thought the two children...," *Luckier than Most,* pg. 240

"When I'm directing a picture...," http://legends.disney.go.com

"Feed the Birds is the first song we completed…," *Walt's Time,* pg. 49

Marc Breaux recollections from www.uni.edu/taft/breauxinterview.html

"Ed was a wonderful man…," Dick Van Dyke on CNN.com 1/27/2009

"With Walt, Bill and Audrey I saw a rough cut…," *Luckier than Most,* pg. 145

"Sorry Pamela, that ship has already sailed," *Disney's World*

"If you look at *Mary Poppins*…" http://www.blackfilm. com/20040514/features/julieandrews)

Larri Thomas recollections to author

Dee Dee Wood recollections to author

Chapter Eleven: The Dean Jones Disney Films (1967-1977)

"I think it was because of the success of the films I was doing there…," www.herbiemania.com

"There's a certain bubble you try to maintain…," *The Times News,* 12/5/1968

"I use Mickey Mouse…," ibid

"I think the studio's operation and success…," *The Deseret News,* 6/18/1971

"The late Bill Walsh…," *The Robesonian,* 4/21/1976

"I didn't want to play Hamlet…," *USA Today,* 10/28/1991

"Dean Jones was one of the top Disney leading men…," Hank Jones, *The Show Bizz Part of My Life*

"Dean Jones—who you saw on film was Dean Jones…," Jan Williams to author

"The morning he came out of the hospital…," Suzanne Pleshette quoted in *Remembering Walt*

Blackbeard's Ghost recollections by Hank Jones from his wonderful book *The Show Bizz Part of My Life* & in response to questions by the author

"After a while I began doing some small acting jobs...," Jan Williams to author

"I seem to recall dong some stunt work...," Dick Warlock to author

"I worked with Peter Ustinov...," Jonathan Daly to author

"My favorite film hand down...," Hank Jones to author

"With the first movie..." www.herbiemania.com

"Robert Stevenson—I think history will probably judge him...," *New Straits Times*, 5/3/1986

"No, we had no idea...," www.herbiemania.com

"The next picture I was involved in was The Love Bug...," Peter Renaday to author

"I also did stunts on The Love Bug and other "Herbie" films...," Dick Warlock to author

"Before we had a script I decided we should find out...," *Williamson Daily News*, 8/8/1970

"One of the pictures...," Peter Renaday to author

"Dean and I became very close friends...," Jonathan Day to author

Snowball Express recollections by Michael McGreevey to author

Shaggy D.A. recollections by Michael McGreevey, Hank Jones, Peter Renaday, Jan Williams, Dick Warlock and Jonathan Daly to author

Herbie Goes to Monte Carlo recollections by Jan Williams to author

"I know that VW backward and forward...," http://d23.disney.go.com

Chapter Twelve: The Studio Post Walt

"I saw him the Monday he came back from the hospital…," Winston Hibler quoted in *Remembering Walt,* pg. 196

"My brother and I ran into Walt in the hall…," ibid, pg. 194

"While we were shooting Blackbeard's Ghost…," ibid pg. 192

"I have lost a great friend…," Sam Goldwyn quoted in *Los Angeles Times,* 12/16/1966

"No eulogy will be read…," Richard Zukor, ibid

"Walt Disney contributed as much…," Jack Warner, ibid

"Walt's warmth…," Mervyn LeRoy, ibid

"The joy he brought the world…," Fred MacMurray, ibid

"I am greatly saddened by this loss…," Julie Andrews, ibid

"I makes me so sad…," Annette Funicello, ibid

"A disaster for the entire world," Maurice Chevalier, ibid

"I knew Walt as a friend…," Pat Brown, ibid

"There just aren't any words…," Ronald Reagan, ibid

"We will continue to operate Walt's company…," *New York Times,* 12/16/1966

"I know a committee form is a lousy form in this business…," *Forbes,* 7/1/1967

"That doesn't mean we will find someone to replace Walt…," *Meriden Journal,* 1/9/1967

"We continue to get offers of merger…," *The Free Lance Star,* 6/19/1967

"We've never before had this much product on hand…," *Forbes,* 7/1/1967

"The system is working out well…," *Toledo Blade,* 6/27/1967

"Walt was like a champion of all his people…," www.laughingplace.com/

"Walt very seldom made a policy decision…," *Miami News,* 6/15/1967

"We all miss the man…," ibid

"Sure, we think of Walt all the time…," ibid

"Bill Walsh was the most important man at the studio after Walt's passing…," Hank Jones to author

"There are all kinds of producers…," *Los Angeles Times*, 12/5/1971

"Walt was alive during Blackbeard…," Hank Jones to author

"I never felt that they went by the idea…," Robert Pine to author

"Years after Mr. Disney died…," Kurt Russell quoted in *Remembering Walt*, pg. 207

The One and Only Genuine Original Family Band recollections by Hank Jones, *The Show Bizz Part of My Life*

"My most difficult directorial assignment…," Michael O'Herlihy quoted in Disney press book

"I had worked first with Michael O'Herlihy…," Hank Jones to author

"Although it was his first musical…," Bill Anderson quoted in Disney press book

The Sherman Brothers on the score for *Family Band*, Disney press Book

"I stared as the dialogue coach…," Peter Renaday to author

"You must have empathy for Disney material…," Norman Tokar quoted in *Lodi News-Sentinel*, 3/14/1972

"A few years later, after Walt had died, I made Rascal…," Billy Mumy to author

"I was interviewed at length by Bill Anderson…," Jonathan Daly to author

"The Computer Wore Tennis Shoes was originally shot…," Michael McGreevey to author

"As usual, Disney had put together a great supporting cast…," Jon Provost & Laurie Jacobson, *Timmy's in the Well: The Jon Provost Story*, Cumberland House Publishing

"Joe Flynn was another great guy…," Dick Warlock to author

"I worked with Kurt Russell…," Peter Renaday to author

"My first picture as Kurt Russell's stunt man…," Dick Warlock to author

"I did a Disney TV program called Ride a Northbound Horse…," Harry Carey, Jr to author

"I worked with Kurt Russell in The Barefoot Executive…," Hank Jones, *The Show Bizz Part of My Life*

"Another one we did together…," Peter Renaday to author

"I've always felt that *The Barefoot Executive*…," Hank Jones to author

"Concocting cartoon comedy…," *The Calgary Herald*, 8/3/1971

"I think that my performance in Michael O'Hara The Fourth…," Michael McGreevey to author

"My favorite of the Medford College trilogy…," Michael McGreevey to author

"A few years later I was cast…," Hank Jones, *The Show Bizz Part of My Life*

"Acting was ok, but…," Jan Williams to author

"Even the smallest part was cast…," Hank Jones to author

The Bears and I recollections by Robert Pine to author

"By the time we did our third of the Medfield College trilogy…," Michael McGreevey to author

"Kurt was level headed…," Jonathan Daly to author

"I worked as an assistant to the producer…," Jan Williams to the author

"I try to make only one film a year…," *Lewiston Evening Journal*, 8/8/1975

"I didn't get to know Don Knotts very well…," Dick Warlock to author

"I really don't remember much about No Deposit, No Return…," Hank Jones to author

"As it turned out…" Alan Young to author

"My final film at Disney…," Hank Jones, *The Show Bizz Part of My Life*

"Cat from Outer Space also had Mel Carter in it…," Hank Jones to author

"The Cat from Outer Space was a Norman Tokar film all the way…," Jan Williams to author

"A more down to earth guy you will never meet is Ken Berry…," Dick Warlock to author

"I worked with Hans…," Jonathan Daly to author

"There's no great statement in *The Apple Dumpling Gang films*…," *Ottawa Citizen*, 7/24/1979

"It's really fun to work together in another comedy…," ibid

Recollections of *The Apple Dumpling Gang Rides Again*, Robert Pine to author

Last Flight of Noah's Ark recollections by Jan Williams to author

Condorman recollections by Jan Williams to author

Selected Bibliography

Annakin, Ken. *So You Wanna Be a Director?* Tomahawk Press, 2001

Ebsen, Buddy & Stephen Cox, *The Other Side of Oz,* Donovan Pub Company, 1994

Funicello, Annette and Patricia Romanowski. *A Dream is a Wish Your Heart Makes,* Hyperion Press, 1994

Gabler, Neal. *Walt Disney: The Triumph of the American Imagination,* Vintage Books, 2006

Gammon, Ronald. *Faith is a Star,* RP Dutton, 1963

Green, Amy Boothe and Howard E. Green. *Remembering Walt: Favorite Memories of Walt Disney,* Disney Editions, 2001

Lawson, Valerie. *Mary Poppins she Wrote: The Life of P.L. Travers,* Simon & Schuster, 1999

Malden, Karl. *Where Do I Start,* Limelight Editions, 2001

Maltin, Leonard. *The Disney Films,* third edition, Hyperion Press, 1973

McGilligan, Patrick. *Film Crazy: Interviews with Hollywood Legends,* St. Martin's, 2001

Mills, John. *Up in the Clouds, Gentlemen Please,* Orion, 2002

Mills, John. *Still Memories: An Autobiography in Photographs,* Hutchinson, 2000

Mosley, Leonard. *Disney's World,* Scarborough House Publishers, 1985

Negri, Pola. *Memoirs of a Star,* Doubleday, 1970

O'Hara, Maureen and John Nicoletti. *Tis Herself,* Simon & Schuster, 2005

Provost, Jon & Laurie Jacobson. *Timmy's in the Well: The Jon Provost Story,* Living Legends Publishing Group, 2009

Quirk, Lawrence J. *Jane Wyman: The Actress and the Woman,* Dembner Books, 1986

Schickel, Richard. *The Disney Version,* Irvin R. Dee, Inc., 1997

Sherman, Richard and Robert. *Walt's Time: From Before to Beyond,* Camphor Tree Publishers, 1998

Smith, Dave. *Disney A to Z,* Hyperion Press, 1996

Stirling, Richard. *Julie Andrews: An Intimate Biography,* St. Martins, 2009

Thomas, Bob. *Walt Disney: An American Original,* Hyperion Press, 1994

Tomlinson, David. *Luckier than Most,* Hodder & Stoughton, 1990

Tranberg, Charles. *Fred MacMurray: A Biography,* Bear Manor Media, 2007

Van Dyke, Dick. *My Lucky Life In and Out of Show Business,* Crown, 2011

Watts, Steven. *The Magic Kingdom: Walt Disney & the American Way of Life,* Hougton/Mifflin Co., 1997

Williams, Pat and Jim Denney, *How to Be Like Walt,* Health Communications, Inc., 2004

Index

CPSIA information can be obtained at www.ICGtesting.com
Printed in the USA
LVOW070142310112

266316LV00005B/91/P

9 781593 936846